DATE			

© THE BAKER & TAYLOR CO.

Political powerlessness

To my mother and father

POLITICAL POWERLESSNESS
Agricultural workers in post-war England

RENÉE DANZIGER

MANCHESTER UNIVERSITY PRESS
Manchester and New York

distributed exclusively in the USA and Canada
by ST. MARTIN'S PRESS, New York

Published by Manchester University Press
    Oxford Road, Manchester M13 9PL, UK
Distributed exclusively in the USA and Canada by
    St. Martin's Press, Inc.,
    Room 400, 175 Fifth Avenue, New York, NY 10010, USA

British Library cataloguing in publication data
Danziger, Renée
    Political powerlessness : agricultural
    workers in post-war England.
    1. England. Agricultural industries.
    Working conditions, 1945–1984
    I.   Title
    331.2'043'0942

Library of Congress cataloging in publication data applied for

ISBN 0-7190-2695-4 *hardback*

Printed in Great Britain
by Billing & Sons Limited, Worcester
Typesetting: Heather Hems, Tower House, Queen Street, Gillingham, Dorset

Contents

Acknowledgements

Few unexpected difficulties were encountered in the course of this study, which originated as a doctoral thesis. On certain occasions my research was impeded by the confidentiality of documents and similar problems arose when a few individuals refused to allow me to interview them. In general, however, I received more help and co-operation throughout my period of study than I probably deserved. In particular, I would like to thank Professor Howard Newby of the University of Essex, whose assistance went far beyond the call of duty. He not only gave me the advice and support that were necessary for getting my project off the ground, but also continued to encourage and advise me throughout the periods of research and writing-up—and this in spite of his many commitments at his own university. I would also like to thank my Oxford supervisor, Steven Lukes, for his constant interest and assistance, and for his many valuable suggestions. I am grateful, too, to John Goldthorpe of Nuffield College for reading and commenting in detail on much of my work. For financial assistance I am grateful to the Economic and Social Research Council, and for personal support I am indebted to Jeremy Coller. I would scarcely have been able to have written beyond the title page had it not been for the unfailing co-operation of the Agricultural and Allied Workers' National Trade Group of the Transport and General Workers' Union (TGWU), whose national officers at Headland House were invariably willing to assist me in my research by providing me with access to vital information and by giving me the benefit of their first-hand experiences of power and powerlessness. Many of the Trade Group's District Organisers also helped me by replying to my questionnaire. Special thanks are due to District Organiser Peter Medhurst for helping me to arrange my field-work. The fieldwork which I carried out in the summer of 1984 proved to be a valuable, and highly enjoyable, experience, thanks to the helpfulness and hospitality of Thelma and Eric Rayner, the late Charlie Collett, Don Pollard and their numerous colleagues and friends in the Suffolk area. Many members of the Trade Group and of the National Farmers' Union (NFU) who sit on the Agricultural Wages Board were kind enough to answer my questions about the Board's operation, as were past and present Independent Chairs of the Board. Many of the NFU's county secretaries also helped me by replying to my questionnaire, and their assistance was largely due to the prior co-operation of the NFU's Director of Administration, Mr A. G. Elliott. Finally, thanks are due to the Members of Parliament, civil servants and other authorities who assisted me by answering my numerous questions and by providing me with useful material. In particular, Diana Rench of the Oxfordshire Ministry of Agriculture, Fisheries, and Food (MAFF) was most kind by making it possible for me to attend a number of Agricultural Dwelling House Advisory Committees (ADHACs) held in Oxfordshire.

Ever since the Industrial Revolution began in England, a popular device in literature, and more recently in the mass media, has been to offset the stark inequalities and social conflict of urban life with the presumed tranquility and harmony of English rural society. The communication media are replete with images of 'the city' as a hotbed of civic strife, torn by the antagonism which prevails between luxury home-owners and slum dwellers, between financial institutions and dole queues, between West End and East End . . . in short, between the haves and have-nots of industrial, urban society. Conversely, the countryside is held up as a welcome retreat from such pervasive conflict, characterised as it is by an innocent preoccupation with the simple things in life which can be shared by all: the rhythm of nature, the village green, the local market and, of course, the country pub.[1]

Whatever social functions this sort of contrast may be intended to serve, it is built upon a severely skewed image of rural England. A cursory glance through English social history reveals that extremities of poverty and wealth shaped the social fabric of the countryside long before the Industrial Revolution began, and that they have continued to do so ever since.[2] Moreover, recent research suggests that the persistent gulf between the rural privileged and the rural deprived has continued to engender a form of social conflict which may differ from urban unrest in kind, but not in degree.[3]

In contemporary England, the poverty of the countryside is well represented by the hired agricultural work-force, while its great wealth is typified by their employers. If one defines poverty in terms of relative deprivation,[4] and if earnings levels are taken as an index of material well-being, it becomes impossible to describe Britain's 130,000 full-time farmworkers as anything but poor. Indeed, their earnings have been considerably lower than those of their industrial counterparts ever since the nineteenth century. In 1886 average agricultural earnings constituted 77 per cent of average industrial earnings; by 1924 farmworkers found that they earned on average just over half of what industrial workers earned; and although the gap between agricultural and industrial earnings had narrowed by 1952 to return to the 1886 level, by 1983 the figure had slipped down again to 65·9 per cent. In 1984, despite their long hours of work—between 46 and 49 hours per week, depending on occupation—agricultural workers were earning a weekly average of £115, which was over £50 per week less than the national average wage.[5]

But is it valid to relate these low earnings to the prevalence of poverty among farmworkers? Unfortunately, there have been few studies which have tested for the possible relationship between agricultural wages and poverty—a fact which may reflect the widespread belief in rural 'contentment'. Nevertheless, the available evidence does suggest quite clearly that farmworkers in England are not only low paid, but are also in many cases living in what can be termed poverty. For example, a small-scale survey conducted in 1975 found that out of 110 farmworkers' families across the country, 43 went without proper breakfast because they could not afford it; 87 had no regular night out, 75 of them because they could not afford it; and 33 had never had a holiday away from home.[6] Further evidence of farmworkers' poverty can be gleaned from their dependence on means-tested benefits provided by the state. In 1983 as many as 12,000 farmworkers with families were claiming Family Income Supplement (FIS) so as to keep above the 'official' poverty line; a further 12,000 were estimated by the Department of Health and Social Security (DHSS) as qualifying for FIS, although they failed to claim it. Farmworkers have for many years been one of the largest occupational groups among two-parent families to claim FIS, a fact which confirms their poverty relative to other occupational groups.

The agricultural worker's deprivation, which stems from the size of his weekly wage-packet, invades virtually all spheres of his life, the most significant being arguably agricultural accommodation. Roughly 50 per cent of the agricultural work-force live in tied cottages which are houses owned by their employers and provided along with the job, either rent-free or for a nominal weekly rent. The provision of this housing is not as advantageous as it may at first seem. Firstly, tied cottages are used repeatedly to justify farmworkers' low wages, thus perpetuating their poverty. Secondly, the tied cottage is invariably situated on, or very near, the farm at which the worker is employed. This arrangement

allows for savings on time and money spent on the journey to
and from work, but by the same token it spells isolation for
the farmworker and his family from other dwellings, and
from essential services and amenities such as doctors, schools,
shops and entertainment. Thirdly, the double dependency of
the worker on his employer for both housing and employment fosters an insecurity to which few other workers are
subjected. This was particularly the case until fairly recently,
for the loss of a farm job was accompanied almost invariably
by immediate eviction. Fourthly, the worker is 'on call' for
virtually twenty-four hours a day, to cover for emergencies
which may arise on the farm. Finally, tied accommodation
has restricted the occupational mobility of those farmworkers who may wish to leave agricultural employment,
since finding a new job requires in virtually all cases locating
suitable new housing. Farmworkers are often prevented from
finding and paying for alternative housing by their isolation
and lack of savings. Yet, despite these many problems attached
to tied accommodation, farmworkers are often compelled to
accept it, because the high prices and rents of private housing,
coupled with the scarcity of rural council housing, make it
the only affordable means of sheltering themselves and
their families.[7]

   Whether they live in a tied cottage on the farm, or in a
private or council house in a nearby village, many farmworkers
find that their opportunities for travel and communication are
severely restricted. Since the late 1950s there has been a
series of cut-backs in the rural bus service which has led to a
decline in the mobility of many farmworkers and their
families, since few of them can afford the expense of running
a car. At the same time, rising costs are forcing village shops
and post offices to close down, pushing agricultural workers
and their families further afield for their essential purchases.
The decline in the number of telephone kiosks, a forecasted
'side effect' of the recent privatisation of British Telecom,
will further curb the agricultural workers' contact with the
world beyond the local village. Yet another problem facing
the rural poor is the scarcity of public information and
advice centres, which tend to be concentrated in towns and
cities. While private professional services and solicitors are
beyond the financial means of most farmworkers, the free
advice of public information services is often beyond their
reach because of the sheer physical difficulties involved in
reaching them. These various forms of social deprivation

mean that for many agricultural workers, the only easily accessible and regular channels of communication with society at large are those which they can select on their television screens.[8]

The principles of orthodox free market theory might lead the observer to assume, on the basis of farmworkers' low wages, that agricultural work is not skilled, arduous or dangerous. For, as Barbara Wootton explains, a central postulate of classical economic theory is that '. . . the monetary and other advantages of any occupation will tend to balance one another so that jobs that involve disagreeable or dangerous work, or inconvenient or long hours, will be more highly remunerated than those that do not'.[9] Agriculture is certainly one sector of the labour market which challenges the wisdom of this 'free market' theory of wages. For, regardless of what wage levels suggest, agriculture ranks as Britain's third most dangerous industry after mining and construction. Dangers to the health and safety of the work-force are rife, ranging from the effects of contact with toxic chemicals to the occurrence of accidents and contraction of ailments during the operation of heavy machinery. Although certain precautions are taken, in 1983 alone a total of sixty-three people were killed in farm accidents, while the number of non-fatal injuries runs at an official rate of 4,000 per year, with unofficial estimates placing the figure as high as 120,000.[10]

Considerable skill is involved in agricultural work, partly because so much dexterity is required to forestall some of the more avoidable occupational hazards. But agriculture demands from its work-force other skills too, and this has been increasingly the case as the industry has become more technologically sophisticated. The National Board for Prices and Incomes (NBPI) acknowledged this fact when it reported in 1969 that the 6–7 per cent a year increase in agricultural output over the previous ten years had been at least partially due to the fact that agricultural workers had managed to 'develop new skills, increase their versatility and adapt their working methods to new machinery and new techniques'.[11] Yet the sophistication and complexity of agricultural work remain, by and large, overlooked, both in pecuniary and status terms. What one observer wrote in 1923 of the typical farmworker still holds today

> his is a skilled trade. It seems absurd that this should have to be
> emphasised, but it is necessary to do so, for it has become the

custom during the last century or so to speak of the agricultural worker as synonymous with the lowest type of worker—this is doubtless attributable partly to ignorance of the nature of his duties and partly to subconscious association with his small cash wage.[12]

Half a century after this was written, agricultural workers were still being denied the rightful recognition of their skill and sophistication, with the mass media continuing to present farmworkers as either 'country bumpkins' or as unskilled farm 'labourers'.

Just as the farmworker has retained in certain circles the image of almost backward simplicity, so the farmer has held on to his high social standing of the nineteenth century. That farmers enjoy a relatively high status is shown in the continued public perception of the farmer's occupation as an admirable and enviable 'way of life' (rather than as just another means of earning a living), and also by the fact that for many people the 'ultimate British aspiration is still normally to be a member of the landed gentry'. And, as in the case of the farmworkers, so too the status of farmers matches, at least to some extent, the level of their material wealth.[13]

The profitability of running a farm is not based solely upon the livelihood that the farm enterprise can provide. It also has much to do with the fact that farming 'brings in its train automatic access to capital gains of a kind which, on the record of post-war years, has headed the league for all major types of assets'.[14] Among the financial privileges enjoyed by many farmers is the receipt of subsidies and grants paid for by the Treasury, at an estimated value of £13,000–£20,000 per farmer per year. Meanwhile, due to a complex system of concessions, farmers pay in return only 10–15 per cent of their income to the public purse in the form of taxes.[15] The strongest evidence of farmers' material prosperity and security is to be found in the willingness of banks to lend vast sums of money to agricultural enterprises for the construction of new farm buildings, for the acquisition of new machinery, or for the purchase of more farmland. Bank loans to farmers rose by 30 per cent in 1979, 25 per cent in 1980 and a further 20 per cent in 1981, when the total amount of agricultural bank loans stood in the region of £4,000,000,000.[16] It should be noted, however, that the country's larger farmers receive the best part of these bank loans. They are responsible for the bulk of agricultural production and they take the lion's share of state grants and subsidies; in turn, this makes them the most 'reliable' investments for the banks.[17]

The wealth of many farmers must also be attributed to the industry's outstanding and ever-increasing rate of output. The increased application of new machinery, chemicals, breeding techniques and other scientific novelties has seen unprecedented rises in agricultural production over the past thirty years. Between 1954 and 1981 yields of wheat to the acre rose by 98 per cent, barley by 62 per cent, sugar by 23 per cent, while in 1981 dairy cows produced on average 48 per cent more milk and hens laid 52 per cent more eggs than in 1945. Although agriculture's contribution to the Gross Domestic Product (GDP) has been declining ever since the Industrial Revolution began (standing at a current rate of 2·3 per cent) and food represents only 17 per cent of consumers' total expenditure, agriculture remains highly productive on its own terms, with little sign of any decline in its output levels. Furthermore, because it provides 60 per cent of all food consumed in the UK (thus saving on imports) while also producing billions of pounds worth of exports every year, agriculture is widely regarded as a valuable national asset. It is largely for this reason that Britain's post-war governments have continued, without exception, to protect the industry by providing it with the grants, subsidies and concessions noted above. The result of this arrangement has been the accumulation of enormous wealth among the country's large farmers—a wealth which is just as striking as is the poverty of their employees. But what is more remarkable than the simple existence of this great disparity in material well-being is that it appears to have been tolerated for so long by the materially disadvantaged whose silence has enabled the popular myth of rural harmony to persist.

A common response to this anomoly is the observation that, because of its scattered and isolated nature, the agricultural work-force has never been able to combine in the way that industrial workers have done in protest against their poor conditions of work. Thus, although farmworkers may indeed resent their poverty, which contrasts so starkly with the affluence of many of their employers, there is little that they can do to improve their situation. While there is a certain validity in this argument, it is worth noting also that farmworkers have at their disposal a potential opportunity for quick and effective industrial action which is denied to most other groups of workers, who instead have had to carry out what are often protracted and costly battles in their pursuit of better wages and conditions. Unlike almost all other industries, agriculture is based upon animate produce which, in the case of livestock, requires around-the-clock attention; or, in the case of crops, demands periodic stretches of concentrated labour. In either case, the effects of a threatened or actual stoppage of work for even a short, but carefully time, period could be devastating.

To argue that this opportunity for action is purely academic in the sense that it would require a degree of organisation which the scatteredness of farmworkers precludes them from achieving is to overlook the fact that their employers are similarly dispersed; and yet, roughly 90 per cent of farmers belong to the National Farmers' Union (NFU), an organisation noted for its record of successful promotion of farmers' interests.[18] It is this discrepancy in the respective capacities of the two groups for effective organisation and action which leads to the conclusion that although isolation undoubtedly contributes to the inability of farmworkers to organise themselves, this is not the sole factor explaining their apparent silence. It is, of course, incumbent upon the observer to justify the assumption that farmworkers would seek improved conditions of work if they were able to do so. But once this assumption is justified (see Chapter 1), the question remains: why have farmworkers refrained so far from demanding and achieving better conditions of work?

The apparent acceptance by farmworkers of their social and material deprivation has been studied in detail by Howard Newby. Newby explored the widespread belief that what has traditionally prevented farmworkers from protesting against conditions which few other groups of workers would tolerate has been the paternalism of their employers and their own reciprocal deference. What Newby found in his study of deference among East Anglian farmworkers was that

The deference which is often attributed to the agricultural worker . . . rest[s] largely upon a fallacious inference made from his largely quiescent social and political behaviour. This quiescence . . . must be seen to result from the agricultural worker's dependence rather than from his deference. The dependence of the agricultural worker upon the farmer for employment, and in many cases for housing in addition, militates against the overt expression of dissatisfaction . . .[19]

Newby's study concludes that it is a complex 'system of constraints', rather than social–psychological properties such as 'deference', which explains the apparent passivity of the contemporary farm work-force in the face of their deprivation. He suggests that their quiescence is on the whole a rational, rather than irrational, response to a situation of extensive powerlessness which stems chiefly from farm-workers' weakness in both the labour and housing markets.

The work-place powerlessness among farmworkers which Newby identified in his research, coupled with the lessons of history, together have provided a stubborn barrier against the use of mass industrial action by the farmworkers' union in its pursuit of improved conditions. The last organised strike by farmworkers took place in 1923. That strike was such a painful lesson in the superior strength of agricultural employers that since that time the farmworkers' union has relied almost exclusively upon its access to formal policy-making institutions and upon external allies in its struggles to improve the farmworkers' lot. For example, the union has negotiated minimum wage rates for farmworkers since 1948 through the centralised machinery of the Agricultural Wages Board (England and Wales), a body whose decisions have statutory backing and on which the workers are guaranteed equal representation with their employers. Similarly, the long-standing campaign for the abolition of the tied cottage has not been fought on the farm; instead, it has been pursued largely by putting pressure on the Labour Party to pass legislation to achieve this end. And in its struggle to gain safer conditions of work, the union has relied upon the support which it can muster from other unions and partly on the pressure which it can bring to bear upon official and semi-official bodies concerned with health and safety at work. In none of these three areas of campaigning has the union leadership since 1923 actively sought large-scale grass-roots involvement in the form of direct action.

In view of the farmworkers' powerlessness at the grass-roots level, Newby regards this dependency on formal institutions and outside help as the only reasonable course of action open to the union. He suggests that the only hope for a 'dramatic improvement' in farmworkers' life chances lies in 'external political action, including legislation' and through the 'decisive intervention of external agencies'.[20]

The aims of this book are in a sense two-fold. Firstly, it seeks to examine the concept of political powerlessness and to formulate an approach to studying that concept (and the related concepts of power and interests) which may prove useful in social analysis. Secondly, it attempts to determine the extent to which farmworkers in the post-war period have in practice satisfied their interests by participating in formal policy-making institutions, and by making use of the assistance of external groups such as the Labour Party. Are these the best means by which to improve farmworkers' social and economic conditions? Or are the farmworkers' political pursuits conditioned by their work-place powerlessness in such a way that they are similarly constrained at both the work-place and the political levels? In answering these empirical questions, the proposed approach to the concept of political powerlessness will be put to use: in this way it can be tested for its validity and its utility in social analysis. The overall purpose is thus to explore the phenomenon of political powerlessness at both a theoretical and an empirical level. In certain respects it is highly distressing that the contemporary agricultural work-force should provide the student of powerlessness with such a perfect case study. But from the academic observer's point of view, the powerlessness which pervades farmworkers' organisational, political, social and economic lives is auspicious in so far as it provides a strong base from which to develop an understanding of that important social phenomenon, the experience of powerlessness.

The book is divided into two parts. The first part provides a theoretical and descriptive farmework for the case study. Chapter 1 sets out to shed light on the many forms and dimensions of political power and powerlessness which pervade social and political life; it then goes on to develop an operational definition of political powerlessness which is later applied to the case study in Part Two. Chapter 2 considers the context of capitalist agriculture in which agricultural labour relations are played out, and looks at the outstanding profitability of the post-war agricultural industry. Of particular interest in this chapter are the effects which government policies since 1945 have had upon agriculture and, more specifically, their implications for farmers' ability to promote and satisfy their occupational interests. Chapter 3 reviews the work-place powerlessness of the post-war agricultural work-force, concentrating in particular on the implications of the work-force's labour market weakness for the workers' ability to pursue their occupational interests through direct action.

Part Two considers the definitions of powerlessness and power which were put forward in Chapter 1 in the light of original and secondary empirical material concerning the experiences of the agricultural labour force. More specifically, this second part analyses the power relations involved in the processes of agricultural wage negotiation; the passage and effects of tied cottage legislation; and the regulation of agricultural health and safety. In attempting to understand the powerlessness of farmworkers and their union in each of these areas, the ideas and concepts which are explored in Chapter 2 are applied to the situation in which farmworkers find themselves.

Two additional points must be made at the outset. Firstly, it is held that the agricultural industry in the post-war period differs so greatly and in so many respects from its pre-war incarnation as to justify the choice of 1945 as the historical starting point for this study. The cut-off point, 1984–85, marks the end of post-war agriculture as we have known it. The Conservative government elected in 1979, and re-elected in 1983 and 1987, has introduced radical changes in British agricultural policy in an effort to bring down agricultural subsidies, reduce agricultural surpluses and make more farm-land available to non-agricultural property developers. The implications of these developments, which represent a break with a forty-year-old trend, are far-reaching, but beyond the scope of this study. In so far as this inquiry is concerned with the timeless issue of political powerlessness, however, these limitations will not impair its findings and conclusions.

Secondly, after much deliberation, the decision was taken to refer throughout the book to the individual farmworker and farmer in the masculine rather than the feminine form. This should not be interpreted as a denial of the importance of the female farmworker, who almost certainly suffers greater powerlessness than her male counterpart. The decision was taken partly on stylistic grounds, but chiefly because the majority of farmworkers and farmers are, in fact, male.

Anyone who has been to the countryside and seen the way in which many farmworkers live will appreciate why this particular case study was chosen. Long hours of hard work in sunshine, rain and snow; difficulties in affording the most basic of commodities; limited contact with the world beyond the village boundaries; a constant fear of redundancy; and finally, an old age marred by disease and ailments which result from a life of working on the land: these are some of the more unpleasant, but nonetheless prevalent, features of the agricultural workers' life. An understanding of farmworkers' powerlessness will hopefully go some way towards finding out how their situation can be improved.

The case study may have a wider interest, too. The job insecurity, low pay and isolation which have been the farmworkers' lot since the late eighteenth century are, as the twentieth century draws to its close, increasingly familiar among many groups of traditionally militant and well-organised industrial manual workers. An insight into the political powerlessness which has accompanied farmworkers' occupational decline and their responses to this powerlessness may provide some salutary lessons for the broader labour movement.

NOTES

1 Shaw, J. M. (ed.), (1979), *Rural Deprivation and Planning*, Geo Abstracts, Norwich, introduction; Newby, H. (1979), *Green and Pleasant Land?*, Penguin, Harmondsworth, p. 13; Jones, G. (1973), *Rural Life*, Longman, London; Norton-Taylor, R. (1982), *Whose Land is it Anyway?*, Turnstone Press, Wellingborough, p. 272.

2 Hobsbawm, E. J. and Rude, G. (1969), *Captain Swing*, Lawrence and Wishart, London; Dunbabin, J. P. D. (1974), *Rural Discontent in Nineteenth Century Britain*, Faber and Faber, London; Fussell, G. E. (1948), *From Tolpuddle to TUC*, Windsor Press, Slough.

3 Newby, H. (1979), *The Deferential Worker*, Penguin, Harmondsworth, p. 1.

4 Townsend, P. (1979), *Poverty in the U.K.*, Penguin, Harmondsworth; Holman, R. (1978), *Poverty*, Martin Robertson, London; Mack, J. and Lansley, S. (1984), *Poor Britain*, Allen & Unwin, London.

5 Department of Employment, HMSO, London, *New Earnings Survey 1983 Part A*. Department of Employment, HMSO, London, *New Earnings Survey 1984 Part A*. Donaldson, J. G. S. and F. (1969), *Farming in Britain Today*, Allen Lane, London, p. 29. MAFF, *Annual Review of Agriculture 1984*, London. Relatively little statistical information concerning the work situation of farmworkers in England has been found in the course of this study. Consequently, although the study is concerned primarily with English farmworkers, it has been necessary in many cases to use figures relating to British farmworkers as a whole. The main source of statistical information has been the Ministry of Agriculture, Fisheries, and Food (MAFF).

6 Brown, M. and Winyard, S. (1975), *Low Pay on the Farm*, Low Pay Unit, London.

7 Newby, H., *The Deferential Worker*, pp. 178-94; Newby, H., Bell,

C., Rose, D., and Saunders, P. (1978), *Property, Patertnalism and Power*, Hutchinson, London, pp. 163–7; Shelter, (1974), *Report on Tied Accommodation*, Shelter, London; National Board for Prices and Incomes (1969), *Pay of Workers in Agriculture in England and Wales*, Report No. 101, January, p. 7; Irving, B. and Hilgendorf, L. (1975), *Tied Cottages in British Agriculture*, Tavistock Institute, London.

8   Rural Voice and The Bus and Coach Council (1983), *The Country Would Miss the Buss*, February; the *Times* 27 June 1984, 'Rural koisks could close'; The National Council of Social Service and the National Consumer Council (1978), *The Right to Know*.

9   Wootton, B. (1955), *The Social Foundations of Wage Policy*, Allen & Unwin, London, pp. 54–5.

10 Winyard, S. and Danziger, R. (1984), *Hard Labour*, Low Pay Unit, London.

11 NBPI, *Pay of Workers*, p. 3.

12 Venn, J. A. (1923), *Foundations of Agricultural Economics*, Cambridge University Press, London, p. 232.

13 Rogers, S. J. (1970), 'Farmers as pressure groups', *New Society*, 5 February; *Public Attitudes Towards Farmers*, a Mori Poll report, commissioned by the National Farmers' Union, March 1983.

14 *Investors' Chronicle*, 23 March 1984, p. 78.

15 Body, R. (1982), *Agriculture: the Triumph and the Shame*, Temple Smith, London; Norton-Taylor, *op. cit.*, pp. 100–101.

16 MAFF, *Annual Review of Agriculture 1984*, London.

17 Body, *op. cit.*; Body, R. (1984), *Farming in the Clouds*, Temple Smith, London.

18 Mackintosh, R. (1970), 'The problems of agricultural politics', *JAE*, 21 (1); Wrong, D. H. (1979), *Power*, Blackwell, Southampton, pp. 135–6; Self, P. and Storing, H. (1962), *The State of the Farmer*, Allen & Unwin, London, p. 37.

19 Newby, *op. cit.*, p. 414.

20 *Ibid.*, pp. 435–6.

PART ONE

Chapter 1

Power and powerlessness

The observation that 'power' constitutes one of social science's most extensively researched concepts has become a commonplace among political scientists and sociologists. Moreover, while it might be difficult to identify two students of power who concur over the meaning of that concept, almost without exception they are found to agree that 'power' merits all of the academic attention which it has so far received.[1] This consensus can be attributed to the common belief that power, however it is defined, is a factor which influences deeply the social and political lives of all people, regardless of their historical, geographical or social location. Yet social life is equally shaped by powerlessness, in spite of which, relatively few social or political thinkers have devoted their energies to analysing the nature of powerlessness.[2]

This inquiry into political powerlessness begins with a review of some of the available literature on power. This is partly because such literature is more plentiful and, in general, more developed than works on powerlessness; but also, and more importantly, because of the close empirical and conceptual relationships that exist between power and powerlessness. Before considering a selection of views on power, however, it should be noted that, for the purposes of this study, 'political' powerlessness refers to all of 'those social processes by means of which values are authoritatively allocated for a community'. Thus, for example, political activity could include wage negotiation and the activities of certain quangos as well, of course, as the activity which goes on in the legislative, executive and judicial spheres of government.[3]

I THE PLURALIST APPROACH TO POWER

According to pluralist analysis, political power is exercised within centres of formal decision-making during a process by which members of the 'political stratum' are held to take concrete decisions over 'routine' and 'key' issues. Locating power is a matter of identifying 'who participates, who wins and loses, and who prevails in decision-making', with the pluralist researcher paying most attention to 'who prevails' because it is this that is believed to reveal which individual or group within the political stratum has the 'most power'.[4]

A central tenet of this school is that in any community with a pluralist system of government, virtually all groups can bring forward their grievances and demands for the attention of elected political decision-makers. This opportunity is available to them largely because the 'independence, penetrability, and heterogeneity of the various segments of the political stratum all but guarantee that any dissatisfied group will find spokesmen in the political stratum'.[5]

However, pluralist researchers have repeatedly observed that in spite of this alleged opportunity to bring their grievances to the notice of political decision-makers, *in practice* few people take any such action. Pluralists note that as a result of this popular political inaction, most issues are generated, developed and decided upon by a small minority of political activists.[6] The pluralists emphasise, however, that this narrow spread of actual political participation is by no means indicative of an 'elitist' political system.[7] Instead, the political abstention of most people in a pluralist society is regarded as the outcome of their own free choice, rather than the effect of living under a 'closed' political system. According to one of the best-known pluralists, Robert A. Dahl, the reason that most people abstain from political activity in a pluralistically governed community is quite simply that 'At the focus of most men's [sic] lives are primary activities involving, food, sex, love, family, work, play, shelter, comfort, friendship, social esteem, and the like. Activities like these—not politics—are the primary concerns of most men and women.'[8] Thus, in a pluralist system, although the opportunity for widespread political participation exists, relatively few citizens choose to make use of it.

A further characteristic of a pluralist system is that, regardless of their personal (lack of) interest in politics, all citizens possess some resources with which to exercise political power in decision-making centres. The political activists have access to, and make use of, more resources than do the politically 'inactive' citizens; and the activists also exercise greater power than do their apolitical counterparts because of the former's direct involvement in the decision-making process.[9] Nonetheless, the apolitical stratum is held to exercise power, too, although in an indirect fashion, through the influence which they exert over their elected decision-makers. This widely dispersed, indirect influence is based upon the elected decision-makers' desire to seek re-election. In order to win the electorate's vote in the next election these decision-makers must behave while they are in office according to how they think the voters wish them to behave. Thus, all citizens of a pluralist system are seen to exercise some power in the decision-making process, albeit in varying degrees, due to the power resource which the vote represents.[10]

The pluralist researcher's main interest is not in the potential or indirect power of the apolitical majority, but rather in the activities of the political minority which is directly involved in decision-making. By studying the actions of this minority during the decision-making process—noting in particular which participants initiate the alternatives which are finally adopted, which participants veto the alternatives initiated by others, and which ones propose alternatives that are vetoed—the researcher is said to be able to discover 'who governs' a given community.[11]

The decision-making process itself is portrayed by pluralists as a competition between different political leaders who represent the interests of numerous organisations, all of whom possess effective resources which they use in their efforts to prevail in the decision-making process. Political resources are varied and can include (among other things)

> an individual's own time; access to money, credit and wealth; control over jobs; control over information; esteem or social standing; the possession of charisma, popularity, legitimacy, legality; and the rights pertaining to public office. The list might also include solidarity: the capacity of a member of one segment of society to evoke support from others who identify him as like themselves because of similarities in occupation, social standing, religion, ethnic origin, or racial stock.[12]

In a pluralist system these resources are neither held to be equally distributed among all political participants, nor are they perceived as being cumulative and concentrated in the hands of a political elite. Instead, the pluralists argue that the distribution of resources in a pluralist system is characterised by the following features:

1. Many different kinds of resources for influencing officials are available to different citizens.

2. With few exceptions, these resources are unequally distributed.

3. Individuals best off in their access to one kind of resource are often badly off with respect to many other resources.

4. No one influence resource dominates all the others in all or even most key decisions.

5. With some exceptions, an influence resource is effective in some issue-areas or in some specific decisions but not in all.

6. Virtually no one, and certainly no group of more than a few individuals, is entirely lacking in some influence resources.[13]

It is this system of 'dispersed inequalities' which is said to guarantee that in a pluralist system the failure of a given group or individual to prevail in one area of decision-making will not imply similar failures by that group or individual in other decision-making areas.

II THE 'SECOND FACE' OF POWER

Shortly after Robert Dahl tested and claimed to have verified the above hypotheses in his empirical study of power, the pluralist approach came under attack by Peter Bachrach and Morton Baratz, who argued that whereas political power has 'two faces', the pluralists were capable of seeing only one.

Bachrach and Baratz concur with the pluralists that the question of 'who prevails in the decision-making process' is an important one which must be answered in any serious study of political power. However, they argue further that a student of power must also devote attention to the 'second face' of power, which reveals itself in the process by which certain demands are selected and others are rejected for formal consideration by the political decision-makers. As Bachrach and Baratz put it

> Of course power is exercised when A participates in the making of decisions that affect B. But power is also exercised when A devotes his energies to creating or reinforcing social and political values and institutional practices that limit the scope of the political process to public consideration of only those issues which are comparatively innocuous to A.[14]

It should be noted that there is nothing inherent in the pluralist approach which prevents pluralists from recognising that certain issues are kept off of the political agenda by individuals or groups whose interests would be threatened by the emergence of such issues. While some pluralists appear to take political issues as 'givens' without inquiring into their creation,[15] others note that not all potential issues reach the decision-making arena. For example, although Dahl argues that the openness of the political system is such as to guarantee to almost any dissatisfied group a political spokesman, he also observes that

> to have a spokesman does not insure that the group's problems will be solved by political action. Politicians may not see how they can gain by taking a position on an issue; action by government may seem to be wholly inappropriate; policies intended to cope with dissatisfaction may be blocked; solutions may be improperly designed; indeed, politicians may even find it politically profitable to maintain a shaky coalition by keeping tension and discontent alive and deflecting attention to irrelevant 'solutions' or alternative issues.[16]

Nevertheless, the clear recognition that certain issues are kept off of the political agenda does not mean that Dahl, or any other pluralist, views this phenomenon as an integral feature of political power. Instead, it is portrayed by pluralists as part of the 'political background', or as the context within which power is exercised, with 'power' being restricted to the relatively straightforward process of 'prevailing in the formal process of decision-making'.[17]

By contrast, Bachrach and Baratz argue that a serious study of power must include an inquiry into both the process of formal decision-making *and* that of issue-selection, or agenda setting, because both of these processes are said to entail the exercise of political power. In an attempt to explain the 'second face' of power more clearly, Bachrach and Baratz refer to E. E. Schattschneider's astute observation that

> All forms of political organisation have a bias in favour of the exploitation of some forms of conflict and the suppression of others because organisation is the mobilisation of bias. Some issues are organised into politics while others are organised out.[18]

According to Bachrach and Baratz, the 'primary method for sustaining a given mobilisation of bias is nondecision-making', where the concept of a nondecision is defined as

a decision that results in suppression or thwarting of a latent or manifest challenge to the values or interests of the decision-maker. To be more explicit, nondecision-making is a means by which demands for change in the existing allocation of benefits and privileges in the community can be suffocated before they are even voiced; or kept covert; or killed before they gain access to the relevant decision-making arena; or, failing all these things, maimed or destroyed in the decision-implementing process.[19]

Bachrach and Baratz then provide a list of the different forms which nondecision-making can take. What they all have in common is that they result in 'non-challenges' to the status quo by those who are disfavoured by it. The first type of nondecision which Bachrach and Baratz mention involves the use of physical force (such as imprisonment or harrassment) to prevent demands for change in the established order from emerging in the formal political arena. A second form of nondecision is the employment of negative or positive sanctions (the deprivation or distribution of valued goods) to dissuade potential challengers to the status quo from raising their challenge within the formal arena of decision-making. Thirdly, nondecision-making can be carried out by invoking an 'existing bias of the political system- a norm, precedent, rule or procedure to squelch a threatening demand or incipient issue'. For example, a demand for change could be denied legitimacy by being branded 'unpatriotic', 'immoral' or 'unreasonable', and could thus be destroyed altogether. Alternatively, procedures could be invoked to crush an issue, such as the referral of the issue to an endless string of committees which spend a sufficiently long time discussing the issue as to reduce its original impact or meaning. Fourthly, nondecision-making may involve re-shaping or reinforcing the existing mobilisation of bias. This might entail the establishment of new rules or procedures with which ensuing demands would have to comply before they could reach the decision-making arena. The object here is to construct rules and procedures which would prevent threatening demands from ever reaching that arena. Finally, there is a situation which Bachrach and Baratz claim is 'closely allied to, but actually is not nondecision-making in the strict sense'. This involves those cases where potential challengers of the status quo refrain from raising their challenge because they anticipate either failure or a hostile reaction from the decision-makers.[20]

By their nature, most nondecisions are difficult to locate, not least because nondecision-makers often take steps to hide their non-decisions from the public eye, or else because they themselves may be unaware of their own nondecision-making practices.[21] Nevertheless, Bachrach and Baratz reject the pluralists' contention that because of this, non-decisions are impossible to identify. They concede that the 'quasi-nondecision' (which involves B's non-action in anticipation of A's reactions) may be impossible to verify empirically. However, they deny vigorously the allegation that all non-decisions are non-events and therefore unverifiable, as they claim that 'although absence of conflict may be a non-event, a decision which results in prevention of conflict *is* very much an event—and an observable one to boot'.[22]

In order to strengthen their defence of the 'second face' of power, Bachrach and Baratz outline a method by which nondecisions can be empirically identified.[23] They suggest that the researcher should begin by studying the political decision-making process of a given community. By identifying 'who participates, who wins and loses, and who prevails' within that process, the researcher is said to be able to ascertain the nature of the particular mobilisation of bias which operates within the given community's political system. More specifically, the observer will be able to find out which groups are disfavoured by the mobilisation of bias and whether those groups' interests are expressed in the political system.

The researcher's next task is to uncover whether and how the existing mobilisation of bias is 'buttressed by non-decisions'.

> Armed with the leads picked up from his study of the decision-making process, he must determine if those persons and groups apparently disfavoured by the mobilisation of bias have grievances, overt or covert . . . overt grievances are those that have already been expressed and have generated an issue within the political system, whereas covert ones are still outside the system.[24]

If the researcher finds that no one in the community has grievances of either an overt or covert nature, then he or she must conclude that nondecisions have not been made. Alternatively, if grievances are uncovered, then the researcher must proceed to identify how and why these grievances have not been raised and/or resolved in the decision-making arena.

This part of the inquiry must be carried out primarily through discussion with the aggrieved. The nondecision-makers themselves will be of little assistance because they may well be unaware of, or unwilling to discuss, their exercises of power through nondecision-making. By contrast, Bachrach and Baratz argue, the aggrieved are always aware that their inability to bring their grievances forward for resolution in the decision-making arena is the consequence of an exercise of power.[25]

By combining the 'pluralist' and 'two faces' approaches to power, the researcher can, in principle, uncover diverse forms of political power at two conceptually distinct but empirically related levels.

The first level concerns those power relations that exist within the formal political decision-making arena, where political participants compete with one another in their attempts to prevail in the decision-making process. Power is exercised here by introducing resolutions to issues which are subsequently adopted (and by ensuring their adoption), and by vetoing alternative resolutions which are proposed by other participants in the decision-making process. As well as these 'direct' forms of prevailing in the decision-making process, there are the 'negative aspects of decision-making' which include, for example, deciding formally not to act or not to decide on particular issues.[26]

The second level at which political power is exercised lies outside the formal arena, but the exercise of such power has significant consequences for what is debated and decided upon within the formal arena. This second level of political power is also known as agenda-setting. It can involve any of a number of different non-decisions, either singly or in combination, which prevent certain demands from becoming 'issues' while allowing others to emerge for formal resolution in the decision-making arena.

III   POWER AND INTERESTS

Bachrach and Baratz's approach to the study of political power marks a significant advance on the pluralists', chiefly because instead of taking political issues as 'givens' they analyse the power relations involved in the (non-)transformation of some social demands into political issues. However,

Bachrach and Baratz are constrained in their study of power by their acceptance of the pluralists' insistence that any hypothesis concerning power must be based on observable phenomena if it is to be academically and socially useful. This behaviouralist inclination prevents Bachrach and Baratz from pursuing some of the most important questions about political power relations. For example, their preoccupation with observability leads them to argue that if the researcher is unable to locate any actual conflict between those who gain and those who appear to lose from the prevailing mobilisation of bias—that is, if he or she can find no party claiming to harbour either overt or covert grievances—then 'the presumption must be that there is consensus on the prevailing allocation of values, in which case nondecision-making is impossible'.[27] Bachrach and Baratz recognise in principle that this presumed consensus may not be a genuine consensus at all, but rather the product of effective nondecision-making. However, they refuse to develop this point, agreeing instead with the behavioural precepts of the pluralists who insist that where a suspected case of 'false consensus' cannot be empirically verified through observation, its existence cannot be legitimately asserted by the researcher who might otherwise attribute grievances where none exist.[28]

In similar behaviouralist fashion, Bachrach and Baratz's definition of a 'power struggle' requires that the victim (although not necessarily the perpetrator) of such a struggle must be aware of its existence. This condition is laid down so as to prevent the researcher from imputing a power relationship where none exists. Bachrach and Baratz acknowledge that a power relationship could, in principle, exist without the victim being aware of it; but they argue that 'for the purposes of analysis' a power struggle can be said to exist only when either A and B, or just B, are aware of its existence and make this awareness known to the observer.[29]

The chief weakness in Bachrach and Baratz's approach to the study of power is contained in these methodological principles, which limit the researcher to studying only what is wholly and directly observable, and so require the researcher to overlook important forms of power and powerlessness. Conversely, it is suggested here that the researcher's inability to induce B to articulate its grievances, or to assert them in some other behavioural manner, does not justify the researcher's conclusion that B has no grievances. It may be the case that B is prevented from expressing its grievances by A's exercise of power, perhaps through the threat of sanctions or even by an exercise of power which results in B's own unawareness of its grievances, as well as in B's unconsciousness of the very power relationship in which it is involved. The point here is that it can be as misleading and dangerous to deduce from the apparent absence of grievances the existence of a genuine consensus as it is to ascribe grievances where none exist.[30] It is, of course, more difficult to analyse those power relations which B is unable to acknowledge behaviourally as a result of the very power being exercised over B, but methodological difficulties do not entitle the researcher to define these power relationships out of existence.

Steven Lukes has developed a view of power in which A exercises power over B in such a way that B is made unaware of the conflict of interests and the power relationship which exist between A and B. A is said to exercise this type of power '. . . by influencing, shaping or determining . . . [B's] very wants'[31] so that B's wants will correspond with A's, but not B's interests. In such an event, whenever B pursues its wants it will be acting in the interests of A and against its own interests. Yet the nature of this power relationship is such that B will not be aware that its wants conflict with its own (but not A's) interests. Nor will B be conscious of the power which A has exercised over it to create this lack of awareness on B's part. In fact, the notable effectiveness of this form of power lies precisely in B's ignorance of its being exercised, for it is this ignorance which prevents B from struggling against A's power.

How could A possibly exercise power over B in such a way that B would unwittingly harm its own interests while serving A's? Having raised the possibility of this insidious form of power, Lukes remains ambiguous as to the mechanics of its exercise. In his discussion Lukes suggests that B's thoughts and wants can be controlled both through the control of information and through processes of socialisation.[32] There is, however, a substantial difference between these two forms of thought control which Lukes does not explore: it is suggested here that only the former fits comfortably into discussions on the exercise of power.

Political socialisation is a complex process which operates through all actors in a given society and through an array of social, cultural and political institutions over an extended period of time. Just as all actors participate to some extent in the socialisation process, so too are they influenced by it: socialisation is, in other words, about the development and maintenance of a society's *Weltanschauung* and the *Weltanschauung* of its component actors. In this respect, socialisation is more relevant to discussions on ideology rather than inquiries into the exercise of power.

A and B can be located in the socialisation framework only in so far as A is that individual or group which benefits from the ideology into which a given community is socialised, while B loses out. A cannot be identified, however, as the agent which is causally responsible for the pervasion of the given ideology, since socialisation is a diffuse phenomenon whose sources and perpetrators range throughout society and history. A discussion on the exercise of power in which the exerciser of power cannot be identified becomes meaningless.

The socialisation variant of Lukes's conception of power is unacceptable also on methodological grounds. Lukes suggests that the exercise of power can be shown to have occurred by looking at how B behaves when A no longer exercises its hypothesised power over B. In the case of socialisation, even if A could be identified, in order to determine empirically that A had exercised power over B it would be necessary to strip B of its *Weltanschauung*. The manufacture of this counterfactual evidence would be an unworkable means for studying the exercise of power over B, in so far as lifting B out of its ideological context would be tantamount to discussing an actor other than B.

By contrast, the control of information corresponds more closely with our everyday useage of the concept of power, and it is a sociologically important conception of power which is amenable to empirical investigation. This form of power is exercised when A manipulates or witholds information from B which B would require if it were to recognise and act upon what its interests really are in a given situation. Counterfactual evidence of this power relationship becomes available when B gains access to the previously withheld information and changes its behaviour, to act in accordance with its own interests instead of A's. However, as long as B remains deprived of this vital information, B will continue to act in a way which promotes A's interests, but not its own, while remaining unaware that it is being made to frustrate or harm its interests.

This kind of power relationship is both common and effective in social and political life. For example, drug companies sometimes withhold information about the side effects of their products so that people will continue to purchase and use them; governments may withhold details about the build-up to a war so that soldiers will be willing to participate in the subsequent carnage in the interests of 'national defence'; behind the scenes deals which corrupt politicians negotiate for personal gain may be kept secret so that the politician will be re-elected; the list of examples is a long one. What all of these examples illustrate is that A may exercise power over B by withholding or manipulating information in such a way that B is made to act against its own interests, but in the interests of A, without realising it is so doing. (It should be noted that this form of power is less effective the more often it is exercised by a given group or individual, for people develop cynical and critical responses to information which is released by groups or persons who were previously implicated in this form of power exercise.)

The examples listed above in which A withholds information from B so as to manipulate B's wants and actions in a way consistent with A's, rather than B's, interests contain certain assumptions about what 'really' or 'objectively' constitutes B's interests. In the drug companies illustration, the assumption is that B would not take drugs with dangerous side effects if B were aware of their existence. In the case of the war, the assumption is that B would not take part in an aggressive (as opposed to defensive) war. And in the example involving political corruption, the assumption is that B would not re-elect a politician if B had been told of that politician's corrupt practices. All or any of these assumptions may, in fact, be entirely misfounded; B may regard the ill side-effects of a drug as an acceptable price to pay for its main effects, or B may be fully prepared to fight an aggressive war, or, finally, B may not think political corruption is a sufficiently good reason to refrain from re-electing a politician.

In spite of this, it can be useful to work on the initial assumption that B's objective interests lie in avoiding the ill side-effects of drugs, aggressive warfare or corrupt political leadership so as to discover through an appropriate counterfactual, whether B's actions were carried out on the basis of A's exercise of power over B. This power might have been exercised through the propagation of false information, or alternatively by other means; the precise manner in which A controls B (if it does so, at all) is a matter for empirical investigation.

Used in this fashion, the concept of 'objective interests' is an analytic device whose primary purpose is to facilitate the development of empirically verifiable hypotheses about power relationships, rather than itself being an empirically verifiable concept.[33] Moreover, if the concept of objective interests is used heuristically rather than normatively, it need not lead the researcher into the attribution of 'false consciousness'. For example, the observer may posit that Q's objective interests are X, but research may reveal Q to be in pursuit of Y instead of X. The researcher's task is to determine whether any obstacles exist to prevent Q from pursuing and attaining X and, if any exist, what their nature is. At the same time, the researcher will be able to study Q's ability (or inability) to attain Y, and to study the nature of any obstacles that may be involved. In this example, although Q's interests are identified as X, the observation that Q is pursuing Y does not entail an attribution of 'false consciousness' to Q. Instead, Y is regarded as constituting Q's more limited interests, in the context of Q's apparent powerlessness to pursue and achieve X. The study can thus include an analysis of Q's possible powerlessness *via-à-vis* X and Y, both of which are Q's interests, although one is posited as being of theoretically greater value to Q than the other.

If extensive research does not provide any evidence of power and powerlessness relating to Q's failure to pursue and attain X, then the researcher must reassess his or her initial interpretation of Q's objective interests. It may be that Y constitutes Q's objective interests, rather than being Q's 'limited' interests, as had originally been thought.[34] In this way, although the researcher's initial assumption as to what constitutes Q's objective interests is necessarily a subjective judgement, such subjectivity will not impair his or her study. On the contrary, this approach can enhance a study of power and powerlessness for it enables the researcher to study those power relations which B may be unaware of, or may be unable to express in any behavioural, observable fashion.[35]

Certain other benefits accrue to a study of power and powerlessness which is based upon a conception of what constitutes B's objective interests. In particular, it becomes possible to use two further ideas introduced by Steven Lukes. Firstly, there is the notion of power being exercised through inaction; and secondly, there is the idea that power can be exercised unconsciously.

It may at first seem impossible to research into 'inaction'

since this would involve studying the slippery notion of 'what has not happened'. However, if the student of power is equipped with a conception of B's objective interests, then he or she need not stop short (as Bachrach and Baratz do) of researching into the exercise of power through inaction. Once the researcher has put forward a view of B's interests and found that these interests are not being satisfied, then it becomes necessary to uncover why B's interests are being frustrated. Where an identifiable group or individual (A)'s failure to act in a certain way is found to have contributed significantly to the frustration of B's interests, and where acting in that way is a hypothetical (although not necessarily actual) possibility with determinate consequences for B's interests, it can be said that A has exercised power over B.[36] This contrasts with Bachrach and Baratz's approach, in which the observer can establish that power has been exercised through 'inaction' only where there is evidence of A deciding not to act on a given issue.

Matthew Crenson's study of power illustrates the utility of including inaction in an analysis of power. The objective interests of the citizens of Gary, Indiana (B) were assumed by Crenson to be the ability to breath in clean air. When Crenson sought an explanation for the frustration of these interests and of efforts to protect them, what he found was that the very inaction of the US Steel Company (A) was a major obstacle preventing Gary's citizens from campaigning against the company's air polluting practices. As Crenson himself put it, 'What U.S. Steel did not do was probably more important to the career of Gary's air pollution issue than what it did.'[37]

Similarly, the notion of an 'unconscious' exercise of power can be employed once the researcher has outlined what would constitute B's interests in a given context. Having hypothesised B's interests, the researcher can include as an exercise of power anything which A does (or does not do) which contributes significantly to the harming of B's interests, regardless of whether A intended to exercise that power, or was conscious of doing so.[38]

It is interesting to note that Steven Lukes does not link the idea of unconscious power exercises explicitly with the notion of B's interests. Instead, he contends that where A could not possibly have known what the consequences of its (in)action would be, then A cannot be held to have exercised power. This contrasts with those situations where

A's ignorance is due to A's '. . . (remedial) failure to find out those consequences, in which case A is said to have exercised power over B'.

It is in close connection with this point that Lukes introduces the notion of 'responsibility' to his study of power. According to Lukes, if it was not humanly possible for A to have anticipated the consequences of its (in)actions, then A cannot be held responsible for these consequences, as a result of which, A cannot be said to have exercised power over B, even if A's (in)actions harmed B's interests. Similarly, where A could not have acted differently than it did and yet harmed B's interests, one cannot hold A responsible for its actions; nor, therefore, can one say that A exercised power over B. Lukes makes his conceptual link between power and responsibility clear when he writes that

> the attribution of power is at the same time an attribution of (partial or total) responsibility for certain consequences. The point, in other words, of locating power is to fix responsibility for consequences held to flow from the action, or inaction, of certain specifiable agents.[39]

It is evident that when Lukes links power with responsibility in this way he is concerned with moral, rather than causal, responsibility. It is true that where 'A could not have acted otherwise and yet harmed B's interests', A cannot be held morally responsible for its harming of B's interests. However, A *can* be held causally responsible for its harming of B's interests, even where A, in practice, could not have acted otherwise (although acting differently must be a possibility which the observer can hypothesise). To this extent, and because there is no necessary or logical connection between power and moral responsibility, A can be said to have exercised power over B, even where A could not have acted otherwise.[40]

The attribution of A's moral responsibility should not be the overriding concern of a study of power. Instead, the 'point of locating power' is to fix causal responsibility for the 'consequences held to flow from the action, or inaction, of certain specifiable agents', so that the observer can locate which agents would have to be challenged for B to be able to restore and defend its interests. Thus, the criterion to be used for establishing the existence of a power relationship is not A's ability to do otherwise, but rather A's harming of B's interests.

IV THE STUDY OF POWERLESSNESS

The foregoing observations on the study of power will be useful in the construction of a working definition of political powerlessness. In constructing this definition and applying it to the case study, it is hoped that some light will be shed on forms and dimensions of political powerlessness which have until now been largely neglected. This neglect has been partly due to social scientists' preoccupation with the more 'macho' concept of power, and partly to the tendency among those who do study powerlessness to concentrate on the nature of powerlessness in a given case, rather than drawing on their case study to explore the concept of powerlessness *per se*.

It is proposed that *Q is politically powerless to the extent that Q is unable to promote or defend its interests within authoritative processes of value allocation in a given community*. An empirical study of political powerlessness based on this definition would require research into whatever factors give rise to and perpetuate the inability of Q to promote or defend its interests within these authoritative processes. For analytic purposes, these factors can be divided into two categories.

The first category consists of conscious and unconscious exercises of power over Q by other groups or individuals (T). These exercises of power can be carried out by action or inaction, their most important feature being that they contribute significantly to Q's inability to promote and defend its political interests. An exercise of power can take a variety of forms, many of which have been noted above. They include: T prevailing over Q in formal decision-making; T's nondecision-making against Q's interests through the use of force, sanctions, existing institutional biases, and the creation of new rules and biases; and T's control of relevant information which prevents Q from recognising what its interests are, in which case T prohibits Q from even attempting to promote or defend its interests.

The second category involves structural or contextual factors, as well as obstacles internal to Q which bar Q from promoting or defending its interests.[41] What these obstacles have in common is that, while they may help to prohibit Q from pursuing its interests, they do not in themselves constitute an exercise of power, nor are they the outcome of power which has been exercised by any specifiable agents.

On the other hand, for this category of obstacles to be effective, T must make use of them in its exercise of power over Q. (It is in this sense that the two categories are analytically, but not empirically, distinct.) This second category of obstacles includes resources of power and the way in which these resources have been socially distributed over time, as well as Q's own historical and structural location which may serve to deny Q those resources which are necessary for the satisfaction of certain of its interests.[42] Obstacles internal to Q include Q's lack of skill or knowledge as to how to use the resources which are in principle available to it, where this lack of skill or knowledge is not caused by the exercise of power by a specifiable agent.

A definition of political powerlessness which includes Q's inability both to promote and to defend its interests enables the researcher to study both levels of political power relationships which were noted earlier. That is, a study of Q's inability to *defend* its interests will involve an analysis of why Q is unable to prevail in the formal political decision-making process; while attention to Q's inability to *promote* its interests will entail an examination of the obstacles which prevent Q from setting the political agenda.

An empirical study of political powerlessness based on the proposed definition must begin with a conception of what constitutes Q's interests. The researcher may then seek to justify or explain his or her conception of Q's interests. The chief objective, however, is not to establish the epistemological or ontological superiority of a given set of interests, but rather to discover whether or not the interests in question have, in practice, been satisfied. Where they are found not to have been satisfied, the researcher's task is to determine whether, and in what ways, this relates to Q's powerlessness.

As well as commencing with a conception of Q's interests, it may also be useful to locate at the outset those groups (Ti) whose interests conflict with Q's, as well as the social context in which Q interacts with Ti. It may well be that Ti has exercised power over Q in defence of its own interests. Moreover, by studying the social context in which Q and Ti operate, the observer will be able to understand which power resources are in principle available, or denied, to each side. However, it must be remembered that Q's powerlessness may be due to the exercise of power by an agent altogether different from Ti, a possibility which can be tested through empirical investigation.

After noting Q's interests and discussing which agents' interests Q's interests conflict with, the researcher might look at what has taken place in those formal channels of decision-making that have a bearing on Q's interests. In particular, it would be important to establish whether Q has ever promoted its interests in these institutions. If Q is found to have promoted its interests, then the question to be answered is why Q has been unable to prevail (i.e. to defend its interests) in formal decision-making procedures. It may be that Q lacks the relevant resources for doing so. To find out whether this is the case would require some knowledge of what the 'relevant' resources are, which can be determined through a close analysis of the decision-making process, including discussions about the process with as many of its participants as possible.

However, the researcher may find that Q has *not* raised what are taken to be its interests in the relevant institutions; instead Q may be seen to have raised demands other than these interests. Rather than dismiss the raising of these demands as symptomatic of Q's 'false consciousness', the researcher must determine the extent to which Q has been able to defend its more limited interests in the formal institutions. As well as studying Q's relative ability to defend its limited interests, the researcher must tackle the question of why Q has been unable to promote what might be referred to as its 'objective', as opposed to its limited, interests in the institutions of formal decision-making. This would involve checking for past or ongoing instances of nondecision-making and paying particular (although not exclusive) attention to the actions and inactions of those actors who benefit from Q's failure to set the agenda. It can also be helpful to discuss with Q whether it recognises any agents or factors which have prohibited it from raising its objective interests in the appropriate institution.

It may be the case that even lengthy and detailed discussion with Q fails to provide the researcher with an answer to the question of why Q has not raised or satisfied its objective interests in the formal arena. The researcher might then explore the possibility that Q has failed to raise these interests because it has not recognised what they are, due to the control of information. Locating power that has been exercised through information control is most easily done from a historical perspective—that is, once the withheld information has become available for Q's use. If Q is found to pursue its interests once the withheld information becomes available to Q, then it can be asserted that power had previously been exercised. Conversely, if the availability of information produces no clear changes in Q's behaviour in relation to Q's objective interests, then the researcher must recognise the inaccuracy of the original conception of Q's objective interests. While this counterfactual method of analysis can be used most successfully in a historical study, it is sometimes possible to uncover T's control of information before Q has made that discovery, by using a comparative, rather than historical, approach.

If after following all of the above guidelines the observer cannot identify any exercise of power or other obstacle to Q's promotion and defence of its assumed interests, then the observer must conclude that the original conception of Q's objective interests was mistaken. In this sense, the hypothesised existence of political powerlessness is falsifiable through empirical analysis.

V POWERLESSNESS, INTERESTS AND THE AGRICULTURAL WORK-FORCE

If the method of studying powerlessness outlined in the previous section is to be followed here, then it will be necessary to begin the study with a clear view of what are regarded as being farmworkers' interests. For reasons which were noted in the preceding discussion concerning the study of power and powerlessness, the approach to interests which will be adopted must be one which enables the observer to identify Q's interests independently of Q's subjective judgements or behaviour. Briefly, this is because exercises of power may be such as to prevent Q from indicating or even recognising what its interests are.

In spite of the objections which the concept of 'objective interests' has raised among some scholars,[43] it is posited here that actors' objective interests can be identified successfully and usefully through what is known as a contextual approach. That is, the observer can identify an actor's interests by reference to the actor's location within a given social context. The possible problems involved in this approach will be considered in due course; here it should be noted that, because actors operate within a host of different contexts (the family unit, occupational groups, religious orders, clubs and so on), any meaningful identification of interests as derived from a contextual approach can only follow on from the prior specification of which context is under consideration.

The context which pertains to the present study of political powerlessness is that of a capitalist economy. In this particular context actors' interests are defined broadly according to the rules of profit maximisation which dictate that, *ceteris paribus*, it is in people's interests to maximise their economic returns and to minimise their costs. It should be noted that these interests are regarded as being objectively valid, irrespective of whether actors operating within a given capitalist economy appear to recognise them or act upon them.[44]

More specifically, the context that concerns the present study is that of capitalist agriculture and the actor under examination is the agricultural work-force. Farmworkers share a complex set of different interests, all of which are determined by, and apply to, the capitalist context in which they operate. The interests which will be focused on in the following chapters are: the earning of high wages for short hours of work; the enjoyment of occupational mobility and independence from their employers in all areas but the cash nexus; and the guarantee of an adequate standard of occupational health and safety. Underlining each of these interests is the principle of maximising economic benefits and minimising costs.

As with agricultural workers, so too the uppermost interests held by agricultural employers, when viewed in the context of running a capitalist enterprise, concern their ability to maximise their economic returns and to minimise their costs. This places agricultural employers in conflict with their workers for, in order to ensure low production costs and high investment returns, employers are required to impinge on their workers' interests as outlined above. Because labour is a relatively costly factor of production, it is in farmers' interests to keep their employment levels, as well as their employees' wages, as low as possible, while still maintaining a productive labour force. Furthermore, it serves farmers' interests to house their workers in tied cottages, as this allows for the continued payment of low wages while also providing employers with a 'captive' labour force. Finally, the use of effective pesticides has seen a dramatic increase in crop yields, as a consequence of which farmers are anxious to continue applying the pesticides to their crops. This practice harms the interests of agricultural workers in those cases where the pesticides injure the health of the workers who apply them. Regardless of how individual farmers and farmworkers interact with one another at a subjective level, in these three areas their relationship is characterised by an unyielding conflict of objective interests.

The advantages of identifying interests contextually in a study of power and powerlessness are two-fold. Firstly, it enables the researcher to overcome the limitations of the pluralist school and its 'second face of power' critics. The observer who uses a contextual approach can go beyond Q's subjective definition of its interests and can determine whether that subjective interpretation is itself the outcome of an exercise of power. This is possible only where the observer has a conception of Q's interests which exists independently of Q's subjective desires. At the same time, when Q's objective interests do not correspond with its subjective desires, the latter need not be brushed aside as invalid or irrelevant. On the contrary, subjective desires are of considerable significance, partly because they may be the product of power exercises; but also because Q's (in)ability to promote and defend its subjective desires is of interest in its own right in a study of powerlessness and power.

The second main advantage which accrues to a contextual approach is best explained by comparing this approach to one which ascribes a set of 'real' (in the sense of ontologically superior) interests to social actors. The problem with asserting the absolute superiority of one particular set of interests over and above all other is that it conflicts with the notion, established earlier, that actors operate within numerous contexts and hold a number of different and sometimes contradictory interests, at both a subjective and objective level. In contrast to a monolithic view of interests, which holds that one set of interests is objectively more significant or more 'real' than all others, the approach proposed here perceives one set of interests as being of overriding importance within a given context, but not as being superior to all other interests is an absolute, all-embracing sense.

In spite of the benefits which derive from a contextual approach, it is not without its internal problems. The chief objection which may be raised against this approach involves the observer's claimed ability to identify Q's interests where Q itself is allegedly unable to do so. How, if at all, can the observer justify or verify his or her conception of Q's objective interests?

Two points should be made in answer to this problem. The first is that, in the final analysis, any conception of interests will be contestable and will be derivative from the observer's own moral and political values. All that the observer can do is set out what are taken to be Q's interests within a specified context and allow others to judge whether his or her interpretation of Q's interests is plausible and acceptable.

Second, and more importantly, in the present study the concept of interests is being used heuristically and therefore does not warrant exhaustive analysis. Although it is held that in the context of capitalist agriculture farmworkers and their employers hold an objective interest in profit maximisation, whether this is in fact the case is of secondary importance. The primary objective of the study is to determine whether farmworkers have been powerless to promote and defend what are taken to be their interests and, if so, to explore the nature of their powerlessness. Where the original conception of farmworkers' interests is mistaken, the attempt to study powerlessness will reveal this misconception, as no evidence of farmworkers pursuing these interests, or of power being exercised to prevent them from doing so will be forthcoming.

The relevance of the context of capitalist agriculture to a study of farmworkers' powerlessness rests upon the fact that farmworkers are studied here as employees of a capitalist enterprise, rather than, for example, as members of the Methodist Church, country clubs or of individual families. Moreover, the specific focus of the study is the relative powerlessness of the farmworkers' union to promote and defend farmworkers' interests. A trade union is a specifically capitalist organisation, in the sense that it is designed and concerned almost exclusively to influence the distribution of valued goods within capitalist society in such a way as to maximise workers' economic gains. It would seem appropriate, therefore, to define the interests of farmworkers and their union in terms of the capitalist principle of profit maximisation.

Having established the context in which this study is set, it remains to explain the choice of farmworkers' interests which will be concentrated on in the study. Capitalism provides the agricultural labour force with a host of objective interests;

here only three are examined. The three which were chosen were selected chiefly because they are areas on which the union has campaigned for many years, with relatively little success. It is posited that a study of these particular interests will reveal a great deal about the nature of the union's powerlessness. In principle, other objective interests on which the union has been entirely silent might have been examined instead, but constraints on time and research facilities made the present course of study a preferable one to follow.

A review of farmworkers' conditions will reveal that in most cases their interests, as defined above, are not being satisfied, nor have they been for many years. Similarly, it will show that over the past forty years farmworkers and their political allies have rarely succeeded in pursuing these interests through the relevant decision-making channels. The objective of the following study is to determine what, if anything, is responsible for this failure to promote and defend farmworkers' hypothesised occupational interests within the relevant political institutions. To begin to understand this phenomenon, it will be useful to consider the social and economic context in which farmworkers and their employers operate and interact with one another, and to outline the power resources which this context makes available to these two groups.

NOTES

1 Dahl, R. (1969), 'The concept of power' in R. Bell. D. Edwards and R. Harrison Walker (eds), *Political Power*, The Free Press, New York, p. 79; Partridge, P. H. (1963), 'Some notes on the concept of power', *PS*, 11, p. 107; Giddens, A. (1979), *Central Problems in Social Theory*, Macmillan, London, p. 68; Wrong, D. H. (1979), *Power*, Blackwell, Southampton, p. 253; Elster, J. (1976), *Some conceptual problems in political theory'* in B. Barry (ed.), *Power and Political Theory*, Wiley, Bath, p. 249; Galbraith, J. K. (1984), *The Anatomy of Power*, Hamilton, London, preface.
2 Gaventa, J. (1980), *Power and Powerlessness*, University of Illinois, Chicago, provides a notable and excellent exception to this.
3 Mokken, R. J. and Stokman, F. N. (1976), 'Power and influence as political phenomena', in B. Barry (ed.), *op. cit.*, p. 48.
4 Polsby, N. (1980), *Community Power and Political Theory*, second edition, Yale University, London, pp. 4–5.
5 Dahl, R. (1961), *Who Governs?*, Yale University, New Haven, p. 93.
6 *Ibid.*, p. 92; Polsby, *op. cit.*, pp. 123–4.
7 Cf. Floyd Hunter's study of power, (1953), *Community Power Structure*, University of North Carolina, Chapel Hill.

8   Dahl, *op. cit.*, p. 279.
9   *Ibid.*, p. 101.
10 *Ibid.*, pp. 163–65.
11 *Ibid.*, p. 336.
12 *Ibid.*, p. 226.
13 *Ibid.*, p. 228.
14 Bachrach, P. and Baratz, M. (1962), 'The two faces of power', *APSR*, 56, p. 948.
15 Polsby, *op. cit.*, pp. 120-1.
16 Dahl, *op. cit.*, p. 93.
17 Polsby, *op. cit.*, p. 191.
18 Schattschneider, E. E. (1960), *The Semisovereign People*, The Dryden Press, Hinsdale, p. 69.
19 Bachrach, P. and Baratz, M. (1970), *Power and Poverty*, Oxford University Press, New York, p. 44.
20 *Ibid.*, pp. 44-6.
21 Bachrach, P. and Baratz, M. (1975), 'Power and its two faces revisited', *APSR*, 69, p. 904.
22 Bachrach, P. and Baratz, M. (1970), *Power and Poverty*, Oxford University Press, New York, p. 46.
23 *Ibid.*, pp. 47-9.
24 *Ibid.*, p. 49.
25 Bachrach, P. and Baratz, M. (1975), 'Power and its two faces revisited', *APSR*, 69, p. 904.
26 Bachrach, P. and Baratz, M. (1963), 'Decisions and nondecisions', *APSR*, 57, p. 641.
27 Bachrach and Baratz, *Power and Poverty*, p. 49.
28 N. Polsby is a particularly strong defender of this thesis.
29 Bachrach and Baratz, *Power and Poverty*, p. 50.
30 Lukes, S. (1974), *Power: a Radical View*, Macmillan, London, p. 24.
31 *Ibid.*, p. 23.
32 See Barry, B. (1975), 'The obscurities of power', *Government and Opposition*, 20, p. 251.
33 Balbus, I. (1970-71), 'The concept of interest in pluralist and Marxian analysis', *Politics and Society*, 1, pp. 168-9.
34 Goldthorpe, J., 'Social Structure, Interests and Political Partianship', xerox; Hindess, B. (1982), 'Power, interests and the outcomes of struggles', *S* 16, (4), p. 509.
35 For further reading on the important debate on 'power and interests' see Lukes, *op. cit.*, pp. 46-50; Bradshaw, A. (1976), 'A critique of S. Lukes' "Power: a radical view" ', *S*, 10 (and Lukes's reply); Benton, T. (1981), 'Objective interests and the Sociology of Power', *S*, 15; Hindess, B. (1975), 'On three dimensional power', *PS*, 24, (especially comments on p. 330); Bloch, M., Heading, B. and Lawrence, P. (1979), 'Power in social theory' in S. C. Brown (ed.), *Philosophical Disputes in the Social Sciences*, Harvester; Saunders, P. (1979), *Urban Politics*, Hutchinson, London; Parenti, M. (1978), *Power and the Powerless*, St Martins, New York.
36 Lukes, *op. cit.*, p. 51.
37 Crenson, M. (1971), *The Un-politics of Air Pollution*, John Hopkins, Baltimore, p. 77.
38 Cf. Flatham, R. E. (1980), *The Practice of Political Authority*,

University of Chicago, Chicago/London, Chapter 7; Wrong, *op. cit.*, pp. 252-3.
39 Lukes, *op. cit.*, pp. 55-6.
40 Cf. Connolly's contention that power and moral responsibility are integrally related concepts. Connolly, W. E. (1983), *The Terms of Political Discourse*, second edition, Martin Robertson, Oxford, p. 131 and pp. 214-5.
41 Lukes, S. (1977), 'Power and structure' in Lukes, S., *Essays in Social Theory*, Columbia University, New York, pp. 9-13.
42 Saunders, *op. cit.*, p. 23; McEachern, D. (1980), *A Class Against Itself*, Cambridge University Press, p. 100; Therborn, G. (1982), 'What does the ruling class do when it rules?' in Giddens and Held (eds), *Classes, Power and Conflict*, Macmillan, Basingstoke, p. 230.
43 See note 35.
44 Newby, H., Bell, C., Rose, D. and Saunders, P. (1978), *Property, Paternalism and Power*, Hutchinson, London, p. 244.

Chapter 2

Farming in post-war England

I FEATURES OF THE CONTEMPORARY AGRICULTURAL INDUSTRY

Patterns of farmland ownership

In England, where private property is a long-established and widely respected institution, the ownership of farmland displays a unique attraction. In one sense farmland is a highly flexible resource for, depending on how it is combined with other resources, it is capable of producing an impressive variety of marketable commodities. On the other hand, land contrasts with the two other chief factors of production, capital and labour, because of its physical immobility and the natural limits set on its availability. These two features of land as a resource—its versatility and natural fixity of supply—have together given rise to a fierce competition over its ownership, particularly among investors who are attracted by the security of a resource which cannot easily be stolen or destroyed.[1]

In spite of the economic and social importance of land ownership patterns there is a dearth of information on this subject.[2] This fact creates obvious difficulties for any attempt to conduct informed debate on the issue, forcing most discussions to rely on conjecture and estimates. There is, however, at least one feature of contemporary farmland ownership which can be commented upon without reservation, and that is its extreme concentration. Almost 80 per cent of England's entire land space is given over to agricultural purposes and this entire area is owned by no more than 2 per cent of the entire population. As much as 90 per cent of this small minority comprises private individuals or groups, with the remaining 10 per cent being constituted by institutions which range from the Church and the Crown, to more recent landed interests, such as insurance companies and pension funds.[3]

The Agricultural Revolution of the eighteenth century initiated a trend towards concentrated land ownership, as yeoman freeholders were gradually forced to sell their land to those who could afford the large-scale investment and technological innovation which marked the beginning of the commercialisation of England's agriculture. The enclosure movement, whose increased momentum in the eighteenth century was another by-product of the Agricultural Revolution and a symptom of agriculture's commercialisation, also influenced the pattern of farmland ownership as it brought about the transfer of common land to the private ownership of established landowners. By the late eighteenth century, and throughout the nineteenth and early twentieth centuries, much of England's farmland was owned by a handful of large landlords who rented it out to tenant farmers who, in turn, hired agricultural workers to work the land.[4]

The second half of the twentieth century has seen a marked movement away from this three-tiered structure of 'landlord–tenant farmer–worker' towards increased owner-occupation, as the large landowners have sold parts of their estates to new owners who often remain on the land to farm it themselves, sometimes with the help of hired labour. In 1950 only 36 per cent of agricultural holdings in England and Wales were owner-occupied, but by 1982 as much as 69 per cent of Britain's holdings were wholly or partly owned by their occupiers.[5] Moreover, numerous studies have shown that the proportion of owner-occupation in Britain is considerably higher than the official figures indicate, standing today somewhere in the region of 75–80 per cent. The explanation for this discrepancy is that in order to avoid high taxation, and to enjoy maximum benefits from public grants to agricultural enterprise, farmers transfer on paper the ownership of their land to trusts, companies and partnerships which, unlike the private farmer, are eligible for grants and greater tax exemptions.[6]

Although owner-occupation has become increasingly widespread over the past forty years, there are signs that the pattern of farmland ownership may return once again in favour of the tenant farmer and away from owner-occupation. The cause for this possible reversal lies in the recent increase in institutional landownership through which land is being leased by what are essentially non-agricultural farm owners to a new generation of tenant farmers. At present, institutional land ownership is a relatively small-scale phenomenon with the only significantly growing trend being the steady purchase of top quality land by financial institutions; roughly half of all farmland placed on the market each year is bought by financial organisations. However, if present rates continue, the re-emergence of tenant farming through increased institutional land ownership will be a slow development; financial institutions currently own only 2 per cent of all farmland and their opportunities for increasing this share are limited, given that only 2 per cent of farmland is put onto the open market each year.[7]

A more immediate and tangible consequence of the City's incursion into the agricultural land market has been, until very recently, a rocketing of land prices and rents.[8] As increasing amounts of capital have been pumped into the land by its new wealthy owners, its price has risen accordingly, for increased investment inflates the value and hence the price of the original resource. This price inflation has been enhanced by the determination of the City institutions to buy more land, almost regardless of the cost. Prior to the Second World War the price of agricultural land sold with vacant possession was £25 per acre; by 1970 it was £250; thirteen years later the price per acre had almost reached the £2,000 mark. Although there are signs in the late 1980s that the quest for farmland may be abating, the effects of the recent agricultural land market boom are still being felt, particularly among tenant farmers. Farmland rents doubled between 1970 and 1976 alone, and rose further each subsequent year to reach a peak in 1978-79 when the average rent increase was 55 per cent. Rents continue to be set at high rates and many tenant farmers are still struggling with the debts incurred through the rapid rent increases of the 1970s and early 1980s. Yet the social and economic attractions of a farming life have so far continued to guarantee to landowners a willing market of both tenants and buyers, despite the recent soaring of rents and prices and the likely recurrence of this pattern in coming years.

Divisions of region, sector and farm size

The price of farmland varies to some extent according to its quality, which is classified by the Ministry of Agriculture, Fisheries, and Food (MAFF) into five grades. The majority of the country's best quality land is to be found in the East,

South-East and East Midlands, while poorer quality land predominates in the highland area. This division of the country in terms of land quality is paralleled by other regional differences which correspond similarly to the two areas on either side of a line drawn between the mouth of the River Tees and the River Exe in the South-West. For example, the lowland zone enjoys considerably more sunshine and less rainfall than the upland zone, a factor which combines with the properties of the area's soil to lend the region to lucrative arable farming. Its profitability has acted like a magnet, drawing large sums of capital investment which have brought in turn an increase in sophistication in the methods of husbandry employed by farmers and farmworkers in the region. Farms in this area tend to be larger than their highland counterparts and are generally more dependent upon hired labour and on modern methods of farm management.

Conversely, the highland farming zone is characterised predominantly by dairy farming, which is less dependent than cropping on top quality soil, and for which the relatively high rainfall levels are less problematic. Farms in this area tend to be smaller and less mechanised than in the East and South-East and the absence of intensive capital investment here has seen the continued reliance upon family labour with non-family workers being hired to a large extent on a part-time or casual basis.

It would be misleading to portray England's agriculture as entirely classifiable along this geographical divide between the highlands and lowlands. There is a sprinkling of dairy farms in the lowlands, just as there are arable farms to be found in the West and North of the country. Moreover, there are variations between farms that cut across these differences of climate, region and farm type; these include the farm's eligibility for grants, its proximity to towns and to food processing companies, and the wealth of its owner. Each of these variables can help to determine what will be grown on the farm, how profitable it will be and, most significantly for the purposes of this study, how much and what kind of labour will be employed. By and large, however, the agricultural pattern which prevailed 100 years ago continues today, with the line between the highlands and lowlands representing a multidimensional divide between these two areas.[10]

Farms differ in what they produce as well as in their sizes and, as the above classification suggests, these two variables are to some extent inter-related. Specialist dairy farms, as well as cattle-rearing and sheep-rearing farms are important among the country's small farms, while very few of the large farms would involve themselves with these enterprises. Conversely, farms with only one or two casual workers and with a relatively limited area of land would seldom engage in specialist cropping which is the stronghold of the large South-Eastern farms.[11] This relationship between farm size and farm type makes a nonsense of generalisations about the 'typical English farm' in terms either of size or of produce. Nevertheless, certain overall trends in farm size can be distinguished, most notably the movement since the 1950s towards fewer, larger farms.[12] The continuing reduction in the number of small farms has been matched by the growing size of those farms which remain, a trend explained by the fact that most farmland purchases are made by existing landowners who wish to expand their enterprises.[13]

Farm amalgamation has gone hand-in-hand with a trend towards farm specialisation. The number of enterprises per farm has been reduced on virtually all types of farm, with the result that it is increasingly uncommon to find a farmer interested equally in cropping and in livestock.[14] The mixed-farm enterprise is rapidly becoming a feature of the past, when farmers were forced to spread their risks. Today, the combination of machinery, technology, biological engineering and financial support from the state has enabled the farmer to concentrate his time, energy and capital on a single enterprise.[15]

Not surprisingly, large farm enterprises have become increasingly important in terms of output. In 1983, for example, the top 13 per cent of farms in terms of size accounted for roughly half of the industry's entire output.[16] This trend has given rise to speculation about what the most fitting future for the 'small farm' should be[17]—a category which still predominates numerically in the UK.[18] (In 1981, 96,000 of the UK's 235,000 agricultural holdings were smaller than 20 hectares, whereas only 30,000 were larger than 100 hectares.) The small farm is commonly divided into two categories: the minority group of highly efficient, intensively run small farms; and the more common small farms which make only a relatively minor contribution to the national production of food. For some commentators, the 'small farm problem' is based on the belief that these comparatively unprofitable enterprises constitute a waste of national resources.

It is held that if these farms were amalgamated into fewer, larger farms, there would be an overall higher volume of agricultural output at an overall lower cost in manpower and capital.[19] This argument assumes that maximum farm output and minimum expenditure of both labour and capital are in themselves desirable features of the production process. While these assumptions are valid in certain situations, in the context of surplus agricultural production and a shortage of alternative employment opportunities for displaced small farmers, they are regarded as being mistaken by at least some participants in the debate. It is this question of interpretation that explains the wide range of proposed solutions to the small farm problem.[20]

One principle on which most people do agree, however, is the influence, for better or worse, of contemporary state intervention in determining the shape of the farming industry. This consensus over the role of the state in Britain's agricultural industry stems from the fact that ever since the Second World War the government of the day has been actively involved in the development of the farming sector, not least through the provision of financial support in an attempt to induce maximum production levels.

II THE POLITICAL ECONOMY OF AGRICULTURE

Government policy 1945–73

The Second World War was highly instrumental in initiating Britain's present agricultural support system. The seige economy and food rationing which the war gave rise to forced the country over a short period of time to replace its heavy dependency on food imports with a greater capacity for self-sufficiency. This development was made possible by the close co-operation forged between the government and the farmers. On the one hand, the government assumed far-reaching control over agricultural production to ensure the expansion of output and the satisfaction of needs which had developed from the war situation. Self and Storing explain that

Compulsory cropping orders were issued, neglected and derelict land was reclaimed, inefficient farmers were evicted. Large numbers of pigs, poultry and cattle had to be slaughtered because feeding-stuffs could not be spared to keep them, although milk production was maintained for nutritional reasons . . . The whole pattern of farming was drastically changed, and unusual efforts and sacrifices demanded of farmers.[21]

On the other hand, farmers benefited from the measures dictated by the war, particularly as these included the introduction of 'fairly generous guaranteed prices' for whatever they could produce.

The emergency measures taken during the war were successful, for the production of food was dramatically increased over a short period of time. (For example, the UK produced over 30 per cent of its wheat in 1946–47, compared with only 21 per cent in 1940–41, and doubled its production of potatoes in the same period.[22]) After the war the urgency of being self-sufficient diminished, although rations continued until well into the 1950s. Yet the country's politicians continued to be haunted by the possibility that a major war or disaster could recur, bringing with it food shortages and the social and political upheaval which food rationing inevitably creates. Consequently, the newly elected Labour government set itself the task of increasing Britain's long-term ability to feed itself. To this end it introduced a system of agricultural support which was in keeping with its more general commitment to the principle of market regulation [23]

The Labour government's chief objectives in the sphere of agricultural policy were embodied in the *Agriculture Act* 1947. This Act required the Minister of Agriculture to conduct an annual review of the economic conditions and prospects of agriculture together with representatives from the industry, on the basis of which the Ministry would set guaranteed fixed prices for a given list of commodities, which covered 80 per cent of total output.[24] The Act committed the Minister to provide

a stable and efficient agricultural industry capable of producing such part of the nation's food and other agricultural produce as in the national interest it is desirable to produce in the United Kingdom, and of producing it at minimum prices consistently with proper remuneration and living conditions for farmers and workers in agriculture and an adequate return on capital invested in the industry.

The support system which the *Agriculture Act* 1947 inaugurated operated in such a way that agricultural produce was bought from the farmers by the state (through the Ministry of Food) at a guaranteed price, and then sold to the consumer at a controlled retail price. The ultimate purpose of this system was to encourage farmers to expand their production levels as far as possible, a task which was facilitated by the fact that farmers were now guaranteed by government fixed prices for virtually whatever they produced. As well as being protected from sudden depressions in the market in this way, farmers were also shielded from drastic increases in production costs, through the annual review which was pledged to take such increases into account each year when it set the fixed price for agricultural commodities.

When the Conservative Party was elected to government in 1951 the comprehensive scheme of state support to agriculture which Labour had introduced came under attack. In a sense the 1947 Act had worked too well. The newly elected Conservative government was disturbed by the rising levels of agricultural output which, by the early 1950s, had reached a point of excess in certain commodity areas. In response to this situation, the government introduced 'standard quantities', a device which limited the Exchequer's commitment to supporting only a predetermined quantum of output of milk, eggs and potatoes. The system worked in such a way that if producers exceeded the specified quantum they were penalised by a reduction in the value of the guaranteed price payable to them.[25] This mechanism acted as an effective brake in production levels, which only a few years earlier farmers had been encouraged to expand.

Of even greater concern to the Conservative government than the over-production of food was the burgeoning cost of agricultural support to the taxpayer. A movement towards decontrol would be in keeping with the government's ideological commitment to 'free' competition and, more significantly, it would help to reduce the rapidly growing financial burden of agricultural support which weighed so heavily upon the Treasury. By 1953–54 the cost of agricultural support to the taxpayer was in the order of £200 million, and by 1954–55 it was approaching £250 million.[26] The new programme of streamlining the state's relationship with the farming industry culminated in the *Agriculture Act* 1957, which provided a mechanism through which the government could gradually reduce its commitment to farm support, without leaving the fate of the farmers entirely to the mercies of the free market. This compromise was made possible by a clause in the Act which stated that the determination of prices would be such 'as to maintain the total value of the guarantees at not less than 97·5 per cent of their total value in the preceding year after allowing for cost changes'. In effect, this meant that the cost of support could be reduced by up to 12 per cent over a five-year period, giving the government a certain release from its earlier total commitment to agricultural support.

The enormous cost which the taxpayer had incurred since the war through the agricultural support system should not overshadow the concomitant expansion in production which had been achieved. In 1938–39 the value of total agricultural gross output in the UK was £295 million; by the end of the year it was £624·5 million; within six years it had risen to £1,071·5 million and by 1961–62 the figure stood at £1,604 million.[27] Production continued to rise throughout the 1960s, which were years of mild turbulence in the farming community as governments made repeated attempts at cutting the cost of the support system in the face of strenuous opposition from the farmers.[28] Apart from periodic disagreements over the appropriate level of support, however, there was broad agreement over the principle of agricultural support which, after twenty years, had become a largely welcomed fact of life for most agriculturalists. The deficiency payments system satisfied the non-farming public to a considerable extent, too, chiefly because it sustained a 'cheap food' policy. The difference between the market price and the guaranteed price of a commodity was paid to farmers by the Treasury rather than through artificially inflated prices, leaving the taxpayer, rather than the consumer, to bear the brunt of the agricultural support machine. In this way, the system had a less 'noticeable' effect on the average person's purse than other means of support might have had.[29]

By the mid-1960s, however, major drawbacks in the deficiency payments system had begun to surface. One problem which affected the farming industry directly was the way in which deficiency payments had created a growing division between large, highly productive farms and the smaller, more marginal ones. The existing gulf between these two groups had been exacerbated by deficiency payments, which favoured the large farms in that payments were made per unit produced, and the large farms tended to produce more units than did the small farms. The imbalance of the system was evident by the early 1960s, when three-fifths of deficiency payments (in terms of value) were being allocated to only one-fifth of farmers. In view of this trend, the 1960s saw piecemeal attempts by successive Ministers of Agriculture to restore a degree of equilibrium to the structure of the industry. In particular, subsidies were paid increasingly in the form of grants rather than deficiency payments, and the small farm became the focus of numerous policy reforms which attempted (without great success) to revive the small-scale end of the industry.

A second problem inherent in the system of deficiency payments to agriculture had significant repercussions on the wider, non-agricultural public. The only way in which the existing system could be maintained by the Treasury was for Britain to enforce some form of controls on the food which it imported from abroad. This was necessary because an influx of cheap foreign food would immediately depress market prices, causing the gap between market price and guaranteed price to widen, which, in turn, would place an increased strain upon Treasury funds. To prevent this sort of situation from arising, the government instituted a 'minimum import price' system which operated in a similar fashion to import tariffs—namely, by restricting Britain's trading policy in favour of domestic products. While this programme succeeded in its aim of avoiding a tremendous fall in the market price of food and a consequent squeeze on Treasury funds, it marked an end to the earlier commitment to supplying the consumer with the cheapest food available on the 'free' market.

The most significant development in British agricultural policy since the passing of the *Agriculture Act* 1947 occurred in 1973 when Britain joined the European Economic Community (EEC). Yet, although Britain's membership of the EEC gave rise to substantial changes in the particular manner by which agriculture was supported, it never at any time threatened the widely held belief that agriculture must receive *some* form of far-reaching financial support from the state. The fact is that since 1947 the principle of state intervention in agriculture has never been seriously challenged in government circles, regardless of which party has formed the government and which the opposition. This continuity of policy and principle is remarkable, not least because a commitment to large-scale agricultural support represents a contradiction to certain basic ideological principles of both main parties. For the Conservatives, extensive state aid to agriculture conflicts with the party's profound commitment to *laissez-faire* economics. For the Labour Party it constitutes a diversion of public money which might be better spent on nationalised industries and other common goods rather than on 'lining the pockets' of private entrepreneurs. Why, then, have successive governments continued to uphold the principle and practice of agricultural support? Part of the explanation lies in the role played by the National Farmers' Union, an organisation whose importance in the farming world merits some analysis.

The National Farmers' Union

The membership of the National Farmers' Union (NFU) covers 80 per cent of all full-time farmers in England and Wales.[30] This is a high proportion of potential members for any voluntary organisation, but is particularly impressive in the NFU, given the great diversity of interests and outlooks that exists among farmers.[31] Unity is maintained within the union through its democratic centralism in which full discussion is officially encouraged at the 866 branches and 49 county branches, but binding decisions are taken by the nationally elected Council once it has considered the resolutions sent in by the branches.[32] Although signs of strain emerge periodically within the organisation, the NFU has so far maintained a cohesive front behind which its annually elected leadership can work for a better deal for 'Britain's farmer'.[33]

Overall, the NFU has achieved considerable gains for its members as well as providing them with a vast range of day-to-day services. It offers them legal advice on all matters relating to the agricultural industry; it monitors the town and country planning system as it affects members; in certain cases it pursues tax problems on behalf of its members; it publicises the 'farmers' case' via the mass media; it studies all legislation of relevance to agriculture, lobbying MPs for changes where they are deemed desirable; and it works closely with the Ministry of Agriculture on various agricultural issues.[34] The NFU, with a staff of over 300, is able to pursue this diverse programme in part because of its financial strength. As well as members' subscriptions (in

1983 they were £28 a year plus 40 pence per acre), the NFU is provided with generous donations from many of its wealthier members. Thus, in 1983, its income was over £8 million, on top of which the NFU enjoys an income from its capital investments, such as a 75 per cent stake in the Fatstock Marketing Corporation, which in 1980–81 had a turnover of £535 million.[35]

The NFU's successful pursuit of its members' interests in high economic gain has drawn a host of comments from observers of the agricultural scene. Graham Wilson views the NFU as '. . . arguably the best and organisationally strongest of western agricultural interest groups'[36] and Howard Newby confirms this image of strength when he refers to the NFU as '. . . undoubtedly one of the most successful pressure groups in Britain'.[37] A similar view is put forward by Wyn Grant, who suggests that, 'The measurement of pressure group effectiveness is a notoriously difficult task, but if one was to abandon academic caution and draw up a short-list of the most effective pressure groups in Britain, the National Farmers' Union would surely be at the top of that list.'[38]

Virtually all commentators attribute the NFU's political and economic success to its close relationship with the Ministry of Agriculture, Fisheries, and Food (MAFF).[39] This relationship is of undoubted importance if for no other reason than that the NFU has concentrated so much of its energy and resources on its cultivation. Over the years the NFU's links with MAFF have developed into a virtually symbiotic relationship, in which the NFU expects MAFF to initiate and implement favourable policies in return for which the NFU co-operates and assists the Ministry in their execution. The strength of this corporatist relationship derives to a considerable extent from its legal and historical foundations.

The *Agriculture Act* 1947 is central to contemporary agricultural politics because it established obligatory annual negotiations over price support levels between the Minister of Agriculture and representatives of the country's farmers. The fact that the NFU was (and remains) the sole representative of farmers provided the NFU with regular and legally sanctioned access to the corridors of Whitehall, a privilege which it retains to this day.[40] The Ministry benefited too from the NFU's role as the farmers' sole recognised representative. Once the Ministry had obtained the NFU's endorsement for its proposed policies, it could be assured of the co-operation of virtually all farmers in their implementation, since the NFU represented and advised the great bulk of the country's farmers. Thus, both the NFU and MAFF drew advantages from the provisions of the *Agriculture Act* 1947 which had paved the way for a close relationship between the two parties. The failure of any government to repeal the 1947 legislation has given the NFU the opportunity to cement its relations with MAFF so that they are no longer confined to the annual review meetings. As Marion Shoard suggeests, 'The Union now has a hand in almost every step the Ministry takes'.[41]

The importance attached by most observers to the NFU's links with MAFF in explaining the continual servicing of farmers' demands by government has often obscured other important sources of political influence which are available to the NFU. For example, although the NFU aims generally to remain 'above party political divisions', it nevertheless becomes involved in pressure politics whenever legislation pertaining to its interests passes through parliament. The NFU lobbies all MPs (and Lords) but concentrates naturally on those who appear to be most sympathetic to its case. Although this tends to be primarily Conservative politicians this is not always the case, as subsequent chapters will demonstrate. At the national level, the NFU has a sophisticated lobbying machine which circulates information sheets to all MPs, putting across the NFU's views on particular issues in clear and forceful terms. The NFU also promotes its interests by discussing them with MPs over lunches and dinners, and in 'Gentlemen's Clubs' where the atmosphere is usually more congenial than it is in the corridors of Westminster. In particular, the NFU enjoys strong links with its 'natural' allies—those MPs and Lords who are themselves farmers. In 1981 there were as many as ninety-two MPs with declared interests in farming and the vast majority of them were farmers and/or landowners.[42]

Just as significant as these links at the national level are the ties which the NFU county and branch officials have established with their (mainly Conservative) local MPs. The use of these ties in securing farmers' interests has proven to be so efficient that the Confederation of British Industries (CBI) has adopted in recent years many of the NFU's lobbying tactics.[43] It comes as something of a surprise then to find that most commentators have neglected the local dimension of the NFU's activities.

While the NFU has proven to be an adept force in the field of pressure politics, none of the points made so far can explain why MPs and Lords of all political persuasions, both rural and urban, have voted so often in favour of policies that are clearly designed to serve farmers' interests, often at the cost of more electorally significant groups. Indeed, in terms of electoral strength, the farmers are a fairly insignificant sector, whose support is, at best, of marginal importance to the main political parties. A perusal of the 1981 Census confirms the downward trend in farmers' voting power which was noted by various writers in 1959, 1962 and 1969. The Census reveals that by the early 1980s only twenty-eight constituencies in England and Wales had over 10 per cent of their normally resident population over the age of 16 years employed (or self-employed) in agriculture, forestry or fishing. In spite of this, farmers' political successes in the 1980s have remained in general at their consistently high level of the 1950s, 1960s and 1970s, suggesting that their political influence is not related in any meaningful sense to their electoral clout.[44]

Although the NFU's relationship with MAFF and its competence in pressure politics have proved to be important resources of power, the NFU's record of political successes is inexplicable until one considers the economic significance of agriculture and the implications which this has had for the NFU's ability to promote and defend its interests.

The role of agriculture in the post-war economy

Ever since the Second World War successive British governments have been anxious to maintain a prosperous agricultural industry. They have shown themselves to be willing to do this by continuing the increasingly expensive policy of agricultural support laid down by the *Agriculture Act* 1947. The original impetus behind the introduction of agricultural support was removed in the 1950s and 1960s by the development of new methods of waging war, which made a conventional international war involving a blockade of Britain a relic of the past. While the proliferation of nuclear weapons removed the urgency of agricultural self-sufficiency in terms of military considerations, state support for agriculture nonetheless continued without serious interruption.

The new justification for agricultural support is based

entirely upon economic arguments. Both main political parties recognise that a high level of domestic food production can provide a significant contribution to Britain's balance of payments, and both parties concur that this is a valuable asset that can and should be exploited. The argument is that as long as Britain's agricultural industry is properly supported, it will continue to produce ever-increasing quantities of the nation's food requirements, thereby saving on imports as well as being capable of providing commodities for export purposes. This fiscal boon assists the national economy by protecting it from what is perhaps the single greatest post-war economic bogy—a balance of payments crisis.[45] Few politicians have challenged the logic or principles underlying this argument, as a result of which there has been little debate since the war between rival policy-makers over the principle of agricultural support.[46]

What is interesting for the purposes of the present study is that this virtually unanimous and unwavering dedication to the goal of maximum agricultural production has provided the NFU with tremendous political leverage. On the one hand, the NFU is able to influence government policy by putting forward proposals that it regards as conducive to increased production. The government may well accept such proposals, given that it shares the NFU's interests in increasing agricultural production. More commonly, the NFU has been able to force governments to withdraw, or reform, their own policy proposals when these proposals are regarded by the NFU as threatening the interests of farmers. This has been done by arguing against the given proposals in terms of their threat to production levels, to the balance of payments and, ultimately, to the national interest. Few governments have withstood such criticism and warning; instead they have usually bowed to what they presume is the NFU's superior knowledge of agricultural matters and withdrawn or reformed their proposed policies accordingly. It is by using their political and economic resources in this way that the NFU has been able to defend and promote its members' interests in maximum profit-making so successfully.[47]

In return for the state's fidelity and its co-operation over farmers' interests, the agricultural industry has fulfilled its obligation to produce an ever-expanding volume of output. From a self-sufficiency level of 30 per cent in the pre-war years, there was an increase to almost double that amount (54 per cent by 1972, despite the fact that there was also a

20 per cent increase in the number of people to be fed over that period). By 1982, home-produced food represented over 60 per cent of all food consumed in the UK as well as providing £7,583 million worth of exports.[48]

In a sense a degree of state aid is essential for maintaining these impressive production levels. Despite technological and scientific advancement, the vagaries of the weather still determine, to some extent, the level of agricultural output. Without strong government support to cover for the possible and actual years of poor harvest (and, to a lesser degree, the periodic outbreaks of epidemics among livestock) farmers would be unwilling to invest their own capital and labour in high input/high output enterprises. As it is, the continuity and reliability of government support provides a stability to the industry which encourages farmers to invest their own resources, to plan ahead, and so to produce commodities on a large scale.

The support which farmers enjoy comes in a wide variety of forms, including tax concessions, rates relief, grants, government subsidies and the free research, advice and training services which are provided by MAFF.[49] These perks and benefits add up to a total value of £4,000,000,000 per year, a hefty sum which helps to explain why agriculture has acted as a magnet for some of the country's wealthiest investors. Capital tends to accumulate where other capital is already available to finance innovations and, as Clutterbuck and Lang note, agriculture provides precisely this sort of investment opportunity.[50] Most notable are the large and numerous bank loans made available to agriculture, usually in preference to other industrial enterprises. In 1983, for example, MAFF reported that the level of bank loans to the farming industry had reached £4,670 million.[51] Farmers, especially those who run large farms, experience few difficulties in securing these bank loans to pay for increasingly expensive land, machinery and farm supplies because their creditors are virtually guaranteed repayment due to the state's protective attitude towards the industry.

The Common Agricultural Policy 1973-84

The most substantial support which governments have provided to agriculture has been in the form of state intervention in the agricultural market. Until 1973 this was carried out by the deficiency payments system, as explained above. After Britain joined the EEC, deficiency payments were replaced by a support system in which the Community 'buys' from farmers all agricultural produce whose price on the 'open' market falls below a predetermined intervention level. Once the market restores the price of the commodity to being above that level the stored produce which the EEC has 'bought' is released onto the market for sale at or above the intervention level. To support this method of price control the EEC enforces a system of high tariffs on non-EEC imports into EEC countries.[52] In effect, the Common Agricultural Policy (CAP) of the EEC provides farmers in Britain with higher prices than those that had previously been guaranteed by the Treasury. The old system had over-loaded the Treasury, which had subsidised Britain's farmers through tax revenue; conversely, the new system has shifted the burden of agricultural support from the taxpayer onto the consumer, who now pays higher prices for food than previously.[53]

A full two-thirds of the EEC's budget is spent on sustaining the CAP, an allocation of Community resources which has relatively favourable consequences for the national populations of countries such as Greece, Italy and France, which have 28·8 per cent, 14·9 per cent and 8·9 per cent of their respective populations engaged in agriculture.[54] By contrast, the policy appears to be less than rational for Britain to pursue, given that only 2·6 per cent of the British population is employed directly in agriculture (including hired farm-workers as well as self-employed farmers). Even if the 5·4 per cent of the population employed in the allied industries is included,[55] then still only 8 per cent of the entire British population can be said to benefit from the £1,300 million spent annually by the EEC on British agriculture in the form of subsidies and grants. Meanwhile, the rest of the population, far from benefiting from the CAP, are paying more for their food than before 1973. It is this imbalance of cost and benefit relating to the CAP that has led some commentators to argue that the CAP is contrary to all British interests except for the farmers', and that a policy more in line with Britain's industrial structure is required.[56]

In practice, not all of Britain's farmers benefit equally from the CAP's extensive funding because, like the deficiency payments system before it, the CAP works primarily to the advantage of the large agricultural producers. Although EEC farm prices are set at a relatively high level so as to help both small and large producers (since all prices are the same for each commodity and all producers receive the same aid per unit produced), the system ends up paying most to the farmers who produce most.[57]

The most controversial feature of the CAP is its creation of food surpluses—the notorious butter mountains and wine lakes, the stockpiles of cheese, beef, wheat, milk and pigmeat.[58] These surpluses are inherent in the present CAP support system which, in order to maintain high food prices in the context of abundant and ever-increasing food production, operates by taking growing quantities of food off of the market and putting it into storage so as to raise artificially the market price of the food. The stored food is then withheld from the market until the prices have risen to above the intervention level. However, because this level is not always reached, the surplus food is often either destroyed or exported to non-EEC countries at 'knock-down' prices so as to prevent it from rotting away altogether in the EEC's storage buildings. The very process of making these food surpluses affordable to non-EEC countries has proven to be a costly operation, costing the EEC £6,000,000,000 in 1980 alone. By 1984 the point had been reached where the promise of a good harvest and high output presented a serious problem for EEC Agriculture Ministers. The absurdity of the situation was underlined by one observer who advised the CAP Ministers that they 'should not consider bankruptcy too soon. Almost anything could happen in the way of drought, flood or disease to reduce the problem to manageable proportions.'[59]

It may be that 1984–85 marked a turning point in the CAP's costly system of overproduction which has so far benefited ostensibly only the Community's farmers. In April 1984 the EEC took its first major step towards reducing the Community's surpluses, when it announced that the Community's production of milk would have to be reduced in each member state by a specified amount. In Britain the quota required a 6·5 per cent reduction on 1983 milk production levels, a stipulation which provoked predictably angry responses from most diary farmers. Their hostility to the measure failed, however, to prevent the national government from enforcing it.

The question which all agriculturalists are asking themselves is whether the milk quota scheme represents the thin end of a wider ranging programme, the aim of which would be to 'rationalise' the EEC's food production policy. The NFU has clearly anticipated such a programme, and indeed pre-empted it in an unprecedented public recognition that

> increasing output through the European Community has made it harder to find commercial outlets and the need to dispose of surpluses of some commodities has put a heavy cost on the Community's budget. The pressure to control spending on the Common Agricultural Policy calls for a reappraisal of the expansionist approach.[60]

Although the NFU made this concession in principle, it joined other European farmers' organisations in expressing its outrage at the EEC's new proposals in 1985 for reforming the CAP. These proposals included a shift in the use of cash resources from price supports to aiding poorer farmers; price cuts in the cereal sector; and changes in the EEC's protectionist policies. The overall aim is clear: a large-scale reduction in the Community's output of food and in the enormous amount of capital that has been spent on creating and then destroying that output. Such a reform, if passed, would lead to other changes, which could include a fall in land prices and a possible return to a more labour-intensive rather than capital-intensive farming industry.[61]

However, there is no guarantee that the EEC's radical proposals will be adopted in the near future. On the contrary, most observers doubt whether it will win the support of farm Ministers, let alone the farmers' lobby. Moreover, if such changes were to be implemented, that in itself would be a costly operation, as the milk quotas of 1984 have shown. The quotas were endorsed in Britain only with the aid of £50 million which had been set aside specifically for paying compensation to dairy farmers who had had to leave the industry as a result of the new regulations. Meanwhile, many hired dairy farmworkers who lost their jobs as a result of the milk quotas received no financial compensation from the EEC, suggesting that farmworkers, unlike farmers, enjoy little political clout in Brussels.[62]

III MODERN FARMING: A SUMMARY AND ANALYSIS

There is little doubt that the tremendous increase in agricultural output achieved by Britain since the Second World War is attributable in large part to the state support which has been given to the industry since that time.[63] In 1947 a virtually infinite market was created for the country's farmers to fill with their produce and for the following forty years successive governments have worked to keep that market open. When existing mechanisms for doing so threatened to collapse, governments responded by reforming the support system in order to preserve it: the *Agriculture Act 1957* and entry into the EEC were two such occasions. As long as government provided agricultural producers with a guarantee that they would 'purchase' everything farmers could produce, farmers had the necessary motivation to expand their production levels as far as possible. In this way the desired result was brought about, with the volume of agricultural output breaking records almost every year. Yet the methods of achieving this advancement generated a new set of problems, most of which continue unabated today.

Chief among these problems—of which the EEC's food surpluses are merely a symptom—is the unending spiral of production in which farmers find themselves. Agricultural support, whether it is provided through deficiency payments or through direct intervention in the market, seduces farmers into producing the maximum possible amount of commodities. To perform in this way, farmers require vast sums of capital in order to pay for more land, better machines, new fertilisers, bigger farm buildings, and other such supplies. One way of paying for these increasingly expensive investments of production is by borrowing from banks and other private funds. These funds are sometimes insufficient for maintaining maximum levels of output and so farmers put pressure on the authorities for increased concessions and grants to help to pay for their necessary inputs. As the cost of the inputs rise, farmers attempt to stretch their output levels still further so as to pay for their costs, while also making a profitable living from their enterprise. However, to expand output further may prove to be impossible without changing basic techniques of production. At this point farmers often bow to the pressures which are upon them to 'cut corners': they bulldoze hedgerows, they burn straw, they rear livestock in intensive conditions and they exploit the labour force as far as possible.

These measures are taken with a view to their implications for production levels rather than with any meaningful regard for their cost to the environment and to other social groups. This is why, for example, farmers have continued to burn straw and to 'factory farm' their animals in the face of widespread public criticism which these practices have drawn. In their exploitation of the hired work-force, farmers have often paid their workers the lowest wage possible, supplementing it frequently with 'free' housing. However, having found that they cannot pay below a certain level without losing their most skilled workers to other farms or other industries, farmers have turned to alternative measures in their efforts to lower the cost of labour. These include the use of casual and contract workers, the growing reliance upon machinery rather than human labour, the 'cutting of corners' in health and safety provisions, and the requirement of workers that they work overtime instead of employing extra labour. In all of these areas the farmer's priority is to maximise production at a minimal cost.[64]

The rocketing of land prices and rents noted earlier forms an integral part of this cycle of high output–high input production. As agricultural output and capital investment in the industry increase, so too does the value of land, with increasing numbers of people eager to have a stake in a uniquely protected industry which boasts exceptional levels of output and profit. As a consequence of this attractiveness of farmland, its owners are virtual masters of the land market, able to charge high prices and rents from profit-seekers. High land prices, in turn, attract only such clients who have access to large capital resources, which usually means financial institutions or those existing farmers who are prospering under the present system. This makes for greater investment in the industry, higher output, and on and on . . .

The demise of the small farmer noted earlier also becomes more understandable in the light of the above discussion. The main beneficiary of the current support system is the large agricultural producer, since each farmer is subsidised per unit produced. If the small farmer is to benefit from the protection afforded to agriculture then he must increase his output, which, in turn, requires high inputs such as complex machinery and chemicals. Yet these agricultural inputs have become increasingly expensive as their producers have carried out their own production processes with the rising wealth of the large farmers in mind.[65] Thus, the small farmer is forced to borrow increasing amounts of capital to pay for the costly inputs which all of his larger neighbours seem to use. But his own comparatively low rate of output diminishes his attractiveness to the banks and other sources of credit which prefer generally to invest in the larger, more secure farmers who are more extensively supported by the state.[66] As a result of this, the small farmer is unable to afford the inputs which other farmers use: it is a matter of time before he is compelled to sell his farm to a larger concern, as it no longer provides an adequate revenue as an independent economic unit. It is the frequency with which this scenario has been acted out in the post-war era that explains the trend towards fewer, larger farms in Britain.

Given the above pressures on the small farmer, one might reasonably expect to find a movement within the community of small farmers towards alternative farming methods which would not require the extensive inputs of mainstream farming. The absence of any such trend is due to the exclusive concentration by all large-scale agricultural research institutions on dominant farming methods (i.e. high input farming). The experience of the organic farming lobby illustrates that alternative farming practices cannot make significant inroads in the industry unless there is first a widespread departure from the current 'maximum output' approach to husbandry, and a concomitant change in MAFF-funded research.[67]

A further and related consequence of the current mode of agricultural production is the transformation of farming into Big Business, or agribusiness as it is commonly referred to. Agribusiness constitutes a tripartite structure of (i) the agricultural supplying operations; (b) the grower-producer (farmer) and (iii) the storage, processing and distributing operations.[68] Both the producers of agricultural inputs and the processers of its outputs have benefited from the existing system of agricultural protection and its related cycle of high agricultural production because they bring rising amounts of capital to these respective operations. As farming has become increasingly capitalised and large-scale in its outputs, these two related sectors have expanded accordingly.

On the input side the main interests are the drug companies, agro-chemical companies and agricultural machinery companies.[69] The drug companies have profited

Figure 1 Maximum output—high input production cycles

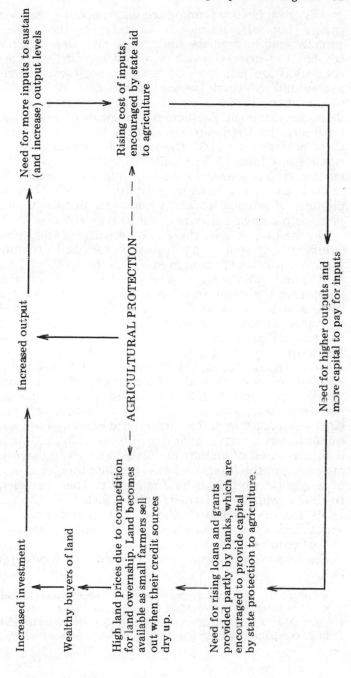

greatly from factory farming techniques. Anti-stress sedatives, energy boosters, hormones to increase the fattening of animals and to regulate their birth rate, and antibiotics to combat the disease which is easily spread in factory farm conditions are just some of the drug products on which the agricultural livestock sector spend £80 million in 1980. Chemical companies have made even greater inroads through their provision of herbicides, fungicides, insecticides and fertilisers. In 1946 farmers spent a few million pounds on these products; by 1982 the value of such sales by ICI alone was no less than £1,350 million.[70] The sale of agricultural machinery has soared to equally impressive levels. Britain's tractor and farm machinery industries sell thousands of millions of pounds worth of goods to British farmers each year, with a single machine costing up to £80,000.[71]

On the output side, there is a network of food processing companies, as well as packagers, storers and distributors of food who have all benefited from the post-war boom in agricultural production. The development of the food companies has paralleled that of the farms in that there has been a trend towards fewer, larger companies which each specialise in certain foods. Three companies account for nearly half of all frozen food sales (Unilever, Nestle and Kraftco); two companies cover two-thirds of the bread market (Rank Hovis, McDougal, and Associated British Foods); and one group sells 60 per cent of all cold breakfast cereals (Kelloggs).[72] Another relatively recent development has been the rise of contractual relationships between these large companies and the larger farmers. The food company agrees to buy a certain quantity of food from the farmer, who is thus ensured of an uncomplicated and profitable outlet for his produce; the food company, on the other hand, is assured of a regular supply of raw materials. Their preference for contracts with large farmers rather than with thousands of small farmers is due to the greater reliability of supplies which such an arrangement allows for, as well as the relative ease of communication and transport.[73]

Clutterbuck and Lang have observed that modern farming is:

> a far cry from orthodox agricultural economics which would suggest that farmers are in perfect competition with themselves, not dominated by outside interests. Rather, they are sandwiched between huge companies on both the input and the output side.[74]

On the one hand, farmers are forced to pay ever-rising prices for the goods provided by chemical and machinery companies, for without them the farm's output would fall and so too would the farmer's income. On the other hand, farmers are in many cases committed to producing food as and when required by the food companies. Howard Newby reveals that

> Most food producers like to retain strict control over the quality of the produce which they purchase and the rate and timing of production. In the case of Bird's Eye peas, for example, the company employs fieldsmen who tell farmers when to sow the crop, who then inspect it, supervise spraying and direct the harvesting operation. Walls also retains considerable control over pig farmers in order to safeguard the quality of their pork pies and sausages. On occasions farmers can be reduced to almost the function of caretakers with most of their major entrepreneurial decisions removed from their hands.[75]

Newby suggests that this relatively new arrangement has so far not seriously disturbed farmers, largely because it has proved to be a highly lucrative method of food production. The point here is that farmers do not have any choice over food production methods, as they must bend increasingly to the demands and strictures of their agribusiness partners.

It is through these tightening bonds between farming and its allied industries, and above all through the agricultural support system which underpins this relationship, that British agriculture has transformed itself from a tradition-bound 'way of life' into Big Business. The many pressures that have helped to bring about this transformation (chief among which has been the escalating need among farmers to maximise their production at minimal costs) have had particularly important ramifications for the hired agricultural work force. Since the cost of inputs such as machinery and chemicals cannot be controlled directly by farmers, economies have instead been made increasingly in the labour sector of farm inputs, in ways which have been noted above.

In the context of the manifold pressures under which farmers have been shown to operate, agricultural employers may be absolved from any moral responsibility for the poor standard of their employees' working conditions. However, employers must be held causally responsible for these conditions, in so far as they perpetuate and uphold the existing system of production which has determined the quality of agricultural workers' lives. The way in which farmworkers have responded to their conditions is the subject of the next chapter.

NOTES

1   Edwards, A. and Rogers, A. (eds) (1974), *Agricultural Resources*, Faber, London, pp. 82–83; Newby, H. (1979), *Green and Pleasant Land?*, Penguin, Harmondsworth, p. 30.
2   Norton-Taylor, R. (1982), *Whose Land is it Anyway?*, Turnston, Wellingborough, pp. 24–9.
3   *Ibid.*
4   Hobsbawm, E. (1968), *Industry and Empire*, Weidenfeld & Nicholson, London, Chapter 5; Scott, J. (1982), *The Upper Classes: Property and Privilege in Britain*, Macmillan, Hong Kong, Chapter 3; Mingay, G. E. (1972), *The Transformation of Agriculture*, in R. Hartwell, G. Mingay, R. Boyson, N. McCord, C. Hanson, A. W. Coats, W. Chaloner, W. O. Henderson and M. Jefferson, (eds), *The Long Debate on Poverty*, Institute for Economic Affairs.
5   MAFF (1968), *Annual Review of Agriculture 1983, A Century of Agricultural Statistics: Great Britain 1866-1966*.
6   Newby, *op. cit.*, p. 39; Norton-Taylor, *op. cit.*, p. 32; Rose, D., Newby, H., Saunders, P. and Bell, C. (1977), 'Land tenure and official statistics', *JAE*, 28 (1).
7   Norton-Taylor, *op. cit.*, pp. 60–3; *Farming News*, 16 March 1984, 'Institutions seen as New Saviours'.
8   *Financial Times*, 7 March 1984, 'British farmland prices reach new highs'; *Financial Times*, 6 June 1984, 'Farmers' problems not reflected in buoyant land values'.
9   National Westminster Bank (1984), *Agricultural Digest*, Number Four, April, p. 7; Body, R. (1984), *Farming in the Clouds*, Temple Smith, London, pp. 39–40; Norton-Taylor, *op. cit.*, p. 107.
10   Beresford, T. (1975), *We Plough the Fields*, Penguin, Harmondsworth, Chapter 8.
11   Britton, D. K. (1988), 'Some explanations in the analysis of long-term changes in the structure of agriculture', *JAE*, 28 (3).
12   MAFF (1970), *The Changing Structure of Agriculture, Annual Reviews of Agriculture 1952-84* (until 1973 these were entitled *Annual Review and Deterination of Guarantees*).
13   National Westminster Bank, *op. cit.*, p. 9; MAFF, *Century of Statistics*, pp. 18-21.
14   Britton, *op. cit.*
15   Newby, H., Bell, C., Rose, D., and Saunders, P. (1978), *Property, Paternalism and Power*, Hutchinson, London, Chapter 2; Phillips, D. and Williams, A. (1984), *Rural Britain*, Blackwell, London, pp. 31-2.
16   MAFF (1984), *Annual Review of Agriculture 1984*.
17   A variety of criteria exist for defining the size of a farm, including the number of hectares that a farm occupies. A useful measure is MAFF's 'Standard Man Days' (SMD) in which 250 SMD is said to provide work for one full-time worker (whether hired or self-employed). According to MAFF (*Changing Structure of Agriculture*,

op. cit.)
    599 SMD or less   = small farm
    600 SMD–1,999 SMD = medium farm
    2,000 SMD or more = large farm.

18   Phillips and Williams, *op. cit.*, p. 31.
19   Donaldson, J. G. S. and Donaldson, F. (1969), *Farming in Britain Today*, Allen Lane, London, Chapter 2.
20   Body, R. (1982), *Agriculture: the Triumph and the Shame*, Temple Smith, London, p. 4; Body, R., *Farming in the Clouds*, pp. 64–9.
21   Self, P. and Storing, H. (1962), *The State and the Farmer*, Allen & Unwin, London, pp. 19--20.
22   MAFF, *Century of Agricultural Statistics, op. cit.*
23   Mackintosh, J. R. (1958), 'The problems of agricultural politics', *JAE*, 21 (1) p. 25; Self, P. and Storing, H. (1958), 'The farmers and the state', *The Political Quarterly*, 29 (1).
24   Beresford, *op. cit.*, p. 18.
25   *Ibid.*, p. 33.
26   MAFF, *Annual Reviews of Agriculture 1954, 1955*; Sharp, G. and Capstick, C. W., 'The place of agriculture in the national economy', *JAE*, 17 (1) p. 2.
27   MAFF, *Century of Statistics, op. cit.*, pp. 76–7.
28   Beresford, *op. cit.*, Chapter 4.
29   Wilson, G. (1977), *Special Interests and Policy-making' Agricultural Policies and Politics in Britain and the U.S.A. 1956–1970*, Wiley, London, Chapter 1.
30   NFU (no date), *The NFU of England and Wales*, NFU Publication, 4-982.
31   See Bell and Newby's typology of British farmers for some idea of the diversity to be found, although as with all such classifications the complexity of farmers' variations is lost to some extent. Bell, C. and Newby, H. (1974), 'Capitalist farmers in the British class structure', *Sociologia Ruralis*, 14.
32   NFU, *The NFU in the 1980s*, NFU Publication Cyclo 259/83.
33   Two especially significant areas of conflict are between small and large farmers; and between 'corn and horn', with the two areas often overlapping.
34   Shoard, M. (1980), *The Theft of the Countryside*, Temple Smith, London, p. 105; *The NFU of England and Wales, op. cit.*,; NFU (no date), *The NFU*, NFU publication, un-numbered.
35   Grant, W. (1983), 'The National Farmers Union: the classic case of incorporation?' in D. Marsh (ed.), *Pressure Politics*, Junction Books, London, p. 129.
36   Wilson, G. (1978), 'Farmers organisations in advanced societies' in H. Newby (ed.), *International Perspectives in Rural Sociology*, Wiley, Chichester.
37   Newby, *Green and Pleasant Land?*, p. 112.
38   Grant, *op. cit.*, p. 129.
39   Wilson, *Special Interests and Policy-making*, p. 45; Newby, *op. cit.*, p. 113; Self and Storing, *Farmers and the State*, pp. 21–3; Self and Storing, *State and the Farmer*, p. 46.
40   Breakaway groups such as the Farmers' Union of Wales and the Smallholders' Association are as yet too small to threaten the NFU's position.

41   Shoard, *Theft of the Countryside, op. cit.*, p. 105. Some observers underestimated the durability of the NFU's links with MAFF and predicted a demise in the NFU's power once Britain joined the EEC. This was because EEC membership entailed an end to the traditional annual review procedure. In practice the NFU has been able to ensure that little of its influence has been lost through EEC membership. It regularly pressurises government and the Ministry to secure favourable EEC policies for agriculture; and it has its own office in Brussels from which to monitor and influence policy-making by the Council of Ministers.

42   Roth, A. (1981), *The Business Background of MPs: 1981*, Parliamentary Profiles, London; Rogers, S. J. (1970), 'Farmers as a pressure group', *New Society*, 5 February, p. 216; Phillips and Williams, *op. cit.*

43   Wyn Grant notes that the CBI has been impressed by a variety of the NFU's pressure politicking tactics, p. 132.

44   For analyses of farmers' electoral clout at various times in the post-war period see Pennock, J. R. (1959), 'The political power of British agriculture', *PS*, 7; Howarth, R. (1969), 'The political strength of British agriculture', *PS*, 17; Self and Storing, *State and Farmer.*

45   Sharp and Capstick, *op. cit.*, pp. 14–15 typify the virtually unquestioned belief that agricultural support, providing that it is kept within reasonable bounds, is justifiable on the grounds that it assists the maintenance of a healthy balance of payments.

46   Richard Body, a farmer and Conservative MP since 1966, is a notable exception, but his apparently eccentric arguments have so far failed to gain significant support. See *Triumph and Shame*, Chapter 8.

47   Rahl, R. (1961), *Who Governs*, Yale University, New Haven, pp. 226–8.

48   Beresford, *op. cit.*; MAFF, *Annual Review 1984*, Table 1, p. 82.

49   Shoard, M. (1980), 'Public money and private vandalism', *New Statesman*, 10 October; Body, *Triumph and Shame*; MAFF, *Annual Review 1984.*

50   Clutterbuck, C. and Lang, T. (1982), *More than We Can Chew*, Pluto, London, p. 72.

51   Body, *op. cit.*, p. 34; MAFF, *Annual Review 1984*; *Guardian*, 20 June 1984, 'Farm loans to rise'.

52   *The Agricultural Policy of the European Community*, European Documentation, Periodical 6/1982, p. 16.

53   Clutterbuck and Lang, *op. cit.*, pp. 56–7.

54   Blake, D. (1984), 'Land of milk and . . .', *New Statesman*, 18 May; Norton-Taylor, *op. cit.*, p. 127; Commission of the European Communities (1981), *The Common Agricultural Policy*, p. 6.

55   NFU (no date), *The National Importance of British Agriculture.*

56   'Sold down the farm', *New Statesman*, 13 April 1984.

57   Norton-Taylor, *op. cit.* .p. 129; EEC Periodical 6/1982, *op. cit.*, p. 60.

58   Shoard, *Public Money . . . .op. cit.; Financial Times*, 13 April 1984, 'EEC butter mountain may reach 1m. tonnes'.

59   *Financial Times*, 9 March 1984, 'Ploughing ahead with crop expansion'.

60 NFU (1984), *The Way Forward: New Directions for Agricultural Policy*, NFU Policy Document, p. 3.
61 *Financial Times*, 2 July 1985, 'Radical reform of EEC farm policy proposed'; *Economist*, 6 July 1985, 'No cash crops now'; *Observer*, 15 September 1985, 'Bitter harvest for farmers as prices are blighted'.
62 *Liverpool Daily Post*, 24 August 1984. This point was repeatedly emphasised by Joan Maynard, the farmworkers' sponsored MP, during parliamentary debates over the milk quotas; *Guardian*, 5 July 1984, 'No cash for farmworkers'; *Daily Telegraph*, 5 July 1984, 'Harsh treatment of sacked farmworkers'.
63 Beresford, *op. cit.*, Chapter 6; Body, *Triumph and Shame*, p. 24; Donaldson and Donaldson, *op. cit.*, Introduction; Selly, C. (1972), *Ill Fares the Land*, Andre Deutsch, London; MAFF (1979), *Farming and the Nation*, February.
64 Clutterbuck and Lang, *op. cit.*, p. 62.
65 MAFF, *Annual Reviews of Agriculture 1960-1980*.
66 Body, *Triumph and Shame*, p. 34.
67 BBC Radio Four Programme, *On Your Farm* transmitted 11 August 1984.
68 Taylor, L. and Jones, A. R. (1965), 'Professionals and specialists in agribusiness', *Sociologia Ruralis*, 5, p. 340.
69 Gold, M. (1983), *Assault and Battery*, Pluto, London, Chapter 4; Body, *Farming in the Clouds*, pp. 22-3; *Farming News*, 6 April 1984, 'Sales booming—but will it last?'.
70 Body, *Farming in the Clouds*, p. 20.
71 *Financial Times*, 13 April 1984, 'Tractor industry achieves turnover of £1.2 bn'; *Farming News*, 16 March 1984, 'Berks takes second look at big bales'; *Farming News*, 9 March 1984, 'Big boys boost sales of Combines'; *Farming News*, 6 April 1984, 'Sales booming'.
72 Clutterbuck and Lang, *op. cit.*, p. 64.
73 Newby, *Green and Pleasant Land?*, p. 64.
74 Clutterbuck and Lang, *op. cit.*.. p. 64.
75 Newby, *Green and Pleasant Land?*, p. 117.

Chapter 3

The organisation of agricultural labour

I AGRICULTURAL LABOUR

Perhaps the most outstanding feature of the English agricultural labour force has been its dramatic numerical decline since the mid-nineteenth century. In 1851 there were 1·48 million agricultural workers employed in England and Wales; one century later only 0·7 million remained;[1] and by 1983 there were only 122,000 regular full-time hired male workers, 11,000 full-time female workers, and 138,000 male and female part-time, seasonal and casual workers employed in the UK agricultural industry.[2] This radical fall in the number of hired farmworkers is attributable to numerous factors, the most important of which has been the increased use, particularly since the Second World War, of labour-saving machinery and work-practices on the farm. The employment of sophisticated machinery has also affected those farmworkers who have remained in the industry. It has seen an increasing demand for skill from these workers, and has placed a growing amount of responsibility on their shoulders. Farmworkers today use complex machinery worth tens of thousands of pounds, often without a work-mate with whom to share the job and the responsibility attached to it.

Although overall trends indicate a dramatic fall in the number of farmworkers as well as increasing levels of skill among those who remain in the industry,[3] not all farms have shed their labour to the same degree. While some farms employ one full-time worker or only casual or part-time labour, others may depend on the labour of as many as twenty full-time workers. At present this latter category of farms forms a clear minority, as Table 1 shows.

Just as farmworkers are unevenly distributed in terms of their labour size groups, so too they are found to be concentrated in certain regions of the country. For example, just over 20 per cent of all workers employed in agriculture in the UK in 1982 were in the cereal-growing regions of the South-East, whereas the North accounted for fewer than

4 per cent of the total work-force.[4]

A third way of viewing the agricultural labour force is in terms of its age structure. Lund *et al.* provide figures for the hired regular full-time male agricultural work force which reveal a trend towards a younger labour force between 1960 and 1980. In 1968, 11·2 per cent of the work-force were 20–25 years of age; 19·2 per cent were 25–35; 47·2 per cent were 35–55; and 20·5 per cent 55–65. The corresponding figures for 1980 were 16·6 per cent; 22·5 per cent, 42·6 per cent; and 17·0 per cent.[5]

Table 1 Distribution of hired regular whole-time workers by labour size groups: England and Wales, June 1982 (N = 2,629)

Labour size group	Proportion of holdings
	%
1 hired regular whole-time worker	26·8
2– 4	44·8
5– 9	20·0
10–14	4·3
15–19	1·8
20 or more	2·3
TOTAL	100·0

Source: MAFF, *Wages and Employment Enquiry*, 1982.

Table 2 Total number of workers in thousands (family and hired) on agricultural holdings in England and Wales, June 1982

| Region | Regular whole-time workers | | | |
	Men	Women	All	All workers[a]
North	6·8	0·5	7·3	12·5
Yorks and Humberside	13·0	1·1	14·1	26·1
E Midlands	15·7	1·3	17·1	31·7
E Anglia	17·6	1·2	18·8	35·0
SE	29·4	4·1	33·5	67·3
SW	20·5	2·0	22·5	44·0
W Midlands	12·0	1·1	13·1	28·8
NW	7·1	0·9	8·0	15·7
England	122·1	12·3	134·4	261·1
Wales	7·1	1·1	8·2	20·9

a Regular whole-time and part-time and seasonal male and female.
Source: MAFF, *Wages and Employment Enquiry*, 1982.

Finally, one might consider the distribution of the workforce according to their occupation. In 1982 the occupational divisions among regular full-time hired men were as in Table 3.

Table 3   Occupational divisions among regular full-time male workers in agriculture, 1982

Occupation	Proportion
	%
Foremen	8·0
Dairy cowmen	7·1
Other stockmen	11·3
Tractor drivers	22·3
General farmworkers	43·5
Horticultural workers	6·2
Other farmworkers	1·6

Source: MAFF, Wages and Employment Enquiry, 1982.

These classifications shed light on certain sociological trends which characterise the contemporary labour force in agriculture. For example, occupational divisions are important variables for explaining agricultural labour mobility. Overall, farmworkers are not a very mobile group within their industry, as shown by the National Economic Development Office (NEDO) survey which Ruth Gasson has drawn upon in her study.[6] Over 40 per cent of the sample were found to have always worked on the same farm and 20 per cent had served the same employer or holding for over twenty years. However, Gasson shows that dairy cowmen and other stockmen form the most mobile occupational group within the industry, while foremen, tractor drivers and general farmworkers remain the longest at the same place of work.[7] Stockmen are also among the most skilled and best paid workers in agriculture, and are the main group to occupy the tied cottage. These factors relate to their occupational mobility for, unlike the numerically preponderant general farmworker, the skilled livestock worker is sufficiently in demand on the agricultural labour market to be earning relatively good wages and 'perks' (such as tied accommodation), as employers have to compete for their relatively scarce skilled labour in this specialist field.

A view of farmworkers' outward mobility presents a rather different picture. Gasson found that 50–60 per cent of all occupational moves in agriculture are to occupations in other industries—most frequently in the transport, building and construction trades and, to a lesser extent, to unskilled jobs such as retailing.[8] Seasonal and casual workers are found to be less inclined to leave the land than are regular workers, and of the latter category it is workers on arable farms rather than livestock workers who are most likely to move to non-agricultural employment.

The overall outflow of agricultural labour rose to sufficiently high proportions in the 1950s to arouse the interest of a number of agricultural economists and rural sociologists. The most notable study to emerge from this development was by W. J. G. Cowie and A. K. Giles who sought an explanation for the farmworkers' 'drift from the land'. From a survey of over 500 farmworkers and ex-farmworkers in the Gloucestershire area, Cowie and Giles found that 'Outstanding among the causes of the movement of workers from agriculture is the level of wages . . .'[9] However, Cowie and Giles's conclusion that farmworkers had left their industry 'voluntarily' (i.e. in pursuit of better-paid work) would seem to contradict the notion that farmworkers have been forced to leave the land by the replacement of their labour by new agricultural machinery. Or, to phrase the issue in the terms of the agricultural economist: has the drift from the land been caused by 'pull' or by 'push' factors?

This question can be answered only if the period of time and the locality to which it is applied are specified. Farm-workers can only be 'pulled', or drawn, out of their industry if the non-agricultural labour market can offer them preferable employment opportunities, a factor which depends on the country's economic climate at a given time. More significant perhaps is the state of the *local* labour market, since farmworkers are unlikely to have the opportunity to travel widely in search of new employment. The relevance of alternative employment opportunities in the explanation of 'pull' is highlighted by Ruth Gasson who found that

> While the causes of dissatisfaction would be likely to operate continuously, actual migration of workers depends on there being other jobs. A close association has been demonstrated at regional levels between rates of movement of labour off farms and employment opportunities in industry . . . In other words, workers are ready to leave the land when industry is booming but understandably cautious when unemployment is rising.[10]

'Push' factors can include incidents such as the imposition of the milk quotas in 1984, or the increased use of family labour. Historically, the most forceful push factor has been the growing reliance by farmers upon labour-saving work practices (e.g. specialisation) and machinery. In so far as farmers have transferred gradually to the use of machines as a substitute for human labour, the 'voluntary' drift of farmworkers into towns and cities in search of improved work conditions (i.e. 'pull') has not seriously disrupted the level of agricultural production. There have been only rare and usually short-lived periods of concern over the past fifty years among agriculturalists over the existence of an apparent scarcity of skilled labour.[11] More commonly, the reverse trend has prevailed; push has outweighed pull, as employers have shed their hired labour at a faster rate than the farmworkers have found preferable alternative employment. This situation has become increasingly marked since the Second World War, as farmers have been compelled to cut their costs of production in every possible way in response to an increasingly intensive high input–maximum output production cycle.

As the number of hired farmworkers has declined, primarily through the influence of push in the agricultural labour market, the number of workers in allied industries has increased. This trend has prompted some commentators to suggest that today's 'farmworker' is the worker who is employed to help in the manufacture of agricultural machinery as much as it is the 'traditional' worker who works in the fields. Our concern here, however, is with the implications of labour market trends for those workers who have remained on the land.

II AGRICULTURAL TRADE UNIONISM

Farmworkers have a long history of trade unionism, indeed longer than have most other groups of workers, for it began as early as 1834 with the 'Tolpuddle Martyrs'. The vicissitudes of agricultural trade unionism since that time have been well-documented by labour historians, many of whom have stressed in particular the obstacles which have confronted the agricultural labour movement since its inception.[12] It has been their inability, so far, to overcome some of these difficulties which explains why, despite its longevity, farm-workers' history is marked as much by set-backs and dis-appointments as by the courage and dedication of its protagonists.

The first spate of organised trade unionism among agri-cultural workers surfaced in the early 1870s when Joseph Arch led the well-known 'Revolt of the Fields'. The farmers' effective lock-out of their workers in 1874 in the Eastern Counties saw the quick collapse of the union movement which was not resurrected in any cohesive form until 1906. In that year farmworkers organised themselves under the leadership of George Edwards, originally to protest and to protect themselves against a series of tied cottage evictions in Norfolk which had been the employers' retaliation for farmworkers' electoral support for the Liberals, rather than for the Tory Party. A brief boom in union membership during the First World War lasted only until 1920—the year the union adopted the name of the National Union of Agricultural Workers (NUAW)—when wages began to fall dramatically and unemployment soared. In September 1921 the government abolished the recently established Central Wages Board, and the statutory agricultural minimum wage went with it. Thereafter agricultural wages plummetted, until in 1923 real wage levels in agriculture fell to below their 1914 level.

The date 1923 marks a watershed for the NUAW, for it was the year of the great Norfolk Strike. The union was compelled to take strike action at this time to end the employers' repeated cuts in wage rates and extensions of working hours. The strike took place in Norfolk, where the union was relatively well-organised, and it lasted for five weeks. With the (chiefly financial), help of urban workers the farmworkers secured some of the gains for which they had fought: most importantly, the farmers' unending move-ment to cut wages and lengthen the work-day was halted, and farmworkers' wages were held at their existing levels. This victory had to be set against the losses incurred by the strike, however, which included a depletion of union funds, a great fall in membership and morale, and the job losses of many of those who had taken part in the strike (in spite of the 'no victimisation' agreement made by employers). On balance, the strike was a costly show of the union's strength, which left a cautious reluctance among many members and officials to attempt industrial action again.

The late 1920s and early 1930s are best described by Reg Groves's chapter heading 'the lean years'. Lower wages and longer hours were repeatedly imposed upon the workers, and unemployment remained high, both in the towns and in the countryside. The mid-1930s saw the start of a slow change in both the farmworkers' conditions and in the union's fortunes, as wages were increased, hours reduced and union membership rose. However, it was the Second World War which saw the largest improvement in farmworkers' conditions and simultaneously in their union's membership figures. Wartime inflation, labour scarcity and wage regulation helped to raise farmworkers' wages considerably (although they remained well below industrial earnings) and these developments were accompanied by a great increase in union membership: by 1947 the NUAW had 162,000 members, which was over three times the 1938 figure.[13]

Although information on NUAW membership levels is based upon estimates, certain trends can be identified.[14] A peak was reached in 1948, after which membership fell slightly, remaining between 124,000 and 129,000 throughout the 1950s. In 1961 the figure fell to 113,646 and although there were some increases during the 1960s, they were followed by falls in the membership level such that the decade closed with only 105,000 members in the NUAW. By 1970 the figure was 94,497 and the 1970s are marked by a continuing drop in the number of union members. The union's profound concern over this trend is evident in its *Annual Reports*. Almost every report provides details of new schemes devised to boost membership levels, but few of these schemes achieved their purpose. In 1971, for example, cash prizes were awarded for the best recruiting efforts by members on both a monthly and county basis; yet in 1973 the Organising Sub-committee was reporting an average annual drop of 10 per cent in the number of union members.

Because the exact number of agricultural workers belonging to the NUAW is unknown, it is impossible to quote what proportion of the potential membership belong to the union. Estimates have varied from 30–35 per cent of the total potential membership,[15] to 40 per cent of the total regular full-time hired labour force in England and Wales,[16] to over 50 per cent.[17] One clear feature is the regional concentration of union members: while Wales only accounted for 2 per cent of total members in the 1970s, 40 per cent were to be found in just three counties: Lincolnshire, Norfolk and Yorkshire.[18]

Overall membership remains low in the farmworkers' union and this has had serious implications for union finances. Unlike the NFU, the farmworkers' union has relied almost entirely upon members' subscriptions for its income. A small membership, which is generally too poor to make generous donations, has meant that the union has had to struggle with a seriously low income ever since its inception. At the same time, this lack of financial resources has prevented the union from pursuing a large-scale and effective recruitment campaign. In the 1970s financial pressures forced the union to shed many of its personnel and facilities for reasons of economy. Between 1970 and 1972 the union's full-time staff was reduced by twenty (including four full-time recruitment officers), its computer system was abandoned and replaced by a manual system of auditing, and contributions to the Labour Party and Trades Union Congress (TUC) were decreased. These economy measures were followed by a predictable, but regretted, failure to increase significantly the declining level of membership.[19]

Moreover, the reduction in staff and services also failed to improve the union's finances. Consequently, the leadership continued to spend considerable energy in search of a solution to the twin problems of low income and low membership. It was obliged to raise members' contributions frequently as a 'last resort' for raising a viable income, but even this strategy could not succeed indefinitely in keeping income in line with expenditure.[20]

The periodic subscription increases were announced in the union's monthly journal, the *Landworker*, accompanied by regretful apologies from union officials, who made clear their awareness of members' personal financial straits.[21] Each time an increase was announced the journal also reminded members of the many services provided by the union. These have ranged from conventional union functions such as wage negotiation, legal aid on work-related problems, the provision of a lively monthly journal and the representation of farmworkers on various organisations and committees, to services more in line with a 'friendly society' than a modern trade union. Such services have included dealing with members' personal and domestic problems, such as winning £6 compensation for a coat lost at a cleaners and £2 compensation for cauliflowers eaten by a neighbour's sheep.[22]

By the mid-1970s these 'friendly' services had become

considerably less prominent in the union's agenda relative to its 'trade union' concerns. Nevertheless, although the pursuit of the miscellaneous and personal problems of members was a costly and time-consuming task, the leadership took the view that this was a valuable 'secondary' service, the importance of which lay in the fact that it 'reflects the traditional "family" relationship that exists within the Union'.[23] The dependency of many farmworkers on the union to solve their non-work related problems may, however, have less to do with their familial feelings towards the union than with their isolation. The relative scarcity of Citizens' Advice Bureaux and similar public advice agencies in rural areas often means that the union is the only agency available to farmworkers to turn to for legal advice and assistance.

The union has not had a high political profile in the sense that virtually all of its time and resources have been devoted to the 'bread and butter' issues of gaining better wages and conditions for its members rather than to conducting more overtly political campaigns. In so far as it has been politically vocal, the union has taken a public stand chiefly on issues which are directly concerned with the agricultural industry: it has long championed land nationalisation (although with diminishing vigour over the years), it opposed Britain's entry into the EEC and it has supported the Labour Party in every election since the Second World War. The union's commitment to the Labour Party was cemented in 1974 when it sponsored the Labour Member of Parliament for Sheffield Brightside, Joan Maynard, a policy which it has upheld ever since that time.

The union's sponsored MP is arguably one of its most important power resources in the parliamentary arena. As with farmers, the numerical decline of farmworkers over the past hundred years has reduced the potantial attractiveness of their vote to most politicians. The number of farmworkers in any given constituency at any time in the post-war period has never been sufficiently high to command any meaningful 'indirect influence'[24] over prospective and existing MPs (who in any case tend to hold safe Conservative seats in the rural areas). At the same time, and in contrast to farmers, farmworkers have no 'natural allies' in parliament to compensate for their electoral marginality. Nor has the union developed strong links with local MPs as the NFU has done so effectively. It is for these reasons that the union's sponsored

MP has been forced to take on the responsibility of being the farmworkers' chief source of influence and power in parliament.

The political colouring of the union's leadership has fluctuated over the years, as a comparison of the *Landworker*'s stance in the 1920s and 1960s and 1970s shows. In 1927, the *Landworker* suggested the following as a topic for discussion at branch meetings across the country

> there *is* a real difference which does divide the workers from the employing class and the wealthy unemployed. The workers are exploited—that is to say, they produce wealth as a result of their labour, but only a part—sometimes a small part—of that wealth is given back to them in the form of wages. The rest is kept by the employers. The employers think this is right and fair—they want it to continue. The workers show that a better arrangement is possible; an arrangement under which all industry shall be carried on by the community for the general good, just as the postal services are, or broadcasting for instance. The workers want to abolish private profit making.[25]

By the 1960s the *Landworker* was publicly disassociating itself from socialist politics, and sought repeatedly to distance itself in particular from the Communist Party. When the journal printed an article in December 1971 by a self-proclaimed member of the Communist Party, the *Landworker* staff apologised and promised its readers a balance in the next edition by printing an article by the Conservative Minister of Agriculture, James Prior.[26]

However, in spite of these political contrasts throughout the union's history and the limited degree of tension to be found between the union's 'radical' and 'reformist' wings, there has been a broad continuity underpinning its policy objectives which is based upon an overriding concern with winning improvements in members' wages; seeing the abolition of the tied cottage and its associated problems; gaining public recognition of the farmworker's skill; and more recently, securing a reasonable standard of health and safety on the farm. A further preoccupation, noted earlier in the chapter, has been with improving the union's membership figures and thereby improving its finances and services.

This concern over recruitment and finances became increasingly prominent in the late 1960s and throughout the 1970s, when it was finally recognised that raising members' subscriptions was an inadequate response to the problem.

Two more far-reaching steps were taken in an attempt to solve the union's difficulties in these spheres. The first of these was in 1968 when the union's Biennial Conference in Aberystwyth voted to change the union's name from the National Union of Agricultural Workers (NUAW) to the National Union of Agricultural *and Allied* Workers (NUAAW). The new title, in fact, merely formalised the trend that had developed over previous years, namely the union's increased recruitment of allied workers into its ranks. (These included forestry workers, roadmen, drainage workers, and workers in food processing companies.) The falling number of agricultural workers in the agricultural industry was reflected in union membership figures, where the ratio of allied workers to farmworkers had been rising steadily.[27] By changing the union's name the Conference gave its recognition to these increasingly important allied workers who were members while at the same time attempting to attract those who remained outside its ranks.[28]

As subsequent *Annual Reports* indicate, the formally closer relationship with allied workers did not significantly improve the union's finances. In 1968 its total funds stood at £682,041 and its expenditure at £366,275; by 1974 the funds had fallen to £575,520 and expenditure had climbed to £551,494; and in 1979 expenditure had outstripped its funds by almost two to one. The union could no longer afford to run its services: a crisis loomed which the leadership recognised could not be solved by repeatedly raising contributions. Consequently, it held a special conference in 1980 to consider possible solutions to the continuing decline in its financial situation. The most promising solution appeared to be the joining of forces with another union. Negotiations were subsequently held with three different unions, and eventually the NUAAW leadership recommended to its members a merger with the country's largest union, the Transport and General Workers' Union (TGWU). In January 1982 a postal ballot of the whole NUAAW membership saw six to one support in favour of the merger among the 52 per cent of the membership who cast their votes. Thus, ever since 1982 the organised agricultural work-force has belonged to the Agricultural and Allied Workers' National Trade Group (AAWNTG) of the TGWU.

The merger demanded certain structural changes from the old NUAAW. (At the time of writing some of these transformations are still in the process of being implemented.)

The branch remains the union's basic unit, but, unlike in the NUAAW, all members of the AAWNTG must belong to branches of fifty or more members. Many old NUAAW branches were amalgamated in order to reach the TGWU's minimum number, with the result that today there are fewer but larger branches than there were prior to the merger.

The NUAAW's District Committees and County Committees have been replaced by new District Committees and Regional Trade Group Committees. In some instances Composite District Committees take the place of District Committees, in which case the District Organiser concerned must deal with workers not only from agriculture but also from numerous other TGWU sections. Sometimes the Organiser concerned may not have an agricultural background, and will have little if any experience of agricultural workers' problems. This lack of experience and understanding of the farmworkers' circumstances at the district level has placed a greater onus upon the AAWNTG's Head Office which, however, lost many of its officers and staff through the merger. Although *Landworker* is currently still produced and there is still a Legal/Health and Safety Department catering solely for farmworkers' problems in these areas, there is a general movement towards a greater integration of the AAWNTG's staff and members with the TGWU's other sectors. Among other things, this integration is aimed at reducing the pressure from the districts on the AAWNTG Head Office, while offering members a net gain in the number of services made available to them by the merger. Further organisational changes have included the replacement of the National Executive Committee by the National Trade Group Committee; of the post of General Secretary by National Trade Group Secretary; and of the week-long Biennial Conference with the two-day Annual Conference which continues to decide union (Trade Group) policy and to place mandates on the full-time officers.

Few members or officials have been willing to pass unreserved judgements on the merger, largely because it is still a relatively new arrangement the full effects of which remain to be seen. Problems of communication are clear, however, for example between officials with a life-time of agricultural experience and those with none. There is also a sense of having been 'swallowed-up' by a large and anonymous union which has no real understanding of rural conditions, attitudes and needs; for example, 'friendly society' services will almost certainly decline as the merger becomes more and more established. In the long term, however, there can be few regrets over the merger which successfully prevented the financial ruin and ultimate collapse of the farmworkers' union organisation. Lay members and officials recognise that other, more positive benefits of the merger may be slow to surface, particularly because of the financial and membership problems which arose within the TGWU itself in the early 1980s. From the AAWNTG's point of view, the enjoyment of the potential benefits of the merger (financial security, a greater variety of services, more industrial muscle and stronger links with allied workers) will depend upon the successful integration of the AAWNTG with the rest of the TGWU, a process that has only just begun.

III   AGRICULTURAL LABOUR RELATIONS

The last organised strike among agricultural workers in England took place over sixty years ago, since which time there has been only one further attempt at taking large-scale industrial action. Apart from its periodic lobbies of parliament and rallies in London (usually in support of the union's annual wage claim) the NUAAW (and, since 1982, the AAWNTG) has been a relatively quiet union.[29] However, on the basis of the definition of farmworkers' interests outlined in Chapter 1 (high wages, non-tied housing and occupational safety) the quiescence of the union—and more particularly of the 60 per cent of farmworkers who do not belong to it— cannot be attributed to the satisfaction of farmworkers' interests by prevailing conditions. How then is the farmworkers' apparent silence to be explained?

It should be noted at the outset that the absence of large-scale and organised opposition to existing conditions is not equivalent to an absence of protest altogether. This point is stressed by labour historians who have shown that in the nineteenth century, for example, prior to the development of trade unionism, workers expressed their dissatisfaction with their conditions of work in subtle and relatively inconspicuous ways. It is true that at times the action taken was fairly widespread and organised as, for instance, in the mid-1930s when the New Poor Law aroused their hostility.[30] But more often than not, farmworkers' protests were less obvious to the onlooker, but nonetheless effective. For a considerable period of time, social protest took highly individualistic forms, such as arson, theft from employers' stocks accompanied by hostile letters, the destruction of fences and the deliberate and violent maiming of animals. Whether opposition was carried out collectively or individually, however, there was a clear expression of dissatisfaction to be gleaned among farmworkers with their work conditions and with the prevailing distribution of rewards between landlords, farmers and workers.[31]

The second half of the nineteenth century saw a decline in the use of isolated and violent methods of protest among agricultural workers. At the same time, farmworkers were often prevented from using newly developed forms of opposition, such as the withdrawal of their labour, which industrial workers had begun to use successfully. The barriers to the farmworkers' use of the strike weapon, many of which persist today, will be considered later; what is of interest here is the response of farmworkers to their constrained situation.

The union's largely successful attempts at taking strike action in the late nineteenth and early twentieth centuries led it to adopt a different strategy for improving conditions, namely the provision of encouragement and assistance to union members for their emigration. Between 1871 and 1881 a total of 200,000 farmworkers left the country with the union's help in search of better fortunes in Canada, Australia and New Zealand.[32] This policy of emigration (and to a lesser degree migration) served two purposes simultaneously. On the one hand, it provided members with an escape route from a situation which they clearly found intolerable, offering them an opportunity to find improved conditions in a different industry or in another country. On the other hand, emigration of substantial numbers of farmworkers placed those who remained in England's farming industry in a stronger labour market position, thus enabling them to put forward demands to their employers more effectively.

Although the farmworkers' drift from the land was a successful, albeit negative, form of protest from the *emigrés* point of view, there were three important problems involved in its useage. First, it deprived the union of many potential members, often the more ambitious and adventurous ones who might have become the union's much-needed leaders had they remained in England.[33] Secondly, farmworkers were able to use this form of protest only as long as there were alternative jobs which they would be able to emigrate or migrate to. The loss of Britain's colonies saw the severe contraction of farmworkers' opportunities for changing their employment through emigration. In the post-war period migration to non-agricultural employment has also become an unreliable and intermittent form of protest which is wholly dependent on the national employment situation and, more specifically, on the state of the local labour market. Finally, the operation of pull factors, in so far as they exist, no longer strengthens the bargaining power of the remaining agricultural workers: push factors have been operating at a rate which has left farmers generally satisfied with having an ever-smaller labour force.

Although historical evidence thus indicates that farmworkers have not accepted passively the conditions imposed on them by their industry, it also reveals that their opposition to these conditions has rarely been vociferous. Moreover, while many farmworkers have protested against their conditions of work by leaving the industry in search of alternative employment, the fact remains that many more have remained tied to the land throughout their working lives. However, the underlying explanation for this continued service to agriculture suggests that neither farmworkers' quiescence nor their loyalty to the industry can be interpreted as a positive endorsement of their conditions.

In his study of East Anglian farmworkers, Howard Newby found that 'the extremely low voluntary quit rate can be attributed in no small measure to a substantial proportion of workers who have lacked the opportunity to move rather than made a choice to stay'.[34] The absence of sufficient opportunities to leave the industry explains not only the 'low voluntary quit rate' among farmworkers but also, as Newby shows, the peaceful labour relations which have characterised their industry so strongly.[35] Farmworkers' quiescence and the resulting industrial peace exist because farmworkers are prevented from using a threatened 'drift from the land' as an effective bargaining tool by their employers' recognition of the emptiness of such a threat.[36]

Some observers have remarked that during those intermittent periods when alternative employment *was* an option for many farmworkers (as in the 1950s) relatively few farmworkers actually made use of the opportunities for leaving the industry which were, in principle, available to them. This observation has been used to argue that the constraints which operate on the farm work-force may not be as severe as Newby suggests.

It is important, however, to consider how far these opportunities for leaving agricultural employment existed in practice. Firstly, the isolation of many farmworkers may have prevented them from taking advantage of potential opportunities to leave the industry. That is, even when the labour market was objectively favourable, it may have been difficult for a farmworker living in a rural area to locate specific job openings in urban centres. Secondly, even if the farmworker did find suitable alternative employment, he may have been unable to accept it because of his housing situation. Where the worker had lived for many years in a tied cottage, he would not have been able to pay for a new house, while the ability to find suitable rented accommodation (in particular where an entire family required housing) could not be guaranteed. (This contrasts with many urban workers who can often remain in their existing accommodation even if they decide to change jobs.) A further consideration may have been the farmworkers' 'job satisfaction'. Although he may have resented the pay and other conditions of agricultural employment, the farmworker may have derived some satisfaction from the outdoor nature of farmwork, in which the worker is more independent than he would be in a factory or in most other areas of work to which farmworkers could hope to transfer.

What all of this points to is that even when the labour market has been relatively loose, many farmworkers have been prevented from changing their employment. It might be argued, however, that in so far as 'job satisfaction' has prevented these farmworkers from leaving agriculture (a distinctly unimportant factor according to Newby), it has been a voluntary, not enforced, decision to remain in the industry. This argument rests upon a definition of 'voluntary' in which the decision to stay in agriculture, where the alternative is perceived as being unacceptable, is regarded as a 'voluntary' decision. Conversely, if the choice between an unattractive option and an unacceptable one is regarded as a 'non-choice', then one can continue to argue that farmworkers have been compelled to remain in agriculture, and to remain there without expressing their grievances effectively.

Regardless of whether one interprets the 'job satisfaction'

element in voluntarist or determinist terms, the important point is that in so far as it exists, job satisfaction among farmworkers has enabled many of them to tolerate conditions of work (such as low pay) which they might otherwise have rebelled against. This factor has strengthened the employers' bargaining position, in that they know that the work-force will accept to some extent relatively poor conditions of employment in return for the 'privilege' of working on the land.

There have been rather more significant factors than job satisfaction which have prevented farmworkers from expressing their grievances loudly and successfully. The most important of these has been the generally tight labour market, although this is not the only one; the very structure of the industry has been a further barrier to protest.

In 1982, over 70 per cent of regular full-time hired workers in a MAFF sample of 2,629 holdings were employed in groups of four or less.[37] Where the hired work-force is this small it is common to find the employer working side-by-side with the workers in the fields. This constant physical proximity often develops into an accompanying social closeness between farmers and their employees which makes militant protest by the workers over their pay and conditions difficult to carry out.[38] As Joan Maynard explains

> Farmworkers have always faced special difficulties . . . In many cases they work in very small numbers and in close relationship with their employers. Farm workers therefore lack the feeling of strength, solidarity and confidence which numbers bring. The boss is not some remote figure it is easy to dislike, he is the man who works beside you most days of the week.[39]

Although farmworkers are aware that it would be in their interests to enjoy improved conditions of work, what is less clear to them is what the most effective means are for pursuing these interests. Whom or what is to be challenged— and how—in order to secure higher wages or better health and safety provisions? The notion of challenging individual employers on these issues is often unacceptable to farmworkers in part because of the friendships which have developed with them over time.

Newby's research shows that the relationship between many farmworkers and their employers has, in general, become closer over the last fifty years.[40] He attributes this largely to the falling number of farmworkers, which has served to lower the ratio of employee to employer on some farms and which, in turn, enables friendly personal relationships to develop between them to an even greater extent than previously. Furthermore, according to Bell and Newby, the close personal relations that exist between farmers and hired farmworkers have also become more widespread due to changes in the nature of the rural village community. The influx of middle class commuters and second-home-owners into scenic rural villages has pushed the traditional 'locals' together in solidarity against this intrusion. This defensive movement towards one another by farmers and farmworkers is not only a social phenomenon; it is also a physical one. The presence of wealthy people in rural areas has pushed up house prices and rents well beyond the farmworkers' means and this is sometimes accompanied by the effective opposition of the 'newcomers' to the building of new council houses. As a result of these trends farmworkers are forced increasingly to accept tied accommodation where it is available. This is significant, for it invariably means that the worker occupying the tied cottage and the farmer who owns it become neighbours in a situation where other neighbours live often a considerable distance away. The ensuing out-of-work-hours contact between farmer and farmworker that can develop may reinforce the friendly relationship which is seen to have evolved during their working hours.[41]

Although friendly relationships exist between some farmworkers and their employers, certain qualifications must be added to this portrayal of agricultural labour relations. It is the close working relationship on the farm which underpins existing 'friendships' and which also distinguishes farmworkers from most industrial workers, whose remoteness from management facilitates the expression of hostility against their employers and their conditions of work. Although farmworkers at present work in what are often small units, the trend towards farm amalgamation and agribusiness enterprises may see a concomitant concentration of labour on large farms, resulting in overall fewer but larger units of hired farmworkers. Some of the country's large farms, mainly those in the South East and East Anglia regions, have come to resemble industrial work-places, in so far as the workforce (in groups of eight, nine, ten or more) works separately from the employer, who is often occupied full-time with the 'paperwork' aspects of the enterprise.[42] Where the workforce reaches this size, the farm is usually a complex, large-scale enterprise, where a foreman and/or manager is often employed to oversee the day-to-day husbandry of the farm. There is consequently little contact between farmworkers and the farmer, and 'friendly' relationships do not, as a consequence, prevail. Instead, '. . . relationships become more universalistic and instrumentally specific and the mode of control is more by reference to impersonal mechanisms operated through a set of formalised procedural rules'.[43] It would, however, be misleading to place a great deal of emphasis on the implications of farm amalgamation for agricultural labour relations. Although as much as one-sixth of the hired regular full-time male work-force is currently employed on only 2 per cent of all holdings, the vast majority remain fairly widely dispersed and isolated.[44]

A second point relating to the allegedly 'close' agricultural labour relations involves the question of how far 'friendly' labour relations represent a pragmatic response by farmworkers to their labour market weakness. Although close personal relationships with the employer are not a guarantee of secure housing or employment,[45] there is a clear temptation to use friendships as far as possible towards this end. Thus, just as the personal 'friendship' between a farmer and farmworker may be a useful device from the farmer's point of view (in that it helps to maintain a co-operative work-force), it may be equally pragmatic from the farmworker's perspective to continue friendly relations in the interests of job security. It is interesting to note in this connection that agricultural labour relations are much closer in the country's more rural and remote areas than in relatively industrialised areas where alternative employment is more readily available.[46] More research would be necessary, however, before the possible instrumentalism of farmworkers in their relations with their employers could be firmly established.[47]

A further issue to note in connection with the close labour relations which characterise farming is raised by Cowie and Giles

> The existence of direct employer–employee relationships is not an unmixed benefit: although vast concentrations of workers in industry give rise to difficult problems in this field, the agricultural employer–employee relationship contains its own peculiar problems. The very closeness of the relationship, which extends outside working hours, necessitates a degree of tolerance, tact and understanding obviously lacking in quite a few instances.[48]

Apart from the possible 'personality clashes' that may arise between employer and worker on the farm, there is also the problem that farmworkers may become frustrated by their lack of diversion, where their only work-mate and neighbour is their employer. Ruth Gasson found that labour turnover is much higher on small farms where farmworkers are in closer contact with their employers than on large farms. She suggests that the explanation for this may lie in the farm-workers' dissatisfaction with their excessively close relations with the farmer and the absence of fellow workers with whom to socialise.[49] Yet another problem in the close relations which are said to exist between farmers and farm-workers relates to what Newby refers to as the 'deferential dialectic'. This places the farmer in a contradictory situation in which he must remain close and friendly with his employees and yet retain their respect for his authority: the farmer must, in other words, balance an element of 'differentiation' from his workers with one of 'identification' with them. The difficulties in achieving this balance are not easily overcome, and agricultural labour relations are conse quently often in a less than harmonious state.[50]

It should be noted also that in so far as agriculture's peace-ful labour relations can be attributed to the physical proximity of the farmworker and his employer, this is not only due to the 'friendly relationship' that may develop between them. Their physical closeness also facilitates the victimisation of employees if they 'step out of line', whether by voting Liberal instead of Tory, as in the early twentieth century, or by joining the union, participating in its activities or organising the local work force, as in later years. It is true that in some cases farmers positively encourage their workers to join the union because of the financial (chiefly insurance) benefits it provides. At the same time, cases of victimisation or of feared victimisation cannot be overlooked. More than one agricultural worker attending union rallies in London has avoided the television cameras for fear of being identified by employers, and many have explained the low turn-out for these rallies by referring to similar fears among the members who failed to attend.

The peaceful and friendly labour relations to be found on many farms in England cannot easily be attributed to a blindness on the part of the majority of farmworkers as to what their occupational interests constitute. Instead, the situation suggests a clear recognition of their powerlessness to pursue these interests through direct action under prevailing conditions. Given the objective obstacles to farmworkers' expression of grievances and the pursuit of their interests, their silence is neither surprising, nor can it be attributed to their employers' 'hegemonic control' over their outlooks or ideologies. Except in the most rural and isolated of cases, farmworkers come into contact with people other than their employers. Thus, even if the latter emphasise the values of friendship, co-operation and subordination, there are alternative influences, sources of information and ideas which compete with those of the employers. The decline of the farmworkers' occupational community over the past fifty years has seen the disappearance of one source of a 'counter culture'; but alternative influences still exist—one example being the workers in allied industries with whom farmworkers have intermittent, but increasing, contact. Equally important is the role of the mass media which have 'nationalised' the previously local cultures of many communities and occupational groups.[51] Television highlights the deprivation of farmworkers relative to other social groups in England and this can provide them with a potentially 'disruptive influence'.[52] What Newby, Bell, Rose and Saunders found in their study of Suffolk farmers was that

> Most farmers implicitly recognise, however, that the extension of . . . a complete ideological hegemony in the work situation is a difficult, and even an impossible, matter. The farm worker, even when living on the farm, is never completely isolated from disruptive influences outside. Indeed, the 'greedy institution' which many employers would like to create of their farm and locality has been successively undermined as the twentieth century has proceeded.[53]

The 'friendship' which is found to exist between some farmworkers and their employers may, therefore, prevent the workers concerned from actively pursuing their occupational interests; but it will not blind them to the existence of these interests, nor to the fact that they are not being satisfied by prevailing conditions.

Rather than the 'ideological hegemony' of employers, Newby found that foremost among the obstacles to farmworkers' expression and pursuit of their interests was their dual weakness in the labour and housing markets.

> The objective deprivation of the agricultural worker compared with other sections of British society is probably as great today as it has

ever been, yet the farm worker displays few outward signs of dissatisfaction: he rarely complains, does not go on strike and does not
indulge in absenteeism. It is easy to regard him as 'deferential'. Yet
perhaps the most important facet of his overall situation is his
relative powerlessness to obtain higher rewards for his labour owing
to the still quite rigid constraints that operate in both the labour
and housing markets.[54]

This argument is supported by Dunbabin's historical evidence
which reveals that in the late nineteenth century, the two
main periods of agricultural labour unrest (1872-74 and
1890-92) were years when labour was in relatively high
demand. This point is corroborated by O. Jocelyn Dunlop,
who found that farmworkers' best chances for improving
their conditions in the nineteenth century always arose when
their labour was scarce. In these situations even a threatened
withdrawal of labour could at times force farmers to concede
to farmworkers' demands, because there was no alternative
labour with which to replace the rebellious farmworkers.[55]

The extensive dependency of twentieth century farmworkers upon their employers for their livelihoods not only
explains the loud silence which accompanies most farmworkers' deprivation; it also sheds light on the discrepant
effects which isolation and scatteredness have had on the
organisation of farmers and farmworkers. The fact that
farmers are extremely well-organised, while only some
40 per cent of farmworkers are unionised is, of course,
partially due to the greater material resources of farmers. The
access to cars, telephones and money, which far more farmers
than farmworkers enjoy, is a clear advantage for union
organisers, both in recruiting new members and in maintaining
a certain degree of communication and activity among existing
ones. What is also significant is the fact that, unlike the
farmer, the farmworker cannot always afford to challenge the
existing 'amicable' labour relations by joining a union and
suggesting thereby the existence of a conflict of interests
between worker and employer. Consequently, rather than
bargaining for better conditions through the union, the
individual farmworker often remains outside the union,
attempting to secure the most favourable conditions possible
through direct and 'friendly' negotiations.

The consequences of farmworkers' low union membership
are far-reaching. Those who remain outside the union's ranks
are unable to press their demands beyond the point where
relations with the employer would be seriously threatened; in

the final analysis, they are obliged to accept the terms offered by their employers. At the same time, these non-members deprive the union of badly needed income. Non-members pay nothing towards the union's costs and yet, in many cases, they derive great benefit from the union's activities. Indeed, according to F. D. Mills, this is a major reason why many farmworkers do not join the union; there are no obvious benefits of paying the cost for doing so since many of the fruits of the union's work can be enjoyed by non-members.[56] However, by free-riding in this way, these farmworkers constrain the union significantly, for they prevent its leadership from being able to claim to speak for all farmworkers in its campaigns: it cannot even claim to represent a majority of farmworkers according to most estimates of union membership. Furthermore, the large presence of non-members inhibits the union from developing plans for taking industrial action. The withdrawal of union labour from the country's farms would leave many farm enterprises working as normal, since many farmers employ only non-union labour; meanwhile, those farmers who usually employ unionised workers could replace any strikers with contract and casual non-union labour—as they did during the Norfolk Strike of 1923. Unlike many other groups of workers, farmworkers have been unable to institute a 'closed shop' to prevent this situation from persisting.[57]

Not all non-members have declined to join the union on the basis of the material costs and benefits which membership involves. A small minority of Newby's sample expressed 'ideological' objections to trade unions and strikes *per se*. Most prevalent among the responses to Newby's questions, however, were 'apathy and the failure of the union organisation to penetrate to their situation',[58] an answer which points again to the web of problems relating to the union's poor financial state and consequent lack of staff, facilities, organisation and membership. Newby illuminates the complexity and circularity of the union's powerlessness in this context

> The problems of recruitment and organisation have inhibited the use of the strike weapon, yet without it the NUAAW renders itself unable to raise the standard of living of its members beyond the level determined by a free labour market. This in turn threatens to make unionisation irrelevant for the individual agricultural worker, who has less incentive to join. In many cases the union can hardly be said to give him a better deal than a friendly chat with the boss.

Hence the NUAAW has become trapped within a vicious circle—its lack of power is based ultimately upon a low level of organisation which in turn stems partly from its weakness in wage bargaining.[59]

Over the past century, and particularly in the last fifty years, the labour market position of the agricultural labour force has been deteriorating, both in response to the increasing mechanisation of farming and to the relative decline of agriculture in the national economy. But in recent years, certain groups of manual workers in England's manufacturing industries have been confronted by a situation similar to that with which farmworkers are by now familiar. A constant threat of unemployment hovers over many of them, as the demand for their labour has been reduced by the use of new labour-saving machinery and by the growing importance of new industries in the national economy (primarily the high technology and service industries). The consequences of this situation for industrial labour relations may be that they will come to resemble those which are found in agriculture, an industry which is notable for the quiescence of its labour force which is too powerless to pursue its interests through strike action. The likelihood of this condition developing in Britain's manufacturing industries was raised by the current leader of the Labour Party, Neil Kinnock, who claimed that the existing high level of unemployment in the country was being used 'to create a nation of order takers, an obedient nation, a compliant nation'.[60]

The already long duration of this situation among the agricultural labour force is a significant factor in explaining the great reluctance among farmworkers to withdraw their labour relative to other groups of workers. The absence of a recent history of protest combines with the structure of their industry to deprive farmworkers of the solidarity and group confidence which still enable other workers to pursue their interests collectively.[61] Farmworkers' traditions of large-scale rebellion lie too far back in time to provide them with pertinent lessons on how action might be taken effectively in the modern agricultural industry. To decide to take industrial action now would commit virtually all of England's (unionised) farmworkers to taking a step into an unknown and apparently hazardous territory. This issue was drawn out by a delegate to the AAWNTG's Annual Conference in 1984. During a debate over whether the Trade Group should undertake industrial action in support of its new wage claim, he remarked on how farmworkers have discussed taking action for over sixty years without ever translating their words into deeds. But once a decision to strike is made, he continued, there will have to be a long period of training and organisational preparation before the action could be truly effective. As he put it, 'You can't go into battle without trained troops'.

It follows from the above analysis that there must be an improvement in farmworkers' labour market position before they can pursue their occupational interests through mass industrial action. Such a development is not likely to emerge in the immediate future, for new farming methods which facilitate the shedding of hired labour continue to be developed and applied.[62] The very possibility or threat that farmers will replace their hired workers with new machines or with contract labour remains an effective barrier to direct action among most farmworkers. What then are the implications of this situation for farmworkers and their union?

The union has responded to the work-place powerlessness of its members in two ways. Firstly, the union leadership and Head Office staff have often taken upon themselves the task of improving members' conditions of work, rather than demanding active participation from the membership towards this end.[63] Instead of waiting for the troops to become sufficiently well-trained for going into battle, the union's full time officers have pursued farmworkers' interests on their behalf through a variety of formal organisations and committees which are authorised to allocate goods relating to the industry.

Secondly, the union has often looked to external groups for support and assistance in its efforts to promote and defend its members' interests. As Peter Self and Herbert Storing noted in 1962, the farmworkers' 'intrinsic economic and organisational weakness requires them to seek allies'. Self and Storing suggest that farmworkers might benefit from an alliance with their employers' organisation, the NFU, for not only is it a powerful organisation, but also the two unions share certain goals. However, in so far as farmworkers' interests and goals *conflict* with those of their employers, it would be irrational for them to depend on such an alliance for the satisfaction of their interests. Self and Storing concede this point

As long as they concern themselves primarily with employer-employee issues, such as wages and the tied cottage, they can find the necessary allies only in the Labour Movement, however unsatisfactory the results.[64]

This has indeed been the path which the union has followed in many of its pursuits: it has sought the assistance of the Labour Party and of other trades unions in its efforts to improve the farmworkers' lot. The NUAAW's merger with the TGWU is symptomatic of this trend.

The question which the following chapters set out to answer is whether, given the current absence of an effective strike weapon among farmworkers, their union leaders can achieve substantial improvements in the farmworkers' conditions of work through their involvement in political (value allocating) institutions and with the assistance of external allies. It is by attempting to answer this empirical question that one is best able to test the validity and the utility of the definitions of political powerlessness and power which were proposed in Chapter 1.

NOTES

1 MAFF (1968), *A Century of Agricultural Statistics: Great Britain 1866-1966*; these figures include farmers' working (unpaid) relatives as well as hired farmworkers.
2 MAFF, *Annual Review of Agriculture* 1984.
3 Newby, H. (1979), *The Deferential Worker*, Penguin, Harmondsworth, p 297; Pierson, R. (1975), 'What about the farmworker? a trade union view', *JAE* 29 (3), p. 237.
4 HMSO (1984), *Regional Trends*; these figures include farmers and hired farmworkers.
5 Lund, P. J., Morris, T. G., Temple, J. D., and Watson, J. M. (1982), *Wages and Employment in Agriculture: England and Wales 1960-1980*, MAFF.
6 Gasson, R. (1974), 'Resources in agriculture: labour', in A. Edwards and A. Rogers (eds), *Agricultural Resources*, Faber, London, p. 123.
7 Gasson, R. (1974), *Mobility of Farmworkers*, University of Cambridge, Dept of Land Economy, Occasional Paper No. 2, Chapter 2.
8 *Ibid.*, Chapter 7.
9 Cowie, W. J. G. and Giles, A. K. (1956), 'An inquiry into reasons for the "drift from the land" ', in *Selected Papers in Agricultural Economics*, 5, University of Bristol.
10 Gasson, 'Resources in agriculture', pp. 124-5.
11 Blythe, R. (1969), *Akenfield*, Allen Lane, London, p. 80; Cowie and Giles, *op. cit.*
12 The most notable account is found in Groves, R. (1981), *Sharpen

the Sickle, Merlin Press, London; See also Dunlop, O. J. (1913), *The Farm Labourer*, Fisher Unwin, London; Fussel, G. E. (1948), *From Tolpuddle to T.U.C.*, Windsor Press, Slough; Hobsbawm, E. and Rude, G. (1969), *Captain Swing*, Lawrence & Wishart, London; Dunbabin, J. P. D. (1969), *Rural Discontent in 19th Century Britain*, Faber, London.

13   Mingay, G. E. (1972), 'The transformation of agriculture', in R. Hartwell, G. Mingay, R. Boyson, N. McLord, C. Hanson, A. W. Coats, W. Chaloner, W. O. Henderson and M. Jefferson (1972), *The Long Debate on Poverty*, Institute of Economic Affairs, p. 52. The Transport and General Workers' Union (TGWU) also organised agricultural workers at this time, accounting for some 15,000 in 1939. While the TGWU was strongest in Scotland, the NUA(A)W organised most unionised farmworkers in England and Wales.

14   Newby, *op. cit.*, p. 228.

15   Mills, F. D. (1964), 'The NUAW', *JAE*, 16 (2), p. 231; Self, P. and Storing, H. (1962), *The State and the Farmer*, Allen & Unwin, London, p. 160.

16   Newby, *op. cit.*, p. 254.

17   This was the estimate of Joan Maynard, the farmworkers' sponsored MP, in the mid-1970s. Hansard Vol. 910, 4 May 1975, Column 1092.

18   Newby, *op. cit.*, p. 254.

19   *Landworker*, March 1972.

20   NUAW, *Annual Report*, 1967.

21   E.g. *Landworker*, October 1957, December 1965, November 1967, and March 1972. By 1981 subscriptions were £24 a year.

22   NUAW, *Annual Report*, 1957.

23   NUAAW, *Annual Report*, 1975.

24   Dahl, R. (1961), *Who Governs?*, Yale University, New Haven, pp. 163–5.

25   *Landworker*, February 1927.

26   *Landworker*, December 1971.

27   According to Mills, *op. cit.*, by 1964 30–35 per cent of NUAW members were employed in the allied trades.

28   *Landworker*, June 1968; NUAAW, *Annual Report*, 1968.

29   The Conservative Minister of Agriculture in 1981, Peter Walker, singled out farmworkers for praise because of their quiet industrial behaviour and for being a group which 'does not strike, has no restrictive practices and does not watch the clock'. *Guardian*, 27 October 1981.

30   Hobsbawm and Rude, *op. cit.*, Chapter 15.

31   The chapter by A. J. Peacock in Dunbabin, *op. cit.*, identifies specially social (as opposed to individual) protest in the behaviour of many farmworkers. See also Mingay, *op. cit.*

32   Dunbabin, *op. cit.*, p. 79; Groves, *op. cit.*, pp. 66–7.

33   Groves, *op. cit.*, p. 67; Self and Storing, *op. cit.*, Chapter 7.

34   Newby, *op. cit.*, p. 162.

35   Newby, *op. cit.*; Mingay, *op. cit.*; see also Giles, T. and Stansfield, M. (1980), *The Farmer as Manager*, Allen & Unwin, London, p. 144; 'Good labour relations' have been emphasised by virtually all N.F.U. members and officials with whom I have spoken, and by

almost all agricultural commentators.
36 Newby, *op. cit.*, Chapter 3.
37 MAFF (1983), *Earning, Hours and Numbers of Persons, including the Report on the Wages and Employment Enquiry 1982*, March.
38 Newby, *op. cit.*, p. 301.
39 Maynard, J. (1974), *A Hundred Years of Farmworkers' Struggle*, Institute for Workers' Control, Nottingham; Newby, H. (1972), 'Agricultural workers in the class structure', *SR*, 20.
40 Newby, *Deferential Worker*, p. 241, Chapter 5; Newby, H. (1979), *Green and Pleasant Land?*, Penguin, Harmondsworth, p. 130; Newby, H. (1974), 'The changing sociological environment of the farm', *Farm Management*, 2 (9).
41 Bell, C. and Newby, H. (1975), 'The sources of variation in agricultural workers' images of society' in M. Bulmer (ed.), *Working Class Images of Society*, Routledge Kegan Paul; Newby, H., Bell, C., Rose, D., and Saunders, P. (1978), *Property, Paternalism and Power*, Hutchinson, London; Newby, *Deferential Worker*, p. 362.
42 Newby, 'Agricultural trade unionism and structural change', in J. Maynard (ed.), *op. cit.*
43 Newby, *Deferential Worker*, p. 303.
44 Lund *et al.*, *op. cit.*
45 See Newby, *op. cit.*, pp. 421–2 on the particular significance of tied cottages in this context.
46 Newby, 'The changing sociological environment . . .', p. 475.
47 See Mann, M. (1970), 'The social cohesion of liberal democracy', *ASR*, 35; Martin, R. (1977), *The Sociology of Power*, Routledge & Kegan Paul, London, Chapter 5; Abercrombie, N. and Turner, B. S. (1982), 'The dominant ideology thesis', in Giddens and Held (eds), *Classes, Power and Conflict*, Macmillan, Basingstoke.
48 Cowie and Giles, *op. cit.*, pp. 106–7.
49 Gasson, R. (1974), 'Turnover and size of labour force on farms', *JAE*, 25 (2).
50 Lloyd, D. H. (1982), 'The leadership function in agricultural management', *Agricultural Manpower Studies*, No. 4; Newby, *Diferential Worker*, pp. 417–35; Newby, H. (1977), 'Paternalism and capitalism', in R. Scase (ed.), *Industrial Society*, Allen & Unwin, London, p. 70; Goffe, R. and Scase, R. (1982), ' "Fraternalism" and "Paternalism" as employer strategies in small firms', in G. Day (ed.), *Diversity and Decomposition in the Labour Market*, Gower, Aldershot; Norris, G. M. (1978), 'Industrial paternalist capitalism and local labour markets', *S*, 12 (3).
51 See Westergaard, J. (1972), 'Sociology: the myth of classlessness' in R. Blackburn (ed.), *Ideology in Social Science*, Fontana, Glasgow on the potentially radical implications of a national, rather than localised, working-class culture.
52 The issue of 'media influence' is a complex and controversial one which is beyond the scope of this study. While some commentators argue that the media simply reinforces the values of the ruling class to the 'receptacles' which watch/listen to it, others regard it as having at least a potentially 'disruptive' impact. The point here is that farmworkers can see clearly through the radio and television that their lot is worse than that of others. This will at some stage prompt them to reflect upon the causes and implications of this

inequality.
53 Newby, *et al.*, *Property, Paternalism and Power*, p. 176.
54 Newby, *Deferential Worker*, p. 366.
55 Dunbabin, *op. cit.*, Chapter 4; Dunlop, *op. cit.*, p. 157.
56 Mills, *op. cit.*, p. 231.
57 This was pointed out by most NFU officers with whom I spoke.
58 Newby, *Deferential Worker*, p. 262.
59 *Ibid.*, p. 256.
60 *Guardian*, 23 July 1984, 'Mass Unemployment "used to create a compliant nation" '.
61 J. Gaventa emphasises the importance of historical traditions in the development of a rebellious work-force. Gaventa, J. (1980), *Power and Powerlessness*, University of Illinois, Chicago; see also Wellstone, P. (1978), *How the Rural Poor Got Power*, University of Massachusetts, Amherst.
62 Norton Taylor, R. (1982), *Whose Lane is it Anyway?*, Turnstone, Wellingborough, p. 283; Clutterbuck, C. and Lang, T. (1982), *More than We Can Chew*, Pluto, London, Chapter 5.
63 Numerous commentators have remarked upon the NUAAW's centralist organisation, but all have also noted the union's essentially *democratic* nature. Newby, *Deferential Worker*, p. 250; Mills, *op. cit.*, p. 234; Self and Storing, *op. cit.*, pp. 159–65.
64 Self and Storing, *op. cit.*, pp. 175–6.

PART TWO

Chapter 4

Power and powerlessness in the determination of agricultural wages

In Chapter 1 a guideline for studying political powerlessness was put forward. It began with a definition of political powerlessness as: 'Q's inability to promote or defend its interests within authoritative value allocating institutions', and went on to suggest that in order to determine the extent of Q's powerlessness it would be necessary to have a conception of both Q's objective interests and its subjective desires. It was posited further that a study of political powerlessness would have to be concerned with two levels of political power relationships. Firstly, it would have to take account of the processes involved in 'prevailing' in formal decision-making. Secondly, it would have to consider whether the issues decided upon formally represented Q's objective interests. Where they did not represent these interests, but represented Q's subjective desires (i.e. Q's limited interests) instead, the observer is called upon to determine what processes have been involved in preventing discussion and decision-making over Q's objective interests from emerging on the given institution's agenda. These 'processes', in so far as they are the (in)actions of identifiable actors which result in the harming of Q's interests, are defined as power exercises, whose diverse forms were explored in detail in Chapter 1.

Chapter 1 was followed by two descriptive chapters which sought to place the empirical case study within its wider context. Chapter 2 looked at how capitalist agriculture has developed since 1945, noting the economic pressures placed upon agricultural employers and passed on to their workers. It pointed also to the resources which have become available to farmers for securing the satisfaction of their occupational interests. Chapter 3 then reviewed the state of contemporary agricultural labour relations, and suggested that farmworkers' labour market weakness has been the main barrier to their successful pursuit of their occupational interests at the work-place level.

Having set the case study in a social, economic and historical context, the objective now is to test the utility of the conceptualisation of powerlessness and the research guidelines put forward in Chapter 1 by applying them to the empirical case study.

In this chapter attention is focused on the process of agricultural wage negotiation. This subject is pertinent to the present study, not only because it represents the greatest and most enduring concern of the farmworkers' union, but also because it demonstrates the validity and the utility of including the 'second face' of power in a study of political powerlessness. By using the concepts of nondecision-making and agenda-setting which were noted in Chapter 1, the present study of agricultural wage negotiation shows that, contrary to pluralist precepts, power relations external to formal decision-making can be more decisive for the (non)satisfaction of Q's interests than the formal process of decision-making itself, because of the profound influence which the former has upon the latter.

For example, certain cases are identified in which farmworkers have attempted to promote their objective interests in earning high wages within the Agricultural Wages Board (AWB), but have been unable to do so with any success. Their powerlessness to set the Board's agenda in some of these cases can only be explained if one recognises how the mobilisation of values can be used outside the formal processes of decision-making to force a group to withdraw its demands altogether from formal consideration by a given institution. Another power mechanism found to have been used to prevent farmworkers from promoting their interests beyond the initial stages of wage negotiation is the mobilisation of procedural routines. This second form of nondecision-making is, like the first, capable of explaining, at least in part, why farmworkers' wages have not been significantly increased by the AWB.

What are perhaps more interesting than these individual examples of institutional bias are the more explicitly 'extra-institutional' power exercises involved in preventing farmworkers from promoting their objective interests by setting the AWB's agenda. In order to appreciate the significance of these power exercises it is necessary to supersede the pluralist approach to studying power, in so far as that approach concentrates exclusively on the power which is exercised overtly within decision-making institutions, relegating all extra-institutional relations and processes to the status of a 'background context'. The evidence of this chapter is that the formal decision-making process of a given value-allocating body is not the sole locus of political power. The case of agricultural wage negotiation suggests the necessity of considering how power may be exercised altogether beyond the formal value-allocating institution in ways that can influence the power, which is then exercised, and the powerlessness, which is experienced, within that institution.

Section I outlines the extent of low pay among farm-workers and argues that the continued payment of low wages to farmworkers satisfies the objective interests of agricultural employers while contravening those of their workers.

The aim of Sections II, III and IV is to demonstrate how closely power relationships outside a decision-making institution can be related to the institution's formal decision-making process. For example, Section II shows how farm-workers' labour market powerlessness is such as to inhibit the AWB's decision-makers from upholding (and often even discussing) farmworkers' objective interests—a factor which renders meaningless the farmworkers' formally equal representation on the AWB with their employers. This section argues further that the influence of farmworkers' powerlessness outside the Board upon the AWB's members is so long-established and far-reaching that, although it is never acknowledged explicitly, it remains the overriding factor in determining the Board's agenda.

Sections III and IV explore in greater detail how 'T' might exercise power outside a decision-making institution in such a way as to enable T to set that institution's agenda. Section III looks at a particular instance of agricultural employers drawing on their parliamentary power resources in order to secure the removal of what they regarded as an unfavourable AWB Chairman. By exercising power outside the Board in this way the employers were able to 're-establish' their control over the AWB's agenda. Section IV highlights the extent and importance of employers' labour market strength for the operation of the AWB. This section considers the minimal impact which the farmworkers' overtime ban in 1984 had on employers' interests, and concludes that this failed attempt at taking industrial action served to reinforce the employers' superior influence in the wages conflict at all levels, including the institutional one.

It was argued in Chapter 1 that, although the concept of objective interests is valuable in social analysis, a study of powerlessness which dismisses as irrelevant Q's pursuit of its limited interests would risk the omission of interesting discoveries concerning the nature of powerlessness. This belief is upheld by the present chapter, which inquires into farmworkers' inability to win even 9 per cent or 10 per cent wage increases through the AWB. An investigation into the formal wage bargaining process shows that this powerlessness to defend their limited interests is largely attributable to farmworkers' deficiency in what is evidently a crucial power resource: access to relevant information.

A study of the AWB from a pluralist standpoint would suggest that farmworkers and farmers exercise similar amounts of power within the wage bargaining process, for they are seen to have prevailed in the AWB's voting process roughly the same number of times over the past two decades. By utilising an approach which incorporates the notion of nondecision-making, however, and which looks further at the impact of power which is exercised altogether beyond the Board upon the AWB's agenda, this chapter suggests that the pluralist approach explains relatively little about the experience of political powerlessness and the exercise of power.

I AGRICULTURAL WAGES: A CONFLICT OF INTERESTS

Agricultural workers have been one of the most poorly paid groups of workers in England for over a century.[1] This continuity does not mean that they live today as they did in 1914, namely on the 'same amount of nourishment which they could obtain in a workhouse or prison'. On the contrary, in absolute terms, the agricultural worker's standard of living has improved beyond any doubt, partly because of the welfare state's provision of health care, education and social security. Yet, in relative terms, agricultural workers remain poorly paid: as in 1914, so too in 1984, '. . . they are the worst paid workers in Britain'.[2]

Ten years after the end of the Second World War farmworkers found that their hourly earnings would have to be increased by nearly one-third to match those of transport workers; by over 40 per cent to match those of building workers; and by just over half as much to catch up with the average worker in manufacturing industries.[3] In spite of agriculture's increasing prosperity over the following decades, farmworkers' earnings remained low throughout the 1960s, 1970s and into the 1980s. By 1984 average gross weekly earnings among full-time male adult workers in agriculture and horticulture were £115, compared to average earnings in manufacturing industries of £158·90. In the same year, general farmworkers found themselves at the very bottom of a list of 178 occupations which the Department of Employment had ranked according to average earnings: they were in the same position that B. S. Rowntree had attributed to them seventy years earlier, namely at the very foot of the occupational earnings ladder.[4]

These low earnings can not be attributed to a comparatively short working week. In 1946 the farmworkers' standard working week (not inclusive of overtime) was 48 hours. It fell to 47 hours in 1947 and remained at this level until 1960, whereas by 1955 the standard working week in almost all other industries had reached 44 or 45 hours.[5] Between 1960 and 1975 the farmworkers' standard week was reduced in six steps to 40 hours, where it remained in 1984. By contrast, the Trades Union Congress (TUC) reported in 1983 that: 'With more than 7 million manual workers covered by agreements giving a 39 hour week or less, any employer still clinging to the 40 hour week is in a small and shrinking minority'.[6] Thus, farmworkers' low wages are accompanied by a relatively long, not short, standard working week.

In 1971 a Wages Structure was introduced in the agricultural industry in an attempt to recognise and remunerate the differential skills among farmworkers and, thus, alleviate to some extent the high concentration of low pay in the industry. So far, however, it has failed to produce the intended uplift in farmworkers' earnings: 85 per cent of farmworkers still earn less than the average manual worker. Under the Wages Structure scheme, craftsmen are entitled to a 10 per cent premium above the statutory minimum for 'ordinary workers'; Appointment Grade II Workers are entitled to 20 per cent, and Appointment Grade I Workers are entitled to a 30 per cent premium. Following an initially low take-up rate among farmworkers, the Wages Structure became somewhat more popular by the late 1970s, as more workers began to take the necessary proficiency tests to qualify as a 'skilled' worker.[7] Between 1979 and 1982 the average number of craft certificates issued per year in England was 2,153, which suggests, however, that the Wages Structure has yet to make significant inroads in the pattern of agricultural workers' earnings.[8]

The main method by which farmworkers have attempted to improve their earnings has been by working as much over-time as is available to them. As Table 1 suggests, the

Table 1 Average weekly hours: full-time males (April 1984)

Category	Total hours per week	Overtime per week
All manual workers	44·3	5·1
Stockmen	49·2	8·2
Agricultural machine operators/drivers	46·6	6·5
General farmworkers	45·6	5·4

Source: New Earnings Survey, 1984.

availability of overtime work in different agricultural occupations helps to explain the existing earnings differentials between agricultural employees. Dairy cowmen are commonly regarded as the 'labour aristocracy' of the farm labour force because their earnings fall well above the minimum rates of pay. In 1982, for example, they were earning an average of £129·21 per week, as compared to £98·49 earned by general farmworkers. Yet, close inspection reveals that dairy cowmen were working 52·5 hours in order to earn these higher takings, compared, for example, with general farmworkers, who worked an average of 45·5 hours per week.[9]

It is sometimes argued that farmworkers' low cash wages conceal their enjoyment of important non-cash benefits. This argument has lost much of its validity over the past twenty-five years. The first type of 'benefit in kind' which farmworkers are said to enjoy is the cheap or free food they receive from their employers. However, in the year ended December 1982, only 21 per cent of all hired men had received milk and/or potatoes from the farmers for whom they worked. Even if other benefits in kind are added to these (such as cheap or free fuel), the total amount received by farmworkers remains of low cash value: in 1982 the average value of payments in kind received by all hired men was just £2·64 per worker.[10] Over fifteen years ago the National Board for Prices and Incomes (NBPI) recognised that one consequence of farm specialisation would be a significant decrease in payments in kind to hired workers. It concluded its report by stating that not only were such payments 'insufficient to require any serious modification to the conclusion reached on the basis of figures for earnings', but also that their value would decline even further over the coming years.[11]

The other main type of 'fringe benefit' which is held to compensate for farmworkers' low cash earnings is the tied cottage. This benefit will be considered in detail in Chapter 5; suffice it to say here that only 50 per cent of farmworkers live in tied cottages (where the maximum payable rent is currently £1·50), while the rest have to pay private or council rents and mortgages. For those who *do* live in tied accommodation, any financial gains must be set against what are often longer hours of work, greater isolation and more acute occupational immobility compared to their non-tied fellow workers.

It cannot be disputed that relative to most other occupational groups, farmworkers are low paid and have been so for many years. What is important for the present study is that this continuous payment of low wages in agriculture represents a contravention of farmworkers' objective interests as they were defined in Chapter 1—namely, the receipt of high wages for short hours of work. The earning of high wages for short hours of work has been not only in the objective interests of farmworkers, but has also formed their union's explicit, albeit elusive, goal ever since its inception (with 'high' wages and 'short' hours being defined as parity with the average industrial worker). The union's loud proclamation of this goal has transformed what might have been a latent or covert conflict of interests between agricultural workers and their employers into an overt one. This is particularly the case at the national level where the union has expressed farmworkers' interests repeatedly and openly, and where it has been challenged equally often by representatives of agricultural employers.

In Chapter 1 it was also noted that in the context of capitalist agriculture, the basic interests of agricultural employers are the maximisation of economic returns and the minimising of their costs. For farmers, this means more specifically producing maximum profits at the lowest possible cost of production. The conflict between farmers and their workers derives from the fact that in order to satisfy their own interests, employers must pay as low a wage as possible to their workers.[12]

Although each side in this conflict has attempted to pursue

and justify its interests through a mixture of polemic and theoretical arguments, the conflict is, in practice, resolved ultimately by the impersonal forces of the labour market, rather than by the persuasiveness of their respective arguments. It is the relative power of the two sides within the labour market that has determined that the 'lowest possible wage' has until now been a low one.

The farmworkers' union has generally resorted to using moral claims in support of its demand for high wages. In particular, it has pointed to the skill, dedication and high productivity of farmworkers, and has insisted that these virtues ought to be rewarded with better wages than have so far been paid to most farmworkers. Not only do farmworkers 'deserve' higher wages, the union has often remarked also that they require higher wages if farmworkers are to keep up with the high cost of living in rural areas.

In reply to the farmworkers' case for high wages, agricultural employers have rarely disputed the claim that farmworkers are a skilled and dedicated group, who deserve high wages. On the contrary, farmers and their representatives in the National Farmers' Union (NFU) often seem anxious to let it be known that they hold their workers in high esteem. How, then, do they explain and justify the payment of low wages to these workers? Most frequently, farmers argue that however much they would like to, they cannot afford to pay high wages. This argument was put forward in an interview with the Chair of the NFU's Employment and Education Committee

> There is nothing we would like to do more in this industry than pay our farmworkers in line with industrial earnings. But as it is at the moment, the majority of farmers in the livestock categories and a lot of the horticultural categories are paying money to farmworkers . . . the majority of which is coming straight from the banks, in the form of bank loans . . . What I'm saying is that there's no point to keep on and on paying astronomical amounts of money, which we'd *like* to pay for sympathetic reasons, and just slowly completely bankrupt the industry.

For farmworkers' interests to be satisfied, where their interests are defined as parity with industrial earnings, they would require roughly a 50 per cent increase in their existing wage levels. When I discussed this proposition with other NFU representatives they replied if these demands were met the industry would collapse and so would the complete structure of employed labour as we know it.

In reply to the workers' claim for £120 I say 'Fine, as long as you don't mind that I won't employ as many workers . . .

We've tried to explain to them [the workers] that if we're forced to raise wages too much then we'll have to keep shedding labour.

At least in my part of the country, the costs of employing labour is making employers cut their labour *and* cut corners.

The employers' main argument against raising agricultural wages to bring them in line with other workers' wages is that they cannot afford to do this without cutting back significantly on the number of workers they employ. At the same time, the farmers claim, they would be forced to reduce production levels which would harm the industry and, by implication, the nation.

The question of whether 'high' pay increases for low paid workers would result in increased unemployment among these workers is at the centre of a wider contemporary debate which has been triggered by the present government's plans to abolish the Wages Councils. Although the details of this important debate cannot be entered into here, a few observations which are pertinent to the case study can be made.[13]

Firstly, there is little doubt than on certain farms wage increases of 50 per cent would represent a great increase in overall production costs. This would be the case especially on small farms and on labour-intensive farms (which are chiefly horticultural), where farmers would be compelled to cut back on their hired labour force at a faster rate than they are currently doing. On these farms it would not be in farmworkers' interests to demand 50 per cent wage increases in so far as this would entail the loss of their livelihoods altogether. (Having noted this, however, it must also be pointed out that if farmworkers' wages were to reach such a low point as to be equal to, or even less than, the level of state unemployment benefit levels, then their primary interest would cease to be the protection of their jobs.)

Conversely, on other farms where the majority of farmworkers are employed, employers have sufficient capital to increase their workers' wages by as much as 50 per cent. In principle this could be done without cutting back on employment levels if, for example, the employers made limited cuts in their capital investment and production levels. Indeed, on some of the larger farms, particularly on cereal-growing farms, labour costs represent a small enough proportion of total costs to enable farmers to raise wages by up to 50 per cent without even requiring a compensating cut in investment and production.[14] In so far as it is possible to win higher wage increases without suffering job losses (as it would be in these theoretical cases) it is in farmworkers' objective interests to demand and to earn high wages for short hours. (This study is, by necessity, concerned with this latter group of farmworkers, whose interests can reasonably be presented as a 50 per cent wage increase. This majority group also seems to be that with which the farmworkers' union is mainly concerned, judging by the nature of its pay claims.)

Nevertheless, even if it could be established firmly that some farmers could afford, in principle, to pay 50 per cent more to their employees, in practice this is relatively insignificant. The theoretical ability to pay more does not mean that farmers *will* pay more, for to do so unless they were coerced to would be irrational, given that their interests are in maintaining maximum production levels and minimum costs of production. Moreover, if farmers *were* coerced to pay 50 per cent more to their hired workers, at least some of them would respond with labour cut-backs and higher capital investment in labour-saving machinery, although *in principle* they would not need to respond in this way.

The conflict between farmers and farmworkers over the payment of wages is settled in practice neither by the social justice nor by the theoretical validity of their respective claims, but rather by their relative power in the labour market. It is their power in the marketplace that enables agricultural employers to continue satisfying their objective interests by paying low wages to their workers; and that enables them to prevent changes to this situation by threatening the work-force with mechanisation and labour cuts if wages are increased by any significant amount.

The crucial role of the labour market in determining the level of agricultural wages is seen in Howard Newby's study of East Anglia. Newby found that although the farmers of that region were among the most prosperous in the entire country, the earnings of East Anglian farmworkers were among the lowest.[15] After examining the situation in further detail, Newby concluded that

what renders the agricultural worker among the most poorly paid in the region is not the inability of farmers to pay higher wages, compared with farmers in the rest of the country, but the lack of competition for labour in what is a predominantly rural area, which in turn enables a sufficient quantity and quality of labour to be obtained at a lower price than elsewhere. Powerlessness in the market situation therefore seems a better predictor of low wage levels than an inability of farmers to 'afford' higher wages.[16]

Similar conclusions can be drawn from more recent evidence concerning the relationship between farm incomes and wages. A study of farm incomes carried out in 1985 by the University of Manchester's Department of Agricultural Economics found that the highest paid farmers in the country live in Northumberland and Cumbria, where average net farm incomes were £25,439. Meanwhile, a separate report published by the Ministry of Agriculture, Fisheries, and Food (MAFF) in 1983 shows that agricultural workers in these very counties were among the country's lowest paid agricultural workers.[17]

Evidently it has not been the formal arguments of either of the two sides in the wages conflict that has determined the continued payment of low wages and earnings to farmworkers. Instead, the structural location of farmworkers in national and local economies (that is, their peculiar labour market weakness as depicted in Chapter 3) is what has ensured the perpetuation of low pay in agriculture. It was this powerlessness to bargain effectively for high wages in the 'free' market that led farmworkers to welcome the formal regulation of their wages by the AWB.[18]

II   THE AGRICULTURAL WAGES BOARD 1948-81

Constitution

Just as measures of agricultural protection were introduced when Britain was faced with military threat during the Second World War, so too the agricultural statutory minimum wage originated as a wartime measure. It was during the First World War that, confronted by a shortage of skilled labour and an increasing need for food production, the government introduced for the first time a legally enforceable minimum wage in agriculture.[19] The *Corn Production Act* 1917 prescribed a national minimum wage for the agricultural industry to be set by the newly established Central Wages Board and District Wages Committees, while also providing guaranteed cereal prices for farmers. Both measures were introduced as responses to the food shortages produced by the military situation, and they led successfully to the expected improvements in both agricultural production and living standards.

Once wartime conditions appeared to be safely over the government repealled the *Corn Production Act*, thereby abolishing guaranteed prices and the minimum wage control. Cheap American grain had become available and the government was no longer prepared to spend the considerable amount of capital necessary to maintain a system of price controls. The return in 1921 to 'free market' agriculture had an immediate impact on wages which were once again determined through 'voluntary bargaining'. The sharp fall in cereal prices saw an increased shedding of labour coupled with repeated cuts in agricultural wages, so that by late 1922 wages were lower in real terms than they had been in 1914. The Norfolk Strike halted this process of wage reductions temporarily, but the severe hardship which the strike brought on the workers compelled the newly elected Labour government to take measures to pre-empt a recurrence of the situation which had led to the strike. It was in this context that in 1924 the government established a Central Wages Board, in spite of Conservative opposition, to prevent agricultural wages from returning to their depths of 1921–24. Under the Board's aegis, newly formed County Wages Committees were authorised to fix minimum wages in the counties. In 1940 this arrangement was modified in the interests of control and uniformity, as the Central Wages Board became empowered to set a national minimum wage which was to be binding on all counties. This power of the Central Wages Board was reaffirmed by the *Agricultural Wages Act* 1948, which established the Agricultural Wages Board of England and Wales (AWB) the main features of which remain intact at the time of writing.[20]

The functions of the post-Second World War AWB go beyond the fixing of minimum wages for whole-time, part-time and seasonal workers in England and Wales, to include the defining and fixing of rates of pay for overtime work; making directives on holiday entitlement and holiday pay; and evaluating the benefits which it regards as part payment of wages in lieu of cash ('payments in kind').[21]

The Board's wide-ranging directives have statutory effect, so that an employer found to be contravening AWB regulations is liable, upon conviction, to be fined and, in the case of underpayment of wages, ordered to pay arrears of up to two years. The number of employers found to be paying less than the minimum rate has fallen dramatically since the Second World War. In 1950, for example, there were over 1,000 farmworkers found to have been underpaid, whereas by 1982 the number had fallen to just over 100 (although allowance should be made for the overall drop in the number of farmworkers employed during that time).[22]

Payment below the statutory minimum is thus no longer a major problem in agriculture. On the contrary, the vast majority of employers pay over the minimum rate: in 1976 94 per cent of full-time male adult farmworkers were being paid over the statutory minimum. (It should be noted, however, that only 43 per cent were paid more than £5 per week over the minimum.) Yet, although most employers are found to be paying over the statutory minimum rate, the AWB's decisions are of great importance to these employers and their employees. This is because of the common practice in agriculture of increasing all workers' wages by whatever percentage the AWB has applied to the minimum rate. However, while this practice is widespread it is not legally enforceable, unlike the minimum rate of pay.[23]

Under the *Agricultural Wages Act* 1948 the AWB membership comprises (i) five 'independent members' appointed by the Minister of Agriculture, one of whom is appointed as Chair of the AWB. These appointments are for three-year terms, normally renewable by the Minister until the member retires from the Board; (ii) eight representatives of the employers, nominated by the NFU; (iii) eight representatives of the workers, five of whom were nominated by the NUAAW and three by the TGWU, until the two unions merged in 1982, since which time all eight representatives have been nominated by the TGWU.

The AWB's formal procedures remained largely unchanged between 1948 and 1981. Each year around September or October, the Workers' Side submitted to the Board a written wage claim, following which the AWB met to receive the claim formally and to discuss it briefly. A further meeting was then called, roughly a month later, to hold a lengthier discussion of the claim as well as to receive and discuss the

Employers' Side's written reply. Shortly afterwards negotiation took place at a third meeting which usually lasted for two to three days. At this meeting the employers would make an offer to the workers which would invariably fall well below the amount demanded in the workers' claim. The task of the independent members was to narrow the gap between what the Workers' Side demanded and what the Employers' Side was willing to concede. The independents would begin their task of conciliation by agreeing between themselves on a reasonable target to aim for, following which they would try and move each side towards this target by attempting to persuade the employers to increase their offer and the workers to reduce their claim. (The manner in which the independents decided upon their target will be considered in due course.) The independents carried this out by negotiating with two or three leading figures from each side in the absence of representatives from the other side. Thus, for example, the independents met first with the leaders of the Workers' Side, then with the employers' leading members, then the workers' leaders, and so on, at each meeting asking the representatives whether they would accept the other side's revised offer and, if not, how close to it they would be willing to move. In this fashion, direct confrontation between the employers' and the workers' representatives was avoided during the most decisive of AWB deliberations, when the actual bargaining took place. Indeed, the two sides rarely saw one another during these critical meetings of the AWB, except when they passed each other silently by on their ways to and from the independents' chamber.

Power and powerlessness

Despite their elaborate approach to conciliation, the independents were rarely able to find a figure upon which both sides would agree. (Between 1963 and 1983 there was only one pay award which was decided upon unanimously.) As a result of this repeated impasse, the independents were forced into the role of arbitrators. That is, once they felt unable to bring the two sides any closer together, the independents pushed through the annual wage increase by voting together with one side to defeat the other. For example, after two or three days of talks with the independents each side would be made aware by the independents that the independent members were intent upon an agreement in the region of 5–10 per cent. If, for argument's sake, the Employers' Side acted upon this recognition by raising its offer to 5·5 per cent before the Workers' Side climbed down to 9·5 per cent, the independents would vote with the employers against the workers and the new minimum wage increase would be 5·5 per cent.

This built-in process of 'calling the other side's bluff' has placed a constant pressure upon each side of the AWB to compromise their position so as to avoid incurring further losses than are necessary by having awards imposed on them. On those occasions that neither side appears willing to modify its stance sufficiently to win the independents' support, the independents put forward more openly their proposed figure and then attempt to win support for it from at least one side, by suggesting that otherwise the award is likely to be even *less* favourable to the side in question. In this situation the representatives of at least one side are eventually compelled to vote with the independents. But, as Michael Madden notes

> The compliance of either Side in supporting the proposals of the appointed members should not be taken as indications of unqualified approval. As a rule these manifestations are induced through realisation that the appointed members are not to be moved by argument or manoeuvre into a decision more favourable to their interests.[24]

The discussions held in the AWB have been based upon the written submissions of each side, but there is some debate among outside observers over the extent to which AWB decisions are based upon these submissions. According to some, the written submissions and the discussions which they generate are of limited significance in terms of the Board's final decisions because the independent members possess their own criteria by which to judge what constitutes a satisfactory minimum wage level. These criteria are held to derive from the original legislation establishing agricultural minimum wage machinery in non-war conditions, which laid down in 1924 that Agricultural Wages Committees would award:

> so far as practicable for able-bodied men such wages as in the opinion of the Committee are adequate to promote efficiency and

to enable a man in an ordinary case to maintain himself and his family.[25]

Regardless of whatever facts and figures each side might procur in support of its claims, the independents are alleged to be preoccupied with the implications of a given award upon the 'efficiency of agriculture' and the 'living standards of its work-force'.[26]

Conversely, there are those who argue that the substance of the written submissions is the decisive factor in AWB decisions and that the quality of each side's submissions has determined in the past the ways in which the independents have voted.

The truth lies somewhere between these two positions. The independents employ certain key principles in making their judgements as to what constitutes a 'desirable' minimum wage level in any given year, and these principles apply broadly to the well-being of the two sides. In this sense, the 'efficiency of agriculture' and the 'workers' standards of living' constitute the independents' main criteria for deciding which figure to aim for in the negotiation process. This has less to do with the prescriptions of the 1924 legislation, however, than with the independents' aim to maintain their 'independence' by serving the interests of both sides.

At the same time, the independents are not oblivious to the two sides' written submissions—perhaps because these submissions are invariably addressed to the issues of agricultural efficiency and farmworkers' living standards. A perusal of previous submissions reveals that the workers have placed most emphasis on the farmworkers' alleged need for, and right to, a higher standard of living; and on the belief that agricultural efficiency is being threatened by the 'drift from the land' for which low wages are allegedly to blame. The Workers' Side has always supported these claims with the argument that farmers are fully able to pay higher wages without risking the industry's efficiency.

The Employers' Side has responded to these assertions by insisting that high wages will threaten the efficiency and profitability of agriculture because of the already high costs of production. Furthermore, they point to the farmworkers' enjoyment of tied accommodation, fringe benefits and 'job satisfaction' in support of their claim that farmworkers' living standards are not in need of major improvements. The two sides' arguments, and the statistical information with which they have been supported, have played a part in determining the independents' decisions, particularly given the independents' non-agricultural backgrounds and their resulting relative ignorance of the industry's changing profitability from year to year.

Assuming then that the independents make their judgements about 'satisfactory' awards according to the broad criteria of 'efficiency' and 'material well-being', and that they employ the statistics provided by the written submissions to adjust their views on desirable settlements according to the conditions prevailing in agriculture during any given year, the remaining question is: how do they define 'efficiency' and 'material well-being'? In other words, how do the independents decide upon the target which they attempt to move both sides towards during negotiations?

This is best answered by studying the manner in which the independents have performed their duties over the past forty years. They have evidently not viewed their task in terms of having to choose the case put forward by one side (for example, a 50 per cent increase) over that presented by the other side (a 2 per cent increase). Instead, they have been concerned to reach a settlement involving compromise and agreement from both sides. It is this aim for compromise which has determined the independents' approach to 'efficiency' and 'material well-being'. These principles are defined according to a sense of balance in which 'efficiency' (the farmers' interests in low wages) is to be satisfied as far as possible without harming 'living standards' (the workers' interests in high wages), and vice versa.

It is in the construction and advancement of this notion of 'balance' that exercises of power and experiences of powerlessness come so forcefully into play. There are evidently no objective criteria by which the independents might determine the 'correct' point at which to balance the demands and interests of one side against those of the other, and past awards reveal that the independents have not approached this problem by splitting the difference between the workers' original demand and the employers' initial offer. What influences the independents most of all in this context is a sense of 'realism' which is shaped by an accurate assessment of the differential power resources available to agricultural employers and workers outside the immediate parameters of the AWB.

The employers have access to what Robert Dahl refers to as a 'primary resource of great potential importance', namely the control over jobs.[27] In the context of the agricultural job market this resource is a very real and particularly effective one, for reasons which have been outlined in Chapter 3. The independents recognise that farmers would never pay 50 per cent or 60 per cent wage increases, because this is counter to their interests *and* because they have the means to avoid doing so, whether by employing contract, casual or part-time labour, or by investing more capital in machinery. The independents are also aware that farmworkers do not have available to them a defensive (strike) weapon with which to prevent their employers from taking steps such as these. Given this imbalance of power resources between agricultural employers and workers in the labour market, the independents, when determining their 'target' figure, are compelled to use criteria of 'acceptability' which fit those held by the Employers' Side. This is the only perceived way of maintaining the operation of the AWB and preserving the existing structure of the agricultural industry. Thus, although the independents impose compromise settlements upon both sides every year, these compromises are invariably more in the Employers' Side's favour than in the Workers' Side: this explains the continuing trend of low wages and earnings in agriculture.[28]

In contrast to the independents' emphasis on 'compromise', the two sides have generally gone into negotiation with an uncompromising stance. One consequence of this incongruity has been that instead of aiming to satisfy each side equally, the independents have come to view their objective in terms of being able to *dissatisfy* them to a similar extent. This dissatisfaction is based on how far short of each side's claim the award actually falls. But how does this aim for 'balanced dissatisfaction' correspond with the fact that the AWB's awards have in practice continued to serve employers' interests to a far greater extent than those of the workers?

Firstly, the employers have responded to the AWB's annual settlements with a shower of rhetoric to match that of the Workers' Side: just as the NUAAW (and latterly the AAWNTG) has complained each year about their 'paltry' pay increases, so too the NFU has condemned each year's award as being 'too high' and 'unaffordable'. The continuing prosperity of agriculture casts a histrionic light upon the NFU's behaviour, but their rhetoric serves a clear purpose: it makes for an equivalence of public displeasure between the two sides and thereby maintains a semblance of balanced dissatisfaction.

Secondly, and more significantly, it is important to notice that every time the Workers' Side submits their claim for a 30, 40 or 50 per cent pay increase, they are compelled to reduce their claim almost immediately during the first round of discussions. The independent members make clear to the Workers' Side that it will not under any circumstances achieve an award in the region of its written claim. The independents do this by drawing attention to historical precedents which show the Workers' Side to have failed repeatedly to win pay increases of 30 per cent or more; and by drawing attention to norms which define wage claims such as those put forward by the Workers' Side as unrealistic and irresponsible. This 'first stage' of negotiations during which the workers are forced by the independents' nondecision-making to reduce their claims substantially has become so much a formality that the independent members have come to judge the workers' dissatisfaction with the final award according to the workers' *modified* claim, rather than their original one. The chief importance of this first stage, however, is that farmworkers' objective interests are mobilised off of the agenda. The subsequent discussions and voting do not concern the workers' objective interests (i.e. 50 per cent pay increases), but rather their enforced and far more limited demands.[29]

It is the combination of the employers' almost ritual complaints and the systematic modification of the workers' demands that enabled the ex-Chairs of the AWB with whom I spoke to refer to their personal satisfaction with their past records of disappointing each side to equal degrees. This claimed capacity for (dis)-serving both sides equally was presented as evidence of the ex-Chairs' impartiality and of their ability always to arrive at fair wage settlements.

Attributing each side's written submission with a degree of credibility combined with an element of hyperbole, the independents have aimed primarily at drawing concessions from each side in the hopes of arriving at a settlement which appears to be equally (dis)agreeable to both. This proclivity for compromise settlements has had different implications for the two sides of the AWB. The Employers' Side is technically more able to compromise with the independents than is the Workers' Side because it is empowered by the

NFU membership to use its discretion throughout AWB talks. Although the Employers' Side is made aware of what the NFU membership anticipates from AWB discussions each year via the Employment and Education Committee which draws its delegates from across the country, it is not bound by that Committee to achieve a set figure through the AWB. This flexibility is useful for the Employers' Side, for in a sense every wage increase marks a compromise on the employers' part. As one of their representatives told me, '. . . we're always in a position of responding to a claim [from the workers] because I suppose if we had our way, we'd never make any offers at all'.

By contrast, the Workers' Side is mandated by the union's conference to achieve a specified goal. As one might expect, the conference's role in deciding the union's annual pay claim has provided it with some of its most lively, and sometimes most heated, debates. The main point of disagreement has been over whether the AWB representatives should be mandated to pursue a 'substantial increase' in farmworkers' minimum wages, or whether instead the conference should attach a specific figure to the union's wage claim. In general, the union leadership argues in favour of the 'substantial increase' option, while the union's 'purists' insist upon a precise target. This division can be explained by the leadership's anticipation of certain defeat if they enter AWB negotiations with the target decided upon by conference delegates.

Conversely, the delegates who prefer a specified target figure want to prevent their AWB representatives from claiming a victory when the given increase in fact falls short of what the delegates believe would constitute a genuinely 'substantial' increase. More importantly, the delegates do not want to enable the NFU to claim that the Workers' Side has been victorious in the AWB. Firstly, the NFU could use this to their own advantage during the following year's negotiations. Secondly, if the workers' claims are rejected year after year (which they will be as long as the claims continue to be in the region of 50 per cent or more), this could destroy the credibility of the AWB and lead to the establishment of a more favourable institution for wage bargaining. Whether these calculations will be borne out in the future remains to be seen. It is unlikely that they will, not least because the workers' claims for 50 per cent increases are mobilised off of the AWB's agenda covertly and almost immediately at the outset of each year's wage negotiations. Nevertheless, it remains true that the task of reaching apparently 'equitable' solutions would be facilitated considerably if the Workers' Side did *not* enter into negotiations with such high demands; and that the final settlements reached by the AWB would be more easily construed as compromises from both sides if the workers' asked for a 'substantial increase'. In either case, however, (whether the union decides to demand a substantial increase or a 50 per cent pay increase) it is clear that the union is fully aware of what its objective interests are, in spite of its enduring powerlessness to place these interests on the AWB's agenda.

The Employers' Side in particular, but also certain independent members, have been outspoken in the past over their displeasure with the relatively high demands raised by the Workers' Side at the outset of most years' negotiations. In their efforts to prevent farmworkers from promoting their interests via the Board, the employers have often drawn upon dominant values and biases so as to discredit, and ultimately destroy, the workers case.[30] Instances of this 'second face' of power were hinted at during discussions which I held with a number of AWB members. Their unanimous preference for a more moderate claim from the workers reveals a desire to make their exercise of power over the workers less overt than it currently is. If the Workers' Side can be swayed by dominant values relating to realism and sensibility not to raise their high demands in the first place, then the employers and independents will not have to oppose these demands overtly within the Board. The employers would thus not be seen to be exercising power over the Workers' Side and the Board would appear altogether more balanced and legitimate.

One employers' representative told me, '. . . it really is totally unrealistic. Most Unions demand something like 15% . . . whereas our chaps ask for something like 115%'. This was reiterated by another employers' representative, 'Three years ago they [the Workers' Side] put forward a claim for, I think, 100%. Well, I think no matter who you are, how independent or how biased you are, I don't think anybody could accept a claim for a 100% increase is sensible [sic].'

When asked whether a 100 per cent increase would be unjustified regardless of the base rate to which that increase would be applied, the representative replied 'yes, that's right'. One NFU official paid particular tribute to the Scottish farmworkers for their 'sensible approach' to wage bargaining

all three Sides around the table agreed, and all voted together for a 5% increase. [This] was a reflection on the Workers' sensible approach in Scotland, coming forward and saying they wanted a 6% increase and in fact they got a 5% increase.

All of these attitudes are summed up by an ex-Chairperson with whom I spoke

Quite obviously, the demand made by the workers was pitched way above what they could ever expect to get. And this, I always felt, constrained the Workers' Side in their negotiations because at the vey beginning of any negotiation they had to cut their demand by 50% before they could start talking. . . Occasionally they were mandated by their conference to demand a 'substantial increase'— well, that's fine, that's flexible. But on other occasions they were mandated to demand £120 per week when the basic wage was £60—well, that's clearly ridiculous.

Voting

Between 1963 and 1983 the AWB's voting pattern took the following shape: on seven occasions independents voted with employers versus the workers; on seven occasions independents voted with workers versus the employers; on three occasions independents imposed an award upon both sides; on one occasion the AWB reached a unanimous agreement; and there was no information available for three occasions. Contrary to pluralist precepts, however, prevailing in the AWB's decision-making is not a good index of power and powerlessness.[31] The voting patterns outlined above obscure the considerable amount of compromise demanded from the 'winning' side, which often agrees to vote for the independents' proposed figure only in anticipation of even greater defeat if it continues instead to insist on its original claim or offer. Moreover, the Workers' Side, in particular, is compelled to compromise extensively each year, because of the sway which the employers' superior labour market strength has over the independents. Given the AWB's procedural bias which is buttressed by the independents' (and employers') nondecision-making, and which precludes any discussion (let alone voting) over farmworkers' objective interests, can the support of the independents be referred to as a 'victory'?

This question is best approached by looking at concrete examples of the negotiation processes which have preceded AWB decisions. Unfortunately, the AWB's own published accounts of its proceedings provide sparse details on the negotiation process, and the Board's Secretary was unwilling to provide me with access to the verbatim reports of the Board's meetings. In any case, however, a degree of conjecture would have been necessary for deciding how far the two sides were compelled to compromise by the independents. This is because the verbatim reports cover only the full sessions of the Board, and not the private talks between the independents and leaders of each side, which is where the substantive negotiations have always taken place.

In August 1970 the Workers' Side presented the AWB with a claim for the adult male minimum rate to be increased to £18 (from the existing £13·35) and for the standard working week to be reduced to 40 hours (from 43) on the basis of a five-day week to be worked from Monday to Friday. The AWB's account of negotiations does not reveal what the Employers' Side offered, it merely states that 'the Employers' representatives replied to the claim on 22 September 1970'. The report continues.

> The matter was further considered . . . on 20 October when the Independent Members moved that, with effect from 4 January 1971, the minimum adult male rate be increased by £1 13s to £14 16s and that the standard hours be reduced from 43 to 42 but not on the basis of a five-day week. This was carried on the votes of the Independent Members and the Workers' representatives, the Employers' representatives opposing . . . [32]

Could this award be deemed a victory for the Workers' Side simply on the grounds that they voted for it along with the independents? The *Landworker* gives some indication of the union's mixed reactions to the award

> Disappointed as we all must be that we did not secure in the recent Wages Board negotiations our full claim for £18 for a 40 hour five-day week, nevertheless it is generally recognised that the award of 33s and a further reduction of one hour in the standard week represents the highest award ever 'squeezed out' of the Agricultural Wages Board. [33]

The journal divulges some of the procedures which were followed before the award was agreed upon

Step by step the Farmers' Representatives . . . improved their offer of cash on the clear understanding that there should be no reduction in hours, and that the award should not operate until twelve months from the date of the last wage increase.

Towards the end of the day, it became clear that there could be no agreement reached between the Employers' and the Workers' representatives. The Independent Members were, therefore, obliged to assume their role as arbitrators. They told us that they were prepared to propose an increase of 40s with no reduction in hours, but that the Farmers' Representatives would certainly oppose an increase of that size, and that, to secure it, the Independent Members would need the support of the Workers' Side.

In private consultation the Workers' Side reached the unanimous conclusion that to withdraw from our insistence on a reduction in hours would be a betrayal of the best long-term interests of our members. So we informed the Independent Members that we were only prepared to be parties to a compromise settlement that day, provided this included a further reduction in hours. Finally, the Independent Members proposed that we support them in an increase of 33s and a reduction of one hour in the standard week, the changes to be effective from the first Monday in January 1971, eleven months after the date upon which the last award took effect.[34]

Believing this to be the best possible settlement the AWB could achieve that year, the Workers' Side voted with the independents for an award which fell far short of their original claim.[35]

The AWB's account of the decisions taken in 1973 is introduced by more patently evaluative comments than usual

1973 was again a year of some significance for the Wages Board. Decisions were taken leading to an award which was something of a watershed—a 40-hour five-day week and a rate for the ordinary adult male worker in excess of £20 per week.[36]

However large these awards may have appeared to the civil servants who compiled the report, they were decided upon in spite of the Workers' Side's opposition (apart from the 40-hour per week clause). This might at first appear irrational, given that the award was heralded as an apparent 'break-through'. However, the workers had gone into negotiations with a claim for £25 per week for the ordinary adult male worker, and for a five-day week from Monday to Friday. The AWB's award was thus considerably lower than the workers' claims—from the Workers' Side's perspective it did *not* mark a significant watershed in their standard of living, making their opposition to it a wholly understandable response.

The AWB's meetings in 1974 diverged somewhat from usual practice. After a proposal which fell well short of the workers' claim for £35 per week had been agreed upon by the independents and the employers, the Workers' Side withdrew from the subsequent discussion as a gesture of contempt for the proposed award. The meeting was then adjourned without the proposals being confirmed. At a new meeting the independents put forward an amended proposal which was carried by the independents' votes with both sides abstaining. The *Landworker* described the thirteen-hour non-stop negotiations as '. . . the longest, toughest and most complex negotiations in which we have been involved'. This was primarily because, for the first time, neither side was willing to follow the AWB's 'normal' practice of compromising with the independents.[37]

The following year was also a departure from conventional practice in so far as the AWB reached a 'unanimous' decision over the following year's wage increase. The workers' claim in September 1975 was for a £40 weekly minimum basic rate. The employers' reply to this was to offer, according to the *Landworker*, a £3·89 weekly increase which would have brought the minimum up to £34·39. At the next meeting the workers' representatives repeated their claim for £40, which was defeated by the employers' and independents' combined votes. Another proposal by the Employers' Side was defeated, following which the employers offered a £6 weekly increase: this was eventually accepted unanimously. However, the term 'unanimous' may conceal the fact that the £6 increase was over £2 higher than the employers had wanted to pay and £3·50 less than the workers' demand. Furthermore, it was not wholly coincidental that the government of the day had provided for a £6 per week upper limit on all pay increases in that year, as part of its campaign to curb inflation. This externally imposed guideline introduced a new point around which AWB members could focus their attention and towards which they could compromise.

The AWB met in September 1977 to discuss the workers' new demand for a £60 per week minimum wage for a 35-hour week. The employers replied negatively to this in October and a few days later negotiation got under way. The AWB report explains that

The negotiations were unique in that, for the first time, the

Employers' Side and the Workers' Side were invited to have discussions together, without the Independent Members being present. These discussions continued for about an hour but broke up when no progress could be made. Thereupon the normal pattern of negotiations, whereby the Independent Members consulted with each Side in turn, was resumed.[38]

After exceptionally long negotiations the independents proposed an award of £43 per week, which was carried by the votes of the independents and the workers, with the employers opposing it. A full £17 per week less than the workers' original demand, this award represented a curious victory for the 'winning' side. The pressure placed upon the workers to vote with the independents is illuminated by the *Landworker*'s description of events. Once the independents made their offer of £43 per week, the workers began to object, saying they had come for £60—an increase of 50 per cent, not 13 per cent.

> But the independent members told the workers they would go no higher. If the workers refused the package the farmers' proposals were all they were likely to get. And the farmers' offer of £3·90 was contingent on the Workers voting for it. If there was a settlement imposed on the workers, it would be £3·70.
>
> Faced with this ultimatum, the workers agreed to support the Independents, and the package was agreed. Reg Bottini [the General Secretary] told the Press afterwards:
>
> 'We only agreed to this after a lot of heart-searching. Average earnings will rise by around 13 per cent. That is not as much as farm workers deserve. There will be profound disappointment among our members.'[39]

'Profound disappointment' with the AWB's awards is an inevitable by-product of the Board's approach to wage negotiation, although this can be easily overlooked if one focuses exclusively on the Board's formal voting. The independents' persistent search for compromise settlements combines with the uncompromising attitudes of the two sides to ensure that neither the employers nor the workers will ever achieve the target which they hope for at the outset of negotiations. However, it is the Workers' Side which suffers the most profound disappointment: the awards which the AWB has settled on have consistently satisfied the employers' aim of maintaining low wages in agriculture, rather than assisting the workers in their efforts to achieve parity with other manual workers. This imbalance in the two sides: respective 'disappointments' is attributable primarily to the affinity of outlook between the independents and the Employers' Side, both of whom regard 'reasonable' settlements ultimately in terms of what employers are willing to pay.

Yet the very nature of the AWB is such that it simultaneously dilutes the anger and disappointment which it gives rise to among farmworkers. Union members may feel inclined to blame their representatives on the AWB for what is perceived as a paltry wage award; to which the AWB representatives reply that the award was imposed upon them by the independents—within the confines of the AWB there is nothing the workers' representatives can do to change this situation. The Workers' Side of the Board is thus relieved of any responsibility for the low wage awards, and union members are forced to complain about the decisions of the other side and the independents, people over whom they have no direct influence.

The AWB reduces the potential anger felt over wage settlements in another way, one which helps to perpetuate the 'peaceful' labour relations which have characterised twentieth century agriculture. One of the employers' representatives explained this function of the Board to me in terms reminiscent of Lewis Coser's observations on the social significance of 'those safety-valve institutions which serve to divert hostility into substitute objects or which function as channels for cathartic release'.[40] According to the employers' representative,

> What is important is that (the AWB) does take all the aggravation out of setting approximate levels of wages away from the average employer and the average worker so that they are able to work together on very good terms which they do do . . . Most farmers and most workers get on well together and work well together and they are able to vent their feelings on the Wages Board which is a group of faceless people—one never know who they are, really—and they can say 'Sorry, Fred, it's only 5%, but it's the Wages Board up there, whoever they are, that are responsible'. Or, similarly, if an employer is paying what he thinks is a disproportionately high increase, he doesn't cuss the worker, he cusses the Wages Board . . . The net gains are considerable, because everyone is a little happier than they otherwise would be, they don't waste their time hating each other as much as they otherwise might do.

The independent members' disproportionate influence over the decisions of the AWB has meant that they in particular have been 'blamed' repeatedly by other AWB members and by the people whom they represent for the disappointment caused by the AWB's annual settlements. There is, however, a marked difference in attitude towards the independent members between the Employers' Side and the Workers' Side. In general, the employers have accepted the 'independence' of the independent members, and they have regarded their decisions as being overall fair and impartial. (One of the employers' representatives with whom I spoke supported this view by pointing to the equal number of times the independents had voted with each side over the past twenty years.) The employers approve also of the independents' semi-permanent role on the AWB. They claim that sitting on the Board for so many years has provided the independent members with the necessary familiarity with the industry for setting its wage levels, a familiarity which can be maintained without having personal ties with agriculture. This, argues the Employers' Side, is a preferable context for wage negotiation than that provided by the Advisory, Conciliation, and Arbitration Service (ACAS) whose members would have no appreciation of agriculture's idiosyncracies.

Conversely, the Workers' Side is generally more critical of the AWB's constitution, and in particular its independent members. The Workers' Side perceives a distinct bias in the independents' attitudes and decisions which it attributes to the independents' social and economic backgrounds. Although it is incorrect to argue that all independent members have come from an employer's background, it may be true, as certain workers' representatives have argued, that the independents have had an 'employer's approach' to the wages issue; or, as one leading member of the Workers' Side argued, the independents have 'all been drawn from one stratum of society'. Even one of the more recent additions to the independent team who was appointed by the Labour Minister of Agriculture, John Silkin, in the interest of 'balance' has been a disappointment to the Workers' Side. The new member is a worker–director in the steel industry and has voted consistently along with the other independent members. This has been attributed to his common social situation with the other independents, in so far as he has a number of people working 'below' him and is thus alleged to be relatively unsympathetic to the least well-off in any industry.

It is impossible to determine how far the independents take the decisions they do *because of* their occupational backgrounds; but the argument that the independents are drawn from a single social and economic stratum is verifiable. Since 1924 there have been ten Board Chairs, three of whom were Lords, three were Knights and the remaining four were professors. The other independent members have been drawn overwhelmingly from the academic, financial and legal worlds. As an ex-Chair remarked, 'You know, we were terribly middle-class, which was a pity.'

The distribution of information: a resource of power in wage negotiation

The perceived bias among the independent members (or 'Appointed' members, as the Workers' Side refers to them) has not prevented the workers from trying each year to convince the AWB that a 'large' increase in the agricultural minimum wage is imperative. However, in attempting to defend their interests through the AWB, the Workers' Side has been confronted by a major obstacle: it has been denied access to a crucial resource, namely the necessary information for arguing and defending their case. Although wage awards have been broadly in the favour of the Employers' Side due to factors which lie outside of the Board itself (i.e. the employers' superior strength in the labour market and the independents' awareness of this), the workers' ability to argue a convincing case within the AWB is important for the defence of their *limited* interests in an award which is at least a few per centage points higher than it might otherwise be. It is with respect to these more limited interests that the workers' restricted access to information has prevented them from negotiating successfully on so many occasions within the AWB.

Between 1948 and 1984 the database used in AWB negotiations has been the *Annual Review of Agriculture*, which the MAFF produces every year. The *Annual Review* is a White Paper which provides data drawn from surveys of farmers across the U.K. concerning the 'economic condition and prospects of the U.K. agricultural industry'.[41] Like most government White Papers, the *Annual Review*'s statistics have been regarded widely as accurate indices of the industry's existing and anticipated prosperity. However, as Barry Hindess has pointed out, official statistics cannot be accepted as 'mere givens to be taken as they are'. Instead, they must be analysed as a product which has been created in a specific context and by certain instruments.

> In the case of statistics we may distinguish between two sets of instruments—the 'technical' instruments of the social survey and the 'conceptual' instruments, the system of concepts and categories governing the assignment of cases into classes.[42]

What the Workers' Side of the AWB has found is that the conceptual instruments employed for the production of the *Annual Review* have been such as to have precluded statistics which could be of assistance to their case for high wages. On the contrary, they have provided abundant information for the Employers' Side to use in order to convince the independents that high wages are undesirable and unnecessary in agriculture.

Given that one of the most frequently raised points of discussion in the AWB concerns the farmers' ability to pay high wages, it is interesting to note what information the AWB provides in connection with this issue. The most important point to notice is that the *Annual Review* fails to distinguish between farmers who employ labour and those who do not. This omission is of great consequence. For example, in the tables which outline average farm incomes, the figure would be considerably higher *if* they were calculated on the basis of only those farmers who employ labour. This, in turn, could be used by the Workers' Side to support its arguments that farmers can afford to pay high wages; but the figures as they are constituted in the *Annual Review*, depressed by the inclusion of farm incomes of those farms which do not employ labour, are of limited use to the Workers' Side. Similarly, farm income statistics in the *Annual Review* are calculated on the basis of averages between England, Wales, Scotland and Northern Ireland, whereas the AWB is concerned only with England and Wales. Once again, the statistics favour the employers' case, because farm incomes are generally lower in Scotland and Northern Ireland. The Workers' Side has been able to establish that at least 50 per cent of the agricultural workers whom they represent work on the 6,000 largest farms in England and Wales, but they remain unable to specify *how* prosperous those farms are because of the *Annual Review*'s aggregated data.

Where the *Annual Review* does provide information on farmers' incomes, it does so in terms of the conceptual category 'net farm incomes'. Once again, this is of greater use to the Employers' Side than to the Workers' Side because it represents farming incomes as lower than they might otherwise be construed. 'Net farm incomes' constitute farmers' incomes *after* the deduction of various items of expenditure and depreciation. For the purposes of the *Annual Review*'s fact-gathering, the farmer's expenses on car maintenance, insurance and licensing, telephones, electricity and fuel, house repairs and water charges, and even seven-eighths of their NFU contributions are all included under the heading of 'business expenditure' and are thus subtracted from the income before the 'net farm income' is determined. This contrasts greatly with the figure provided by the *Annual Review* for agricultural workers' 'average pay' from which all expenses have to be paid, even where they are work-related, such as the maintenance of cars which are required in order to get to work.[43] Thus, the statistics as they are presented in the *Annual Review* inflate farmworkers' pay relative to farmers' incomes by the differential treatment of the two groups' expenditure and incomes.

It is also significant that the *Annual Review* provides plenty of detail on the state of each agricultural sector, but that the only information on farmworkers among its twenty-seven or twenty-eight tables concerns the numbers employed, their average hours and earnings and the rate of labour productivity. Information on their cost of living, their prospects for alternative employment, their dependency on Family Income Supplement (FIS) and other forms of social security is omitted; yet conceptual categories such as these would be of use to the Workers' Side of the AWB.

There is no statutory obligation on the part of the Workers' Side of the AWB to utilise the *Annual Review* in presenting its case to the AWB. However, the union's limited resources for researching independently into this area and the secrecy which pervades the topic of income levels generally[44] have prevented them so far from producing an acceptable alternative database. So, although the Workers' Side has not invested MAFF's statistics with a 'status of reality which they do not warrant',[45] it remains obliged to use them as far as possible in support of its wage claims in the AWB.

III   THE AGRICULTURAL WAGES BOARD 1981–84: CONFIRMING FARM-WORKERS' POWERLESSNESS I

In 1981 the Independent Chair of the AWB retired from his post, having held it for nine years. Professor Miles explained his resignation by referring to his belief that the Chair must always be aloof from the Board's other members and relatively unpredictable. He felt that after nine years, the two sides of the Board had acquired the ability to predict his actions and reactions, and that consequently it would be in the interests of all concerned if he retired.

On 14 May 1981, Gordon Dickson, Professor of Agriculture at the University of Newcastle upon Tyne, was appointed as the new Independent Chair of the AWB. On taking up his new post Professor Dickson claimed to have few preconceptions about the nature and role of the AWB; yet, soon after his first meeting with the Board's members he decided that the Board would benefit from certain reforms.

In particular, Dickson believed that the AWB and the agricultural industry generally would prosper if a 'progressive wages policy' were to take the place of the existing practice of passing annual piecemeal wage awards. Dickson argued for a long-term but relatively flexible strategy which, once the two sides of the Board agreed upon it, could become the common objective of the entire Board. Thus, for example, the Board might decide to aim for a 40 per cent increase in agricultural wages over the coming three or five years. In the context of this commonly held aim the two sides of the Board would be able to meet annually to discuss 'how', rather than 'whether', to implement this wage increase. This plan of Dickson's never took off in the AWB. Those on the Employers' Side were opposed to it, ostensibly on the grounds of 'impracticality'; they insisted that a 'long-term strategy' was incompatible with the unpredictability of the agricultural industry. The Workers' Side agreed with the programme in principle, but did not see how it could be implemented through the existing machinery of the AWB.

Having failed in this particular attempt to establish a means by which the AWB could begin to take corporate decisions, Dickson sought some other mechanism through which the AWB could develop a 'corporate identity or responsibility'.[46] He decided to try to develop the face-to-face negotiations between workers and employers which had been attempted under the previous Chair in 1977, but which had foundered after one hour. Dickson refused to follow his predecessor's practice of separating the two sides of the AWB and discussing the issue of wages with each side in the absence of, and in a sense on behalf of, the other side. Instead, he kept the two sides together in the same room and forced them to negotiate openly with one another, limiting the independents' role to that of asking for points of clarification. Under Dickson the AWB's wages bargaining process began to resemble the direct employer–employee wage negotiation which characterises most other industries. Only towards the end of the three-day talks was Dickson obliged to separate the two sides in order to enforce a final settlement upon them. In this way, Dickson hoped the AWB would be able to reach 'genuinely agreed' settlements rather than the compromises which had been imposed in the past on one or both sides by the independents.

Dickson departed from what was expected of him in other ways, too. Compared to his predecessors he took a more high profile approach, addressing various agricultural meetings and making speeches which pertained to his role as AWB Chair. During many of his speeches Dickson remarked that he would like to see the AWB taking a more 'corporate' approach to the issue of agricultural wages because this, he believed, would be the only way in which the gap between agricultural and industrial wages could be narrowed.

What was arguably Dickon's greatest innovation occurred in 1983. At the end of 1982 the farmworkers' minimum wage was increased by 7·1 per cent. Then, in February 1983, the *Annual Review of Agriculture* was published, revealing that 1982 had seen an average 45 per cent increase in net farm incomes. This revelation was more of a surprise to the Workers' Side and independents than to the employers, who had already had some idea of how profitable the industry had been during the preceding year—particularly given that the NFU's members and officials provide much of the data from which MAFF compiles its statistics. The Workers' Side responded by demanding an interim award, a demand to which the independents would not at first agree. A further change, and one with more long-term implications, was then demanded by the Workers' Side in the light of the recent events: they called for an adjustment in the timing of the annual wages negotiation from autumn to spring so that the material in the *Annual Review* could be available to *both* sides of the AWB. The independents, under Dickson's leadership, viewed this as an acceptable request. In February 1983 the independents and the Workers' Side voted against the employers in favour of initiating new wage negotiations, with any increase that was decided to apply for up to one year, and all future negotiations to be held likewise in the spring rather than autumn. The workers then withdrew their interim claim and submitted a fresh application to cover the change-over period.

As a result of these changes the Workers' Side won a 5 per cent increase in May 1983, which took effect in September and lasted until spring 1984, when new wage negotiations began. The Workers' Side hailed these events as a great victory. This was not so much because of the second award which they had gained in the space of twelve months (for wages still remained £30 less than other manual workers' wages), but because, as their Trade Group Secretary put it

> The farmers are running scared because, for the first time, we shall now have exactly the same access to government information on farm incomes which they have kept up their sleeves all these years when we negotiated and settled before publication of the Annual Farm Review.[47]

The AWB's subsequent negotiations in April 1984 entailed an even greater departure from 'normal' proceedings. After confirming the new pay increase of 4·5 per cent Professor Dickson announced under Any Other Business that he had been dismissed from his post as Independent Chairperson by the Minister of Agriculture, Michael Jopling.

The dismissal of Professor Dickson was explained initially to the media by the Ministry of Agriculture which insisted that three years was long enough for any public appointment—even though the previous AWB Chairperson had served for nine years and had left at his own request. This 'official' explanation was countered by a host of alternatives, starting with the explanation which Dickson himself had been offered personally by the Minister and which he passed on to the Board: that the employers had expressed a loss of confidence in the Chair. The vehement objections to this allegation by the NFU representatives on the AWB were accepted by Dickson who read in the press shortly after the AWB meeting that the 'real' reason he had been dismissed was that he had claimed publicly on numerous occasions that he wished to see the pay gap closed. Dickson rejected this explanation because, as he remarked so disarmingly,

both the workers *and* the employers had voiced the same
desire in public on many occasions. As Dickson put it,
expressing such a desire was entirely different from establishing a commitment to achieving this end regardless of its costs.

There is, however, a more plausible explanation for
Dickson's dismissal which has been provided by confidential
sources. It would appear that the Conservative government
of the day expressed strong disapproval of the AWB's progress
under Dickson and, in particular, over the 'double award'
of 1983, which conflicted with the government's policies of
keeping wages as low as possible so as to curb inflation.
However, when Dickson was cautioned by a senior civil
servant and told of the Cabinet's displeasure at the farmworkers' 'extra' pay award, he insisted that he could not be
truly 'independent' if he were compelled to observe government guidelines, whatever they might be. He explained to the
civil servant that he would prefer not to carry out his duties
as AWB Chair than to carry them out under external pressure.

Given that Dickson's position as AWB Chair was a government appointment and that the AWB, as a statutory body,
would be influenced to some extent by contemporary
government economic policies (as it was in 1975), it would
be reasonable to assume that the government's dissatisfaction
with Dickson's performance was a major factor in MAFF's
decision not to reappoint him as the AWB's Chair. However,
given also that the awards passed between 1981 and 1984
achieved nothing in terms of narrowing the earnings gap
between agricultural and industrial workers, what is unclear
is why the government should be so unhappy with the way
in which Dickson had discharged his duties. This apparent
anomaly can be explained through an analysis of the NFU's
activities during 1981-84 in regard to the chairing of
the AWB.

The NFU's AWB representatives may have been genuinely
astonished when Dickson announced his dismissal in April
1984, for they themselves had not made any representations
to MAFF in this connection. What *had* happened was that
the NFU's County Committees had begun to send in resolutions to NFU headquarters complaining about Dickson's
performance and, in particular, his public speeches and
comments concerning the need to improve agricultural
wages. The NFU's headquarters decided not to take this
matter any further, however, because they knew that if they
secured the dismissal of the AWB Chair they would provide

the Workers' Side with evidence that 'independent' members were not appointed independently, and that the Board was biased in the employers' favour.

The County Committees, unhappy with their headquarters' silence, began to voice their complaints through other channels. Specifically, they began to lobby local Conservative MPs, who eventually formed themselves into a cohesive group which then brought the issue forward for the attention of the Agriculture Minister, Michael Jopling. The Minister, anxious to placate his backbenchers (particularly since in so doing he would be supporting the government's policy of securing low wage increases) decided that the dismissal and replacement of Dickson would solve more problems than it would create. To minimise the complications which Dickson's dismissal could give rise to, the Minister found a replacement for Dickson before telling Dickson that he would not be reappointed. This was intended to decrease any possible reluctance on the part of the new Chair to take up a position which might later be surrounded by controversy. Jopling then waited for four months after choosing the new Chair, and three months after dismissing Dickson, before announcing the new appointment publicly. This careful juggling of private negotiations and public announcements was aimed at defusing the furore surrounding the dismissal before new negotiations were due to begin.

The NFU's ability to secure the dismissal of an allegedly unsympathetic Independent AWB bears witness to the NFU's outstanding capacity for promoting and defending its members' interests. This capacity, which contrasts so starkly with the farmworkers' powerlessness to influence the AWB, is due partly to the NFU's superior access to relevant power resources and partly to its extremely skilful use of these resources.

In the incident described above, the relevant power resources were the NFU's extensive ties with MPs. The NFU used its parliamentary allies in order to reassert its control over the AWB's agenda, as derived from the independents' customary, albeit tacit, recognition of the employers' superior labour market strength. The NFU had been under the impression that Professor Dickson was challenging the NFU's long-standing control over the AWB's agenda, through the 'deviant' reforms which he had proposed and which might, some time in the future, actually allow for the promotion and defence of farmworkers' real interests. By overseeing

Dickson's dismissal, the NFU regained its ability to set the AWB's agenda and so to ensure that the AWB would operate as it always had done; namely, in the interests of agricultural employers and against the interests of agricultural workers.

What makes this exercise of power by the NFU so interesting is not simply that it illustrates the NFU's ability to take action outside of the formal decision-making arena in order to influence what occurs within it.[48] A certain interest also derives from the peculiar skill with which the NFU made use of its power resources. The NFU's national officers recognised the damage that could be done to their union's public image if they were seen to approach central government in order to complain about what was, after all, an 'independent' appointment. Consequently, they left this task to the County Committees, who not only had strong links with local MPs, but who also would not be criticised in the same way for complaining about an 'independent' appointee. The national officers must be credited with at least some responsibility for the dismissal of Dickson, however, in so far as it was their very inaction which guaranteed the NFU's successful exercise of power. The net effect of the incident was to reaffirm the farmworkers' powerlessness to promote their interests through the AWB.

The NFU's opposition to Dickson was based chiefly upon what he *said* rather than what he *did*, for the wage increases which he oversaw failed to improve farmworkers' relative earnings by any significant amount. Yet, even Dickson's proposed changes to the AWB did not constitute the threat that some NFU members may have perceived. His desire for a 'corporate identity' was simply a logical extension to the AWB's established approach to wage settlements which had been based on compromise and agreement. Dickson sought only to eliminate the enforced nature of the AWB settlements and in this way to expand the 'consensus' element of AWB negotiations. Nevertheless, his proposals and his public statements in favour of eventually narrowing the gap were regarded as a threat to the status quo by some NFU members, and for this reason they filed their objections to his Chair via NFU County Committees and local Conservative MPs.

Yet any allegations of Dickson's 'partiality' towards the Workers' Side were profoundly misguided. Not only did farmworkers' earnings fail to improve in real terms between 1981 and 1984, but confidential correspondence between union officials suggests that they were far from happy with

Dickson's approach, which was so weighted in favour of consensus as to preclude any substantial increases in farmworkers' wage levels.

Both sides were impressed by Dickson's introduction of face-to-face negotiations, and expressed hopes that these would continue after Dickson's departure. Beyond this innovation there was little in his performance to make his dismissal in itself a greatly regretted affair by either side. For the Employers' Side he was too radical, with his verbal challenges to established AWB practice. For the Workers' Side he was 'more of the same', unwilling to force through genuinely substantial pay increases and excessively concerned with compromise, consensus and corporatism. As an Independent Chairperson of the AWB, Dickson may have looked upon this disfavour which he drew from both sides as a sign of his success and impartiality.

IV   THE FARMWORKERS' OVERTIME
     BAN 1984: CONFIRMING FARM-
     WORKERS' POWERLESSNESS II

The dissatisfaction of the farmworkers' union with the AWB's operation has, on occasion, led certain members of the union to contemplate taking industrial action in support of its wage claims. The purpose of doing this would be two-fold. Firstly, it would, if successful, bring about an immediate improvement in farmworkers' wages. Secondly, the longer term effects of such action would be to strengthen the Workers' Side of the AWB for, as the union recognises, unless and until farmworkers can assert at least some strength in the labour market, the Employers' Side will continue to enjoy the tacit support of the independent members in the process of wage negotiation. However, as this section shows, any attempt at flexing the farmworkers' industrial muscle is likely to fail, unless the union first reverses the existing reluctance among its members to take direct action in support of the union's claims.

This reluctance was highlighted most recently by a survey conducted in late 1984 by the Northern Regional Trade Group of the Agricultural and Allied Workers' Trade Group of the Transport and General Workers' Union (AAWNTG). The survey sought to gauge members' attitudes towards taking action in support of the union's 1985 wage claim. Copies of the questionnaire were sent to the Regional Trade Group's 153 branches in Humberside, South Yorkshire and North Lancashire, and 33 of the branches responded. The results were as in Table 1.

Table 1 Responses to Survey concerning 1985 wage claim

Question	YES	NO
	%	%
Should we hold a national wages rally?	18	74
Should we hold a regional wages rally?	18	74
Should we organise a one-day stoppage?	8	92
Should we organise an Overtime Ban?	8	92
Should we organise a Work-to-Rule?	20	80
Should a wages settlement (agreed by the AWB) be subject to a ballot?	58	33
Should a call for rejection of settlement arising from such a ballot be interpreted as a vote for industrial action?	26	74

When the NUAAW merged with the TGWU in 1982 there was an initial sense of optimism regarding the possibilities of taking industrial action. Union officials hoped that once the agricultural work-force took limited action, other TGWU members would join in with supportive action. This would, in turn, encourage farmworkers to go further in their own endeavours and would bring their action to a successful end. Of particular importance in such a scenario would be the TGWU's organised lorry-drivers and milk tanker-drivers whose prompt collections and deliveries are crucial to the purchase and sale of fresh farm produce. However, even amidst the optimism which accompanied the merger, doubts were expressed over whether farmworkers would be willing to take the necessary steps for initiating such events. The union's experiences in 1984 showed that misgivings such as these were well-founded.

In May 1984 the AAWNTG's Annual Conference carried a resolution instructing the National Trade Group Committee to 'seek an ordinary minimum wage of £130 for a 35-hour week at the next wage round'. More significantly, it carried an addendum to this resolution which called for a vigorous campaign in support of the £130 target, in which each Regional Trade Group Committee was asked to draw up plans for possible action. The union thus found itself committed to breaking a sixty-year tradition of industrial quiescence.

Prior to the union's Annual Conference, the Region One Trade Group Committee had already agreed to advise its members in East Anglia and South East England to take direct action in support of a campaign for higher wages. It was felt that there was no alternative to such action, apart from continuing to complain, largely without effect, about farmworkers' low wages. Yet, although direct action was regarded as a desirable and necessary course of action, the Regional Trade Group Committee viewed an all-out strike as a physical impossibility for the near future, because of the extensive preparation and organisation it would require. In view of these constraints, the officers of Region One decided to call on their members to take part in an overtime ban for the duration of one week, to begin on the August Bank Holiday of 27 August. The planned action was then announced and publicised as widely as possible. Union leaders described it as the union's response to the recent pay increase of 4·5 per cent, as well as a gesture of support for the new pay claim of £130 for a 35-hour week.

Although a week long overtime ban would not have the same impact in terms of industrial disruption that a full-scale strike would have, it was chosen in preference to strike action for a number of reasons. The Regional Trade Group Committee's main consideration had been members' lack of experience in industrial action, and their anticipated reluctance to participate in any seriously disruptive action. Region One officers believed that the membership would have dismissed as adventurist nonsense a proposal for all-out strike action, given the low concentration of union members. Conversely, an overtime ban would have the attraction of being a moderate, but meaningful, gesture of support for the union's wage claims. Furthermore, it would represent from the activists' point of view a 'first step' towards a more far-reaching campaign of action: many officers hoped that a successful overtime ban would provide members with sufficient confidence to take further action in the coming years.

As only a 'first step' into a long-term campaign, the overtime ban was not intended to harm seriously the farms on which union members were employed. For this reason it was scheduled to coincide with the *end* of the main harvest so that for the most part crops would not lie rotting in the ground. Moreover, the union gave clear instructions to live-stock workers to ensure that animals came to no harm, by making arrangements for relief workers to take their place when they took part in the action. Nonetheless, the overtime ban was not to be without any impact at all. Even in the last stages of a harvest, human labour is a vital resource; farmers could stand to lose valuable crops if they were not harvested in time. The primary impact of the overtime ban, however, was symbolic. For the first time in many decades farm-workers were to take the August Bank Holiday as a day of rest and they would only work for eight hours per day for the following week—regardless of their employers' needs or desires. It was to be a sign from farmworkers that their good-will towards their employers would no longer continue unless it was reciprocated by better wages. At the same time, it was to serve as a message to fellow farmworkers that the barriers to industrial action could be overcome if the will to do so was strong enough.

Following the National Conference's endorsement of Region One's plans, two other Regional Trade Group Com-mittees voted to participate in the overtime ban. As in 1923, however, it was the union's best organised areas which became most involved in the action on behalf of the entire membership.

Between June and August numerous letters were sent out by national and regional officers to branch secretaries to inform them of developments in the plans for the overtime ban. The branch secretaries then relayed these messages to their members, either during their monthly collection of Union dues or during branch meetings where a national or regional officer was often present to answer any queries. Some of these meetings were characterised by an enthusiasm for the forthcoming action; but in the majority of cases, members voiced profound doubts about its chances of success and about their own involvement in the action. The doubts ranged from a fear of victimisation; to the lack of impact an overtime ban would have compared to a strike; to the anticipated substitution of union labour by contract workers. Many members agreed in principle to the overtime ban; but they refused to take part in it because of what they perceived to be practical considerations. This attitude was exemplified by a letter sent to Region One officers by a Hertfordshire branch secretary

Dear Brother Jim,

I write on behalf of the above branch re: the overtime ban between August 27 and September 1st, as discussed at our Branch meeting on Tuesday 4th May.

Our members accept the 4½% wage award and can see no point in the overtime ban now that the new wages award has been settled. And the number of Union members are so thin on the ground that it will not affect farms at all in this part of the County.

Yours fraternally,

Bill Collinson, Branch Secretary

[Fictitious names]

In the view of some union members, the very fact that industrial action was being discussed by farmworkers marked a breakthrough for the union. For the first time in sixty years union members had begun to consider seriously a course of action which had been neglected since the Norfolk Strike. As one Sussex Branch Secretary told me

There are some of the most heartfelt, most serious comments coming out now. It shows that the willingness is there . . . most people I've discussed it with support it in principle; but they can't see how to do it practically . . . As far as I'm concerned, it's really stirred things up, both inside and outside the Union. It's a major step forward.

This optimism over the overtime ban's immediate objectives of disrupting agricultural production and encouraging further action by farmworkers proved to be misplaced. Few workers participated in the action and there were no complaints of ruined crops from farmers. In the language of the popular press, the overtime ban was a 'flop'.

In the areas of Suffolk where I carried out fieldwork prior to and during the overtime ban, the most outstanding obstacle to large-scale participation in the action had been the farmworkers' fear of reprisals from their employers. Of the twenty-six farmworkers with whom I spoke, all but one said that they would not be taking part in the overtime ban: their overriding concern had been the insecurity of their employment and the risk that industrial action would entail in this connection. The one worker who expressed enthusiasm for the action in the event declined to take part because, as he pointed out, there would have been little sense in taking action on his own. A number of national, regional and district officers subsequently agreed that the fear of job losses had been a major factor in the overtime ban's low turn-out.

Within the NFU there had been a conscious decision among certain officials to play down the overtime ban in the months which led up to its planned enforcement. Their decision to remain silent over the event was explained to me by one officer (who was also a practising farmer) '. . . The more one reacts to these kinds of issues the more we build up the kudos of the other side . . .'. The officer, who was a leading figure on the NFU's Employment and Education Committee, believed that reactions to the overtime ban might be hostile on individual farms if the workers came out in support of the union's policy. In his view, '. . . it's only human nature that there's going to be hostility towards this'. When he was asked to clarify the form which this hostility might be expected to take, the official replied, 'If they want to take industrial action, that's fine. But don't come running to us in a year or six months time, saying there aren't the jobs in agriculture that there used to be.'

The 'silent approach' to the overtime ban was also adopted by some farmers at their places of work: in the months before 27 August these employers avoided any confrontation with their workers over the issue. One of the Regional Trade Group Secretaries involved in the action explained that on the farms where employers failed to discuss the overtime ban with their workers there was often a reported 'change in atmosphere' between employers and workers. In these situations farmworkers sensed a need to 'tread carefully' if they were to avoid their employers' anticipated anger and the possibility of reprisals. And in many cases the anticipation of anger and reprisals was sufficient to prevent the workers from taking part in the action.

The threat of job losses proved to be a pervasive one during the build-up to the overtime ban. In some cases the NFU's silence was broken in order to emphasise the insecurity of farmworkers' employment. Of particular significance was the well-publicised circular issued by the NFU head office in June, headed 'Agricultural Workers Proposed Industrial Action'. The circular included the following passage

Obviously employees would not be entitled to wages in respect of hours they do not work as a result of this action. Apart from this however the only other recourse open to the employer would be to consider dismissal but this would hardly seem appropriate in the circumstances. *However the brief outline of the legal situation set out below might be useful.* [my emphasis]

Legal advice was thus provided by the NFU to its members informing them that a ban on overtime could in certain cases constitute a breach of contract and could thus qualify the worker for fair dismissal. Most workers were aware of this legal constraint, even if they did not know about the NFU circular. For many of them their contract of employment specified the worker's obligation to work overtime 'as required'. The legal interpretation of this stipulation is done on the basis of previous years' experience. Thus, if the farmworker had worked overtime during the week of 27 August in previous years then he was obliged by contract to do so in 1984. Farmworkers knew that a failure to fulfil the duties set out by their contracts of employment entailed a risk of dismissal and few of them were willing to take this risk.[49]

It was not only the fear of losing their jobs that prevented farmworkers from becoming involved in the overtime ban. An important constraint lay also in their poverty which meant that many farmworkers were dependent on any overtime work which was available during the harvest season. In some cases this work provided them with a vital source of income which would help to pay for essential expenses incurred during the winter months when overtime work would be less plentiful and fuel bills higher. Farmworkers' reliance on overtime pay was highlighted in another way in 1984. In some cases farmers broke their silence over the planned action, by threatening to withdraw the opportunity to work overtime ever again if the worker failed to work overtime during the union's week of action. As one might expect, threats such as this ensured that farmworkers carried out the required overtime work between 27 August and 1 September.

The isolation of farmworkers also proved to be a barrier to successful organisation. One farmworker who said that he would not be taking part in the overtime ban told me of a successful local strike which he had participated in 'many years ago'. But there had been twenty-two workers on the farm then: today there were only four. It was not possible to build up the confidence and solidarity which would be necessary for taking action against the employer. It would be fair to assume that this situation was a common one on many of the farms where workers were employed in groups of four or less.

Many farmworkers also pointed out that even if union members participated in the overtime ban it would have little impact. Employers could cope with the situation easily by employing contract labour to replace striking farmworkers. From the farmworker's point of view this meant that he would be taking risks for no purpose: on this basis the worker rationalised his or her non-participation in the overtime ban.

There was, in general, a sense of powerlessness among farmworkers and a consequent unwillingness to participate in the overtime ban. No farmworker believed that he was being paid high enough wages. But equally, they could not conceive of any means of challenging the situation. They had little reason to believe that the withdrawal of their labour in 1984 would be any more successful than it had been in 1923. On the contrary, the extent of their labour market weakness and their greater isolation compared to the situation in 1923 suggested that they had less chance of success in the 1980s. In anticipation of failure, most farmworkers refused to put their employment at risk by demanding better remuneration for it. Yet, by declining to take direct action *en masse* in support of their wage claim, the agricultural work-force cemented the extensive power which their employers continue to exercise over them in the AWB.

V CONCLUSIONS ON POWER AND POWERLESSNESS IN THE DETERMINATION OF AGRICULTURAL WAGES

Having noted how the bias of the AWB prevents farmworkers from promoting and defending their interests in earning high wages, it must also be said that the AWB does, to some extent, serve other interests of farmworkers. This seemingly contradictory situation is explained by the fact that although the Board precludes 'high' wage settlements, without its statutory regulation of agricultural minimum wages, and in the absence of a national minimum wage, the agricultural work-force would be even worse off than it currently is. Without a statutory minimum wage for agriculture, the farm work-force would have experienced between 1948 and 1984 difficulties comparable to the hardship it suffered between 1921 and 1924, when wages plummeted to the point where they were scarcely enough for workers and their families to live on.

The abolition of the AWB today would almost certainly bring a similar decline in the wages and conditions of many farmworkers, particularly those with the most limited bargaining power, who are currently paid the minimum wage as prescribed by the AWB. This prediction is supported by evidence drawn from the aftermath of the abolition of the Wages Councils in other industries which took place between 1960 and 1983.[50] Many of the workers who lost their Wages Council during this period experienced a serious deterioration in living standards, which had been kept previously at least marginally above the poverty line. As Chris Pond remarked, 'Although the councils had performed abysmally, they at least afforded some minimum protection for the most vulnerable workers.'[51]

However, the AWB's minimum protection for the industry's most vulnerable workers is in itself problematic for the union. It has been seen in this chapter that the AWB serves farmers' interests to a relatively large extent. Not only does the AWB perpetuate low wages in agriculture, it also legitimises them in so far as wages are decided 'together with the workers' and under the guidance of 'independently appointed arbitrators'. Furthermore, the AWB '. . . has removed from the arena of the farm what is customarily the most sensitive issue of all between employers and employees and the one which is most capable of highlighting any conflict of interests . . .[52]' The resulting 'peaceful labour relations' helps farmers to satisfy their interests in maintaining high output levels while depriving farmworkers of a focus for their demands.

While the Board is thus of considerable value to agricultural employers, the employers do not have to take any positive action to ensure its continued survival. This is because the farmworkers' union values too highly the AWB's protection of its weaker members to campaign for the Board's total abolition. The harsh lessons of 1921–24 remain vivid enough for farmworkers to recognise that the situation could become even worse than it is at present. They are consequently forced to support an institution which enables the employers to defend their interests to a far greater extent than the workers can defend theirs.

This imbalance in the AWB's performance is attributed by the Workers' Side to the peculiar institutional bias of the AWB and, in particular, to the manner in which the independents have approached their responsibilities. The union's recent demands for the replacement of the AWB by direct employer–employee negotiations in the form of a Statutory Joint Industrial Council (SJIC) is based on the belief that in the absence of the AWB's independent members the workers would not be compelled to compromise to the extent that they are at present. Any impasse within an SJIC would be settled by arbitration through the Advisory, Conciliation, and Arbitration Services (ACAS), which would, the union believes, produce more genuinely balanced compromises than the independents have done.

The belief that an SJIC would bring about more favourable wage settlements to farmworkers than the AWB has done is misplaced, for it fails to take adequate account of the fact that the bias of the AWB's decision-making process is related above all to the context in which it operates, rather than to particular features of the AWB *per se*. As this chapter has shown, the vastly superior power of the employers over their workers *outside* the AWB has been the overriding factor which has determined their power within the Board.

The independents have steadfastly supported the employers' rather than the workers' interests, largely because they believe that the employers could and would respond to high wage awards by replacing even more men by machines, thereby increasing prematurely the capitalisation of agriculture. At the same time, the independents recognise that the workers would be unable to halt or reverse such a programme of labour cutbacks because of their relative weakness in the labour market. Rather than risk mass redundancies (and a possible fall in production levels which they believe would result from high wage awards), the independents have chosen instead to support the status quo by overseeing consistently low pay increases. There is little reason to believe that members of ACAS would not be influenced similarly by the employers' labour market strength.

The Overtime Ban of 1984 confirmed the employers' superior position within the labour market and cemented at the same time their power within the AWB. The dismissal of Professor Dickson as AWB Chair revealed that, should their economic power prove insufficient to maintain the employers' control over the AWB's agenda, the agricultural employers are equipped with other power resources which can be used to ensure the continued payment of low wages in agriculture. The political resources which the NFU utilised in 'regaining' control over the AWB between 1981 and 1984 were, like the employers' labour market strength, located outside of the Board; and yet by using them, the employers determined what would and what would not be discussed and decided upon within it. This means of controlling the agenda suggests that one cannot discover 'who governs' merely by studying the formal decision-making process in isolation from its economic and social foundations.[53]

This is not to deny the importance of those exercises of power identified in this chapter which relate specifically to the internal workings of the AWB. The systematic mobilisation of values and of historical precedents by the independents and by the Employers' Side of the AWB were shown to force farmworkers to pursue very limited claims, rather than their greater interests in high wage increases. Certain procedural biases were found to have been created and mobilised by the independents for similar purposes. Until 1982 the independents kept the two sides apart from one another throughout the negotiation process. This facilitated the evolution of compromise and the covert exercise of power, since nobody would 'see' the pressure upon the Workers' Side to reduce its claims and to relinquish its pursuit of farmworkers' objective interests. The independents recognised that face-to-face negotiation would serve to harden attitudes and would necessitate the overt exercise of power through the imposition of 'reasonable' pay awards.[54]

A further bias in the AWB, and one which would arguably not necessarily exist within alternative wage negotiation machinery, concerns the inequality of bargaining resources. The AWB's negotiations are such as to enable the employers to use their abundant information resources to the full. These include the *Annual Review* and a first-class Economics Department staffed by a number of ex-employees of MAFF. Meanwhile, the AWB's procedures highlight the workers' relative lack of access to relevant information and other bargaining resources. As a result of this inequality the farmworkers are often powerless to defend their very limited interests.

A host of different forms of power, exercised at a number of levels and within different arenas, coupled with an in-

equitable distribution of power resources and the farmworkers' unfavourable location within the labour market,
have ensured that farmworkers' interests in earning high
wages have been frustrated throughout the post-war period.
The power that employers have exercised over farmworkers,
both within and beyond the AWB, directly as well as through
their influence over the independents, has been such that
each year farmworkers have had to accept wage settlements
which have entrenched their position as one of the country's
lowest paid groups of workers. Their labour market powerlessness has been compensated for by the AWB to the extent
that they are not on starvation wages. But the AWB has not
brought farmworkers' wages in line with those of other
workers, and this is chiefly because the powerlessness for
which the AWB was set up to compensate, has itself
determined the low level of its settlements.

NOTES

1   Donaldson, J. G. S. and Donaldson, F. (1969), *Farming in Britain
    Today*, Allen Lane, London, p. 29.
2   Rowntree, B. S. (1914), *The Labourer and the Land*, with an
    Introduction by D. Lloyd George, J. M. Dent & Sons, London,
    pp. 3 and 10.
3   *Landworker*, November 1955.
4   Department of Employment, *New Earnings Survey Part A 1984*,
    HMSO, London.
5   *Landworker*, November 1955.
6   Quoted from the Agricultural and Allied Workers' National Trade
    Group's Submission to the AWB, April 1983.
7   MAFF, *Report on Wages in Agriculture 1972*, p. 8.
8   MAFF, *Report on Wages in Agriculture 1982* Appendix VI.
9   MAFF (1983), *Earnings, Hours and Numbers of Persons Including
    the Report on the Wages and Employment Enquiry 1982*, March.
10 *Ibid.*
11 National Board for Prices and Incomes (NBPI) (1967), *Pay of
    Workers in Agriculture in England and Wales*, HMSO, p. 17.
12 Martin, R. (1977), *The Sociology of Power*, Routledge & Kegan
    Paul, London, p. 100; Saunders, P. (1979), *Urban Politics*, Hutchin-
    son, London, pp. 45-7.
13 For brief reviews of this debate see: Beckerman, W., 'Pay: Lawson's
    Faulty Thesis', the *Times*, 3 June 1985; Huhne, C., 'The Rich
    Push the Poor out of Work', the *Guardian*, 11 April 1985.
14 See Nix, J. (1984), *Farm Management Pocketbook*, Wye College,
    Farm Business Unit, September.
15 Newby, H. (1972), 'The low earnings of agricultural workers: a
    sociological approach', *JAE*, 23 (1).
16 Newby, H. (1979), *The Deferential Worker*, Penguin, Harmonds-

worth, pp. 175-6.
17 Russell, N. P. (1985), *An Analysis of the Distribution of Farm Incomes in England and Wales*, University of Manchester, Department of Agricultural Economics, Bulletin No. 200, April; MAFF (1983), *Earning, Hours and Numbers of Persons . . ., op. cit.*
18 Madden, M. (1956), 'The NUAW 1906-1956', Oxford University B.Litt. Thesis, p. 208.
19 Groves, R. (1981), *Sharpen the Sickle!*, Merlin Press, London, pp. 150-1.
20 A separate Wages Board exists for Scotland; See Winyard, S. (1982), *Cold Comfort Farm*, Low Pay Unit, London, for a brief history of the AWB.
21 The functions of Agricultural Wages Committees, of which there are twenty-four in England, are comparatively limited. They are: to consider applications for the revaluation of individual tied houses; to issue craft certificates; and to consider applications for permits to pay employees less than the statutory minimum rate where the employee in question is physically and/or mentally disabled.
22 MAFF, *Report of Proceedings under the Agricultural Wages Acts for the period 1 October 1937 to 30 September 1950*; MAFF, *Report on Wages in Agriculture*, 1982.
23 Phillips, D. and Williams, A. (1984), *Rural Britain*, Blackwell, Oxford, pp. 68-9.
24 Madden, *op. cit.*, p. 261.
25 The 1948 legislation does not in fact reiterate these 1924 guidelines.
26 Madden, *op. cit.*, pp. 262 and 275; Wootton, B. (1955), *The Social Foundations of Wage Policy*, George Allen & Unwin, London, pp. 84-7.
27 Dahl, R. (1961), *Who Governs?*, Yale University, New Haven, p. 250; Crenson, M. (1971), *The Unpolitics of Air Pollution*, Johns Hopkins Press, Baltimore, Chapter 2.
28 Westergaard, T. and Resler, H. (1975), *Class in a Capitalist Society*, Heinemann, London, p. 147.
29 Gaventa, J. (1980), *Power and Powerlessness*, University of Illinois, Chicago, pp. 137-8; Crenson, *op. cit.*, Chapter 7; Bachrach, P. and Baratz, M. (1970), *Power and Poverty*, Oxford University Press, p. 45.
30 Bachrach, P. and Baratz, M. (1975), 'Power and its two faces revisited', *APSR*, 69.
31 Polsby, N. (1980), *Community Power and Political Theory*, Second edition, Yale University Press, London, pp. 3-5.
32 MAFF, *Report on Wages in Agriculture*, 1970.
33 *Landworker*, December 1970.
34 *Ibid.*
35 MAFF, *Report on Wages in Agriculture*, 1970.
36 MAFF, *Report on Wages in Agriculture*, 1973.
37 *Landworker*, December 1974.
38 MAFF, *Report on Wages in Agriculture*, 1977, p. 5.
39 *Landworker*, December 1977.
40 Coser, L. (1956), *The Functions of Social Conflict*, Routledge & Kegan Paul, London, p. 41.

41 MAFF, *Annual Review of Agriculture 1983*, p. 1. Prior to 1973 the publication was known as *Annual Review and Determination of Guarantees.*

42 Hindess, B. (1973), *The Use of Official Statistics in Sociology*, Macmillan, London, p. 12.

43 Confidential copy of the Workers' Side's Submission to the AWB, March 1983.

44 See Wootton, *op. cit.*, pp. 28–35 on the secrecy which has traditionally shrouded people's incomes levels, particularly those in the higher brackets.

45 Rose, D., Newby, H., Saunders, P. and Bell, C. (1977), 'Land tenure and official statistics', *JAE*, 28 (1), pp. 75–6.

46 *Farmers Weekly*, 13 November 1981, 'Wages Chief Plans to Rejig Board', p. 40.

47 *Landworker*, May 1983.

48 Pluralist analysis which looks only at the decision-making arena, (dis-)regarding the rest as part of the 'background' against which power is exercised. See Polsby, *op. cit.*, pp. 191–9.

49 Gaventa, *op. cit.*, p. 87. See also Lukes, S. (1974), *Power: a Radical View*, Macmillan, London, on the use of inaction in the exercise of power. This relates to the employers' use of silence as a means of responding to the farmworkers' planned Overtime Ban. See also in this connection Crenson, *op. cit.*, pp. 77–80.

50 Craig, C., Rubery, J., Tarling, R. and Wilkinson, F. (1982), *Labour Market Structure, Industrial Organisation and Low Pay*, Cambridge University Press.

51 Pond, C. (1980), 'Low pay' in N. Bosanquet and P. Townsend (eds), *Labour and Equality*, Heineman, London, p. 93; see also Craig *et al.*, *op. cit.*, for a study of the effects of Wages Council abolition in six industries.

52 Newby, *Deferential Worker*, p. 178.

53 Polsby, *op. cit.*, Chapter 7; Dahl, *op. cit.*, p. 66; Hindess, B. (1976), 'On three dimensional power', *PS*, 24.

54 Bachrach, P. and Baratz, M. (1963), 'Decisions and nondecisions', *APSR*, 57, p. 641; Bachrach, P. and Baratz, M. (1962), 'The two faces of power', *APSR*, 56, p. 948: The mobilisation of bias in the AWB provides a perfect illustration of how, in the words of Bachrach and Baratz, '. . . A devotes his energies to creating or reinforcing social and political values and institutional practices that limit the scope of the political process to public consideration of only those issues which are comparatively innocuous to A.'

Chapter 5

Farmworkers and the Labour Party: a powerful alliance?

The Case of the Tied Cottage Campaign

The purpose of this chapter is to explore further the notion examined in Chapter 4 that the power which is exercised outside formal decision-making procedures can be of greater significance for Q's objective interests than that which is exercised in the formal decision-making process itself. In showing this to be the case, this chapter draws once again on the concept of nondecision-making. It goes further than this, however, by investigating in detail a second idea raised in Chapter 1, namely the pluralist belief that the social distribution of power resources is neither cumulative nor concentrated. This chapter shows that, contrary to this pluralist principle, the NUAAW's powerlessness to set the agenda of important value-allocating institutions is due largely to farmworkers' deficiency in a number of crucial power resources, which contrasts starkly with the relative abundance of power resources which the NFU can, and does, make use of.

By focusing upon the alliance with the Labour Party which the NUAAW had forged in a bid to set Parliament's agenda on tied cottage reform, this chapter is able to address itself to a number of other issues which have been raised in earlier chapters. As well as nondecision-making and the social distribution of power resources, the relationship between power and responsibility is discussed, as is the importance of identifying both Q's objective and limited interests in order to distinguish between a real and false consensus. The chapter is also able to investigate, and largely refute, the proposition raised in Chapter 3 that farmworkers' work-place powerlessness might be compensated for by their union's political alliance with external agencies. Finally, a study of the consequences of the union's relative powerlessness to set the agenda for tied cottage reform serves to confirm the conclusions of Chapter 4: that the 'second face' of power has crucial implications for Q's objective interests. In reassessing this point, the present chapter underlines the inadequacy of the pluralist approach, which focuses solely upon who prevails in formal decision-making.

Section I analyses the social and economic issues raised by the agricultural tied cottage system, as well as the conflict of interests between agricultural employers and workers which the tied cottage system is said to entail at both a subjective and objective level.

Section II explores the extent to which post-war Labour governments have been able and willing to compensate for farmworkers' powerlessness to achieve their goal of tied cottage abolition. This section concentrates chiefly on the Labour government of 1974–79, looking in detail at that government's exercises of power over the NUAAW.

The Labour Party is shown to have exercised power over farmworkers initially by taking steps to prevent tied cottage abolition from emerging on the Parliamentary Labour Party's (PLP) and Parliament's agenda. What is interesting is that the PLP's insistence on tied cottage reform, as opposed to abolition, was agreed to with scarcely any protest from the NUAAW. This consent, to what is effectively a transgression of farmworkers' objective interests, is explicable only if one recognises that the union lacked the necessary electoral and economic resources with which to oppose the party's line, and so to withstand the party's exercise of power. The resulting alliance between the government and the union was thus based on a 'false' rather than a 'real' consensus, in so far as it aimed at satisfying farmworkers' *limited* interests in tied cottage reform rather than their *objective* interests in the wholesale abolition of the tied cottage system. This important distinction can only be made if the observer begins with a conception of 'objective interests' which is independent from actors' subjective desires: as the case study shows, subjective desires and consensus can both be products of exercises of power.

The chapter follows the guidelines set out in Chapter 1 by inquiring not only into the satisfaction or frustration of farmworkers' objective interests in tied cottage abolition, but also by looking into the NUAAW's ability to promote and defend farmworkers' limited interests in tied cottage reform. The importance of not dismissing limited interests as irrelevant in a study of powerlessness is borne out in this chapter. By following the farmworkers' pursuit of their limited interests in tied cottage reform, it is possible to identify further exercises of power and so to determine further the nature of powerlessness. Research reveals that the

National Farmers' Union (NFU) exercised power over farm-workers via the Labour government in such a way as to frustrate even farmworkers' limited interests in achieving security of tenure within the tied cottage system.

What Section II underlines is the importance of how power resources are distributed and used in any given power relation-ship. The NFU's manipulation of information, combined with its access to and use of parliamentary, organisational and economic resources, are shown to have compelled the government to reduce further its commitment to assisting the NUAAW. Once again, the NUAAW's lack of power resources ensured its powerlessness to counter these power exercises and to influence the agenda in its own interests. Consequent-ly, the tied cottage reform, which was eventually discussed and decided in Parliament, served only farmworkers' very limited interests, in spite of the fact that their allies 'prevailed' in the formal decision-making process.

Section III examines the main changes introduced by the government's *Rent (Agriculture) Act* 1976. What this section argues is that the Act achieved less for farmworkers' interests, as they are defined in Chapter 1, than the rhetoric which accompanied it might suggest. Moreover, while serving only farmworkers' very limited interests, the legislation is shown to have left agricultural employers' interests wholly intact; indeed, in certain respects their interests are better served than they were prior to 1976. This situation is attributed not to the decisions which were taken in Parliament; but rather to the power which was exercised over farmworkers outside of Parliament prior to the Bill's formal parliamentary passage, for which both the government and the NFU are held causally, if not morally, responsible.

I THE TIED COTTAGE DEBATE: A CONFLICT OF INTERESTS

'Tied accommodation' consists of housing which is provided 'free of charge' along with a job; or, to put it slightly differently, it is accommodation which is tied to employ-ment. In the agricultural industry tied housing has a long history the starting point of which is a matter of dispute between scholars. According to some, the agricultural tied cottage system has its roots in the feudal era, when the great pre-capitalist lords of the manor of pre-capitalist England were dependent upon a bonded, or tied, labour force to ensure an abundant supply of labour to work on their vast estates. In return for the provision of this labour, the serfs gained the right to live on the lord's land and to cultivate certain areas for their own subsistence. This method of payment in kind virtually guaranteed the serf's obedience and diligence, for he was wholly dependent on the lord for his basic needs, including food and shelter. Although feudalism thus ensured the serf's subjugation to the lord, it also provided the serf with a degree of security in his housing and sustenance. For, as G. M. Trevelyan put it, although it was true that '. . . the peasant could not strike and could not legally emigrate without his lord's consent, . . . neither could his lord evict in fact, whatever may have been the case in theory'.[1]

The development of capitalism in general, and the enclosure movement in particular, saw a fundamental transformation in this reciprocal, if inequitable, relationship. Serfs were replaced by a new class of landless wage labourers, while lords of the manor lost their supremacy to a new class of wealthy and enterprising tenant farmers who sought economic profit from agriculture. These capitalist farmers paid low wages to their labourers and, as a measure of further economy, they included the worker's house which was provided on the estate, as part of the worker's wage. This placed the farm labourer in a position of great insecurity, for he was dependent on the farmer not only for employment but also for housing (and food and fuel). As in feudal times, these benefits were tied to the labourer's employment, but unlike previously, employment could be terminated at a moment's notice, leaving the worker both jobless and homeless.[2]

The late nineteenth century saw further developments in the tied cottage system. According to some scholars, this period marks the true beginning of the agricultural tied cottage system.[3] The decline of farm service (in which workers lived in the farmhouse itself) combined with legislative restrictions on the use of labour gangs to create the future possibility of an agricultural labour shortage. It was with this threatening eventuality in mind that many farmers began to build new dwellings on their land, so as to ensure a continuous pool of labour for themselves: as long as they could provide housing, farmers were confident that they would not be short of hired workers. Many new cottages have been built since the late nineteenth century, but the broad principle behind their construction remains unchanged: it is still a means of attracting and controlling an adequate supply of labour for the farm enterprise.

As in feudal times, the modern farmworker often has little choice but to accept the accommodation which his employer offers him. It is the nature, rather than the extent, of this dependency which differs today from the feudal era. In pre-capitalist England, the landlord's provision of housing to his serfs was one element in the prevailing social relations of production; by contrast, the contemporary farmworker's reliance upon tied housing is linked primarily to the nature of the modern rural housing market.

Rural housing has been subject to special pressures which have combined to close off most non-tied housing to farm-workers. These pressures, which have increased in number and intensity since the Second World War, include the steady purchase of country homes by wealthy urban commuters, by urban dwellers seeking a 'second home', by ex-urban retired people, and by companies or individuals who rent out their rural cottages to tourists, thereby reaping hefty profits. The high demand for these rural retreats in England's green and pleasant land has swallowed up much of the rural housing stock, and has, at the same time, pushed up the rents and prices of those few houses which are put on the open market, placing them well beyond the means of most farmworkers. Thus, for example, in the mid-1970s, the pressures on the housing market were such that rural housing prices were, on average, 60 per cent above the national average, yet farmworkers' earnings were only 67 per cent of the all-industry average.[4]

In this situation one would expect farmworkers (and other rural low-income groups) to turn to the public sector for housing. In fact, the severe shortage of council accommoda-tion has closed off this option for many farmworkers. For reasons which a number of writers have speculated on, rural areas contain a considerably smaller proportion of council housing than do most urban areas, despite there being a comparable demand for such housing in the two areas.[5] In the late 1970s only 22 per cent of all properties in pre-dominantly rural districts were council-owned (as compared to the national average of 32 per cent) and yet council house waiting lists in rural areas have been known to include as many as 2,000 names.[6] Nor is there any sign that this trend is being reversed. Although roughly 50 per cent of all houses built in England between 1974 and 1979 were provided by councils and housing associations, only 24 per cent of these were in rural areas.

Agricultural workers' restricted access to private sector housing and the failure of the public sector to compensate for this have combined to force a growing proportion of the farm labour force to turn to tied accommodation wherever it is available. Whereas in 1948 only 34 per cent of farmworkers lived in a tied cottage, by 1976 the proportion had risen to 53 per cent.[7]

The standard of housing provided in the tied cottage sector varies from region to region, and often from farm to farm, which makes generalisations on this topic difficult. The most comprehensive study of agricultural tied housing to date was carried out in 1974 by Barrie Irving and Linden Hilgendorf, whose survey covered 804 farmworkers and 281 farmers in Britain.[8] They found that 4 per cent of tied cottage inhabitants lived in houses less than ten years old, whereas 60 per cent were in houses built over fifty years ago. This compares with 13 per cent and 36 per cent respectively among farmworkers in non-tied accommodation. Irving and Hilgendorf also compared the amenities provided in tied and non-tied houses occupied by farmworkers. Their conclusions were that 'the only significant difference between the two groups is that people not living in tied cottages are more likely to have central heating than those living in tied cottages'. A more significant difference emerged, however, when the authors compared the distances which the two groups had to travel in order to reach public amenities and services. It should be noted that because tied houses are situated on, or very near, the farm at which their inhabitants work, tied cottage dwellers have a shorter distance to travel to and from work each day than do their non-tied cottage counterparts: 79 per cent of the tied cottage sample had to travel only half a mile or less, as compared with 36 per cent of the non-tied cottage respondents. However, distances to public amenities present a reversal of these advantages, a factor with particularly severe implications for the farm-worker's family. For instance, 71 per cent of the tied cottage dwellers in the sample had to travel half a mile or more to reach the nearest shop, compared with 42 per cent of the non-tied cottage respondents. Only 1 per cent of tied house inhabitants lived within half a mile of the nearest secondary school, compared with 19 per cent of non-tied farmworkers. And, finally, the mean distance to the nearest shopping town for tied cottage dwellers was 6·36 miles, compared with 3·8 miles among non-tied respondents.

Only two-thirds of all farms in Britain have agricultural dwellings on them, and of these 170,000 houses, half are occupied by tourists, members of farmers' families, and other persons not employed in agriculture. The remaining 85,000 houses and the farmworkers who inhabit them are characterised by certain notable trends. For example, over two-thirds of farmworkers in South-East England and Scotland live in tied housing, whereas little over one-quarter do in Yorkshire and Lancashire.[9] Moreover, tied cottage accommodation is linked to some extent with the inhabitants' occupations, as suggested in Table 1.

Table 1 Percentage of regular whole time farmworkers receiving a house or cottage as payment in kind: England and Wales 1982

Category	Proportion
	%
Dairy cowmen	67·8
All other stockmen	51·8
Tractor drivers	56·9
General farmworkers	39·0
Horticultural workers	14·0

Source: MAFF, Wages and Employment Enquiry, 1983.

Another interesting feature of the agricultural tied cottage system is that inhabitants of tied houses tend to receive higher than average wages for their industry. This is largely because the majority of tied cottage dwellers are stockmen who form the most skilled, most sought-after (and, hence, best paid) sector of the farm labour force. Where a tied cottage becomes available the farmer is likely to offer it to a stockman, or similarly skilled worker, as a means of attracting his labour, rather than to a general farmworker whose bargaining position is such that he would probably accept a job without the bonus of 'free' housing, often making do instead with substandard accommodation.

A second possible reason for the tied cottage dweller being paid above-average wages is that the worker who lives in a cottage is likely to stay on the job longer and thus acquires a valuable knowledge of the employer's farm. The employer rewards the worker for this specialised knowledge with higher wages, so that the worker has incentive to remain on the farm. However, it is worth noting the corollary to this factor: in so far as the worker's well-being depends on a specific relationship with a given farm, his mobility in the labour market will be restricted.[10]

Although it may appear to an outsider to be uncontroversial, the agricultural tied cottage system represents far more than simply a means of accommodating 50 per cent of the country's farm labour force: it can be found at the heart of many of the most bitter and intense conflicts in the history of agricultural labour relations. The attitudes held by farmers and farmworkers to the tied cottage system are in some cases diametrically opposed, as Giles and Cowie suggest, 'The employers defend the system as essential to the efficient operation of their business, whilst the workers attack it as demoralising, degrading and unnecessary.'[11] Although such extreme views are not held uniformly by the country's entire population of farmers and farmworkers, the tied cottage has nevertheless provided a unique source of division in agricultural labour relations. The irreconcilability of the tied cottage conflict and the importance attached to it by each side have made the tied cottage the single most contentious issue in agricultural labour relations for seventy-five years.

The importance of the tied cottage issue to each side is attributable to its close bearing upon the objective interests of agricultural employers and workers as defined by the capitalist economy in which they interact. For the employer, the tied cottage is a valuable instrument for ensuring adequate supervision of valuable livestock, as well as being a means of controlling the labour supply. Conversely, for the worker, the tied cottage represents a tool for depressing agricultural wages, restricting labour mobility to other industries, and sharpening the worker's sense of insecurity and isolation. Given their importance to each side in the dispute, these economic nerves which the tied cottage cuts through deserve closer scrutiny.

The agricultural employers' case in favour of retaining the tied cottage system rests on two principal arguments. Firstly, employers insist that it is important to have skilled stockmen on the farm premises continuously in order to provide more or less constant cover over the stock, in case of emergencies such as calving or the outbreak of disease. Secondly, employers claim that without the ability to offer farmworkers free or subsidised housing, farmers would be unable to attract the necessary quantity and quality of farm labour required for the efficient running of farm enterprises.

The first of these arguments has been weakened in the post-war period by the increased use of telephones and transport systems which have enabled farmers, in the event of emergency, to contact stockmen who can report to work virtually at any time, regardless of where they live. Nevertheless, some farmers have continued to insist on the need, or at least the convenience, of having a man on the spot in case of emergencies. In general, however, it is the second argument which has been emphasised over the past forty years; unlike the first, its credibility has been greatly increased by recent developments. The fact that tied cottages are provided rent-free, or for a nominal rent set by the AWB, is important in the context of the lack of rural council housing and the inability of most farmworkers to pay the market rent for the decreasing number of non-tied private houses available on the market.[12] It is this context which has greatly strengthened the farmers' case in favour of the tied cottage system, for their opponents are hard-pressed to suggest an alternative means by which to house the farm labour force.

In spite of the severe housing problems which many farmworkers would face if farm cottages were no longer available to them, most agricultural workers have maintained a rigid opposition to the tied cottage system. They have based their arguments on three broad points, each of which relates to their objective interests which were outlined in Chapter 1. Farmworkers contend that the tied cottage system restricts agricultural labour mobility; it gives rise to insecurity and industrial quiescence; and it has the effect of depressing agricultural wages.

The first of these contentions is based on the observation that, for the tied cottage dweller, finding a new job has meant finding new accommodation at the same time—a task which can prove to be difficult, particularly when the worker has a family to support. In this situation, the worker's mobility is usually restricted to new employment in which another tied house is available, usually another agricultural job. Movement outside the industry is made difficult by the fact that agricultural wages are often too low for the farmworker to accumulate savings which could be used to purchase, or rent, non-tied housing.[13] Thus, in many cases the tied cottage dweller is caught in an effective trap in which any new employment must provide yet another tied house.[14]

The second plank of the farmworkers' argument against the tied cottage system concerns the tied cottage dweller's insecurity, which derives from the awareness that the termination of his employment (whether through illness, injury, dismissal, resignation or retirement) carries with it the likelihood of eviction and homelessness. Until the 1960s, the tied cottage dweller could be evicted from his home with little, if any, advance notice being given by the employer. The farmworker was left homeless, as well as jobless, and was dependent on the mercy of friends or relatives to provide temporary accommodation. Following legislation passed in the 1960s (the subject of the following section) the farmworker was given, at least in principle, a period of up to twelve months in which to find alternative accommodation for himself and his family before being physically evicted from the cottage. In practice, it was not until 1976 that farmworkers were really freed from the fear of being made homeless at the virtual whim of their employers. Until that year, insecurity was part of the tied cottage dweller's life, regardless of how fortunate people may have told him he was for having a 'free' house in which to live.

The farmworker's union journal, the *Landworker*, is replete with emotional accounts of tied cottage evictions which give the onlooker a taste of the distress caused by evictions to farmworkers and their families.[15] There is, for example, the experience of Brother Williams in 1960

> It was in January that Bro. Williams injured his shoulder in an accident at work, and he had no sooner returned to work after a couple of weeks off than he went down with pneumonia. Towards the end of February he was given notice terminating his employment and this was followed by a summons for possession of his cottage, which was heard in the County Court at the end of April. The Union arranged his defence, but there was no real answer to the claim and an Order was made for possession in 28 days. However, the employer undertook not to issue a Warrant for eviction before the end of June.

Brother Williams was a family man with nine children and a keen sense of responsibility. In spite of his poor health he travelled '. . . all over the country in search of work and a house. There were times when he slept rough in order to be able to carry on the search in that area on the following morning'.[16]

As agricultural employers have been quick to point out,

the number of evictions which took place each year was relatively small. Prior to 1976 there were roughly 1,000 possession orders granted by the Courts to farmers each year, but the number of evictions was always much smaller than this, rarely over twenty a year.[17] (In many cases workers found somewhere, often temporary shelter, to move into before the bailiffs arrived to enforce an eviction.) Nevertheless, apart from the very real misery which this 'relatively small' number of evictions represents, tied cottage evictions were of profound significance for *all* tied cottage dwellers, not simply the twenty or so who were evicted each year. As the union's sponsored Labour MP and one-time Vice President, Joan Maynard, explained

> eviction is merely the tip of the iceberg. It is not whether a person is evicted, it is whether the power is there to do it. That is what counts. That power has hung like the sword of Damocles over the heads of our people for many years.[18]

It was the possibility that they might be evicted which brought to many farmworkers a strong sense of insecurity and vulnerability. Moreover,

> It is not a simple concept, this insecurity. Being in a tied cottage colours one's attitude to many of life's vicissitudes . . . Illness is something to be feared more than normally because being laid off for any length of time involves the risk of being dismissed. Old age is viewed with great apprehension: retirement brings nearer the day when some alternative accommodation must be found; loss of physical strength may necessitate the abandonment of agricultural work some years before retirement, adding the task of finding other work to that of finding other accommodation. Redundancy also poses similar difficulties should it arise. The occasional news of some fellow-worker's plight under any of these vicissitudes . . . keeps such fears alive.[19]

The insecurity brought upon farmworkers by the tied cottage system compounded their fear of losing their jobs which their labour market weakness carried with it. This dual weakness forced many farmworkers into positions of quiescence and apparent deference towards their employers who were also their landlords.[20] Rather than join the union and oppose their employers' extensive power over their livelihoods, many farmworkers have chosen instead to 'play it safe' by cultivating harmonious relations with their employers-cum-landlords.[21] Giles and Cowie found in their survey of farmworkers in Gloucestershire some evidence of this instrumental submissiveness and friendliness.

> A few confess frankly to feeling obliged to be careful in their demeanour, to experiencing a sense of dependence on their employer's goodwill. The vehemence with which most deny any such feelings, however, suggests an automatic face-saving reaction to a question which challenges their self-respect.[22]

It would be disingenuous to argue that the traditional quiescence and lack of militancy among farmworkers has been due wholly to the insecurity that tied cottage accommodation has placed upon them, especially since the proportion of farmworkers living in tied houses in the post-war period has rarely exceeded the 50 per cent mark. Nevertheless, most historians agree that the tied cottage has played a significant role in retarding trade unionism and labour militancy among agricultural workers.[23] Furthermore, it should be noted that although only half of the work-force live in tied cottages, many of these workers are drawn from the sector which has the strongest bargaining position in the labour market. Yet, as tied cottage dwellers, these stockmen and skilled workers would have been more reluctant than otherwise to flex their industrial muscle, for fear of losing their homes as well as their jobs if they failed.

The insecurity promoted by tied cottage accommodation has thus cemented the powerlessness experienced by farmworkers in the labour market. They have confronted formidable obstacles on two fronts, which helps to explain their reluctance to demand more forcefully the payment of higher wages. The tied cottage system is related to farmworkers' low pay in other respects. Although many tied cottage dwellers are paid higher rates than those farmworkers who do not live in tied accommodation, they are nevertheless paid poorly in comparison with similarly skilled workers in other industries. Employers often justify the payment of these low wages by pointing to the 'free' accommodation which they provide for their employees. Moreover, while this 'free' housing which some workers are provided with saves them from having to pay high rents, the cost of this perk is the inability to move from the tied house into other housing because of the low cash wage paid to the worker concerned. 'Free' housing is thus balanced by relatively low wages, a lack of independence from employers and labour immobility— factors which explain why tied cottage accommodation is regarded by many farmworkers as being a dubious privilege, and why it is, in practice, a contravention of their objective interests as defined in Chapter 1.

One solution to the problems relating to tied accommodation which has been put forward in the past, and which takes due account of the employers' argument that farm cottages are essential in view of the rural housing shortage, might be the abolition of 'privileged rents' for tied houses.[24] According to proponents of this claimed solution, the houses would remain as physical entities for farmworkers to live in, but the tied system *per se* would be abolished. Once farmworkers were compelled to pay market rents for the farm cottages, their employers would be obliged to pay higher wages which, in turn, would provide farmworkers with a greater choice as to where they lived and worked. However, for the time being, and particularly in the existing context of the rural housing shortage, even some of the most highly skilled farmworkers have to accept low cash wages where they are accompanied by a 'free' house. The tied cottage is, in effect, the 'carrot which will tempt the agricultural worker to accept a low wage'.[25]

It is worth noting further that the tied cottage system has been used to depress the wages of the agricultural workforce as a whole, rather than just those of the tied cottage dwellers themselves. The tied cottage is often pointed to by the Employers' Side of the AWB when they argue against any significant increase in the agricultural minimum wage. The employers' provision of 'free' housing is used to justify the payment of low wages across the board, in spite of the fact that roughly half of the work-force pays council or private rents and mortgages and many of these non-tied workers are paid *less* than the workers in tied houses.

Some commentators and participants in the tied cottage dispute have claimed that although the workers' case has been argued strongly and consistently by their union, it is not a view which is held by the majority of farmworkers.[26] Clearly, there have been some cases where farmworkers have felt relatively secure in their tied houses, where their employers have paid comparatively good wages and where they have, therefore, felt no immediate desire to see the tied cottage system abolished.[27] In other cases, farmworkers may express a wish to retain the tied cottage system because they see no viable alternative to it, particularly given their low wages and the rural housing shortage.[28] However, such support for the tied system of housing is of a distinctly negative nature: tied cottages are regarded as desirable because they are seen as the only available option. The notion that workers' support for the tied cottage system is a negative support is borne out by the absence of any union resolutions at branch, regional or national level in defence of the tied cottage system, which contrasts with the long string of resolutions calling for its abolition or reform to be found throughout the union's history.[29] Furthermore, inasmuch as the mass of farmworkers have been relatively silent on the tied cottage issue, this must be attributed, at least partially, to the very insecurity and fear of industrial conflict which is generated by the tied cottage system itself.

Above all, the tied cottage system runs counter to farm-workers' objective interests in the ability to bargain freely for higher wages and better conditions of work. By the same token, the tied cottage system satisfies the interests of agricultural employers in keeping labour costs low, while at the same time maintaining peaceful labour relations.

The two sides of the tied cottage conflict thus represent antithetic views and opposing interests at both objective and subjective levels. The employers benefit from the tied cottage system not only because it allows for the close supervision of animals and the proper housing of good workers, but also because it provides them with the ability to control the labour force, both numerically and in terms of labour relations, and this in turn serves their interests in efficiency and profitability. Meanwhile, the workers attack the system for tying them to the land, depressing their wages and enforcing their subservience to their employers. Although both sides of the dispute often obfuscate the issues involved through their use of misleading rationalisations and emotive language, in the final analysis each side is found to be pursing a valid case. The employers want to protect their interests in low labour costs, the workers seek the freedom to demand better conditions without fear of reprisals. Stripped of its rhetoric, the tied cottage debate represents a '. . . conflict of interest between capital and labour with each side pursuing its legitimate interest to the detriment of the other'.[30]

The agricultural tied cottage has generated a profound bitterness among employers and workers, which contrasts somewhat with the relative uncontentiousness of tied housing in other industries. This is largely because those industries with large-scale tied accommodation networks (such as mining, the railways and the metropolitan police) also have sufficient resources to enable employees to remain in their tied house for a lengthy period of time after the termination of their employment, during which time alternative housing can be found. Conversely, in agriculture, although there is tied housing on a large scale, it is distributed among many thousands of employers who each have, at most, only a handful of service houses. In the majority of cases, agricultural employers have been compelled to evict their workers promptly, although often regretfully, so as to offer new workers 'free' housing before stock and crops begin to suffer.[31]

There is a further reason for the particular emotiveness of the tied cottage issue in agriculture. The conventionally divisive issue of wage negotiation has been removed from the farmyard, having become the responsibility of the anonymous AWB whose decisions are imposed upon farmers and farmworkers alike. As Howard Newby observed, 'only the tied cottage has remained to epitomise the conflict between capital and labour'.[32] This conflict is all the more intensive because of the otherwise 'friendly' relations which exist between farmers and farmworkers. On a day-to-day basis, many farmers and farmworkers work co-operatively and they enjoy what are frequently referred to as 'good labour relations'. However, tied cottage evictions, when they occur, underline the ultimate priorities of agricultural employers, which are maximum production and economic profit, as opposed to the fulfilment of personal obligations to employees of many years' standing. The peculiarly friendly nature of agricultural labour relations are thrown into painful disarray by each economically motivated or threatened eviction which workers either experience or hear about. In this way, the tied cottage serves to remind farmworkers that behind their 'good labour relations' lies a skilful instrumentality on the part of their employers which sometimes obscures the conflict of objective interests which exists between the two parties.[33] Above all, it is a conflict which the employers appear to be better equipped to pursue.

II   THE NUAAW'S ALLIANCE WITH THE LABOUR PARTY: POWER OR POWERLESSNESS?

In view of the harm inflicted upon farmworkers' interests by the tied cottage system, the farmworkers' union committed itself to a long and vigorous campaign for tied cottage abolition. The issue was politicised as early as 1909 when George Edwards, the leader of the Eastern Counties Agricultural Labourers' and Smallholders' Union (a predecessor of the NUAW) addressed a Trades Union Congress (TUC) in Ipswich. At the meeting, Edwards called upon Labour MPs to

> take up at once the issue of eviction of workmen and their families from their homes during trade disputes and do everything possible to pass into law a measure which would put an end to this cruel method of warfare.[34]

Ever since that date, the union has conducted its campaign for tied cottage abolition by pressing the Labour Party to 'take up the issue of eviction' on its behalf. This approach to the issue was adopted partly because the changes which the union sought were specifically legal ones, the hoped-for effect of which would be the curbing of employers' power over their workers, which derived from their role as landlords. As the *Landworker* explained

> A change in the law can only be made by parliament, and the issue therefore automatically becomes a political one. The Tory Party has said quite plainly, 'We believe in the tied cottage system, and we intend that it shall remain'. There is only one other political party in the country which can hope to form a Government—the Labour Party.[35]

A further, and in a sense related, reason for the farmworkers' dependency on the Labour Party was that, as Peter Self and Herbert Storing have noted, the union did not in practice have the option of 'going it alone' because of its 'intrinsic economic and organisational weakness'. In a political campaign directed against the interests of agricultural employers (as the tied cottage campaign was) the Labour Party was the only effective ally to whom the union could turn.[36]

The following narrative and analysis suggest that the union's dependency on the Labour Party for assistance in its tied cottage campaign had important ramifications not only for the course which the campaign took, but also for the very determination of its goals. For, although numerous issues of *Landworker* suggest that many union members and officers favoured, in principle, the wholesale abolition of the tied cottage system, in practice, the union is found to have aimed almost exclusively for tied cottage *reform*.[37] This discrepancy is attributed to the consistent unwillingness of the Parliamentary Labour Party (PLP) to place tied cottage abolition on the political agenda for reasons of political expediency. The PLP's rejection of the abolition option was usually implicit, being carried out most often through its inaction, that is, by the PLP's failure to discuss the possibility of placing abolition on the agenda.[38] On a few occasions, however, abolition was mobilised off of the agenda through decisive action, although it remained covert. This occurred, for example, in 1975, when a minority proposal to consider tied cottage abolition was swiftly stifled by numerous Labour MPs who branded the proposal 'unrealistic' and politically dangerous, thus squashing its legitimacy within the PLP.[39]

Meanwhile, the NUAAW lacked the necessary electoral, organisational and economic resources with which to sway Labour's attitudes on this matter. Recognising its own powerlessness and its dependency on Labour's support for the achievement of any change, the union was compelled to campaign for tied cottage reform.[40] The resulting consensus between successive Labour governments and the NUAAW over the goal of tied cottage reform should therefore be recognised as being an enforced consensus which resulted from Labour's exercise of power over the union through its persistent refusal to place farmworkers' higher interests in tied cottage abolition on the parliamentary agenda.

The NUAAW's heavy dependency on the Labour Party and its relative powerlessness to influence the party's attitude *via-à-vis* tied cottage reform thus explain why the union concentrated on defending its members' relatively limited interests in tied cottage reform, rather than attempting to promote their greater interests in abolition. However, even within the framework of farmworkers' limited interests, certain reforms were more satisfactory than others for the farmworkers. The particular reform which the Union sought from the Labour Party was the introduction of the same security of tenure for tied cottage inhabitants as that enjoyed by other, non-tied tenants. If achieved, this reform would remove the fear of eviction and homelessness which had plagued the tied cottage dweller for so long. It was true that apart from this improvement the tied cottage system would remain intact, along with its many problems which were not related directly to the eviction aspect of the system. Yet providing the farmworker with a secure house and home represented such a significant and desirable breakthrough that this version of tied cottage reform was referred to frequently, but misleadingly, in numerous union documents and press releases as tied cottage 'abolition'. For the purposes of this study the distinction between reform and abolition is an important one to bear in mind.

Labour governments 1945-70

In spite of a string of promises made by the Labour Party to the agricultural work-force during every General Election campaign between 1945 and 1970, the Labour Party was reluctant to involve itself in any concrete way in the tied cottage campaign. The Labour government of 1945-51 took no action at all on the tied cottage issue. The Labour governments of 1964-66 and 1966-70 did pass legislation which had some bearing on tied housing; but the significance of this legislation lay chiefly in the fact that it brought the tied cottage system to the statute book for the first time, not in any substantive reform which it introduced.

Labour's failure to introduce major reform to the tied cottage system between 1945 and 1970 can be explained by a range of different factors. During Labour's time in office between 1945 and 1951 the chief obstacle to tied cottage reform lay in the Minister of Agriculture, Tom Williams's, concern to ensure a safe passage through parliament for the Agriculture Bill. The concept of extensive state support to agriculture in a non-military context was a novel one, and many farmers were worried about the possible interference in their business which state support was (wrongly) expected to bring with it. Having secured the reluctant agreement of the NFU to co-operate in the new agricultural support system embodied in the *Agriculture Act* 1947, Tom Williams was unwilling to jeopardise this delicate arrangement by introducing contentious tied cottage legislation.

The NUAAW secured three Acts of Parliament from the Labour governments of 1964-66 and 1966-70. These were the *Protection from Eviction Act* 1964; the *Rent Act* 1965; and the *Agriculture Act* 1970. The chief innovation in the

Protection from Eviction Act lay in its requirement of land-lords that prior to carrying out an eviction they obtain a court order permitting them to do so; and in its provision that courts had the right to suspend the execution of an eviction order for up to twelve months. The *Rent Act* 1965 changed the twelve month period to 'a period to be deter-mined by the Court'. The *Agriculture Act* 1970 granted the tied cottage occupant a period of six months security of tenure following the end of the occupant's formal right to occupy the cottage.

None of these reforms brought the tied cottage dweller significantly closer to enjoying the security of tenure which tenants of non-tied housing possessed. What was most galling for the NUAAW was that even the minor changes introduced by these Acts were rendered meaningless by the requirements, contained in the Acts, that the law courts consider the effects of their judgements on agricultural production levels before pronouncing on individual cases. Thus, if the court had reason to believe that agricultural output would suffer if an eviction were stalled by six or twelve months, then the court would be empowered (and expected) to waive the twelve month suspension period laid down by the *Protection from Eviction Act* and the six-month security of tenure established by the *Agriculture Act*. The continuing stream of tied cottage evictions between 1964 and 1974, recounted in the pages of *Landworker*, bears witness to the courts' respect for the exigencies of agricultural production.

Labour's failure to live up to its promise that 'there would be no eviction from a farm cottage without suitable accommodation first being made available'[41] can be explained by a number of factors. Firstly, tied cottage abolition, or a total overhaul of the existing tied cottage system, was ruled out by the continuing rural housing shortage which made farmworkers dependent on their employers for the provision of accommodation. As in the 1940s, it was argued in the 1960s that the abolition of tied cottages would leave farm-workers homeless and therefore worse off—not, as some suggested, better off.[42]

Secondly, extensive tied cottage reform was blocked by the organised opposition of the NFU.[43] Even the limited measures which the Protection from Eviction Bill proposed 'generated much heated argument in and out of Parliament' and led the NFU to circularise all MPs with forboding warn-ings of the likely detriment which the Act would cause to

the farming industry.[44] The NFU's pressure on the government was successful, not only because it was well-organised,
but also because the government's commitment to maximum
agricultural production meant that it took seriously the
NFU's threats about the negative implications of tied cottage
reform for agricultural efficiency. The government thus held
conflicting allegiances to agricultural employers and agricultural workers, resulting in a temporary confusion during
the passage of the Bill. This was reflected in Housing Minister,
Richard Crossman's, explanation of the court's new duties
under the *Protection from Eviction Act*

> They should not forget that women and children might be thrown
> onto the streets, but also that a pedigree herd might be ruined.
> How one measures between the two, I do not know.[45]

As the final wording of the *Protection from Eviction Act*
showed, the government ultimately decided that evicting
families was a lesser evil than harming pedigree herds, since
such a step would at least leave agricultural production levels
intact. This priority was reflected again in the *Rent Act* 1965
and the *Agriculture Act* 1970, both of which offered
protection to tied cottage dwellers only in so far as this was
not, in the view of the courts, 'prejudicial to the interests of
the farm enterprise'.

This preference for maximum production over farmworkers' security of tenure which was embodied in Labour's
legislation illustrates the impact of the third factor which
militated against tied cottage reform. This was the government's belief that only an 'efficient' agricultural industry
would be capable of providing sufficient food to feed the
urban working class at a relatively low cost. Rather than
question the validity of the NFU's argument that tied cottage
reform would seriously harm agricultural production, the
government assumed that the NFU had sufficient expertise
to make such predictions. On the basis of this assumption,
the government decided to protect the interests of farmers
and industrial workers (the government's 'natural' constituency) at the comparatively low cost of disappointing the
agricultural work-force. The farmers had the necessary
economic and organisational resources with which to promote
their interests, and the urban working class had the necessary
economic and electoral resources for doing this; by contrast,
farmworkers lacked these relevant resources, as a result of
which they were unable to see their interests in extensive tied

cottage reform promoted in Parliament. Thus, by 1970 Labour's efforts to reform the tied cottage system scarcely left agricultural employers any worse off than they had been in 1964; by the same token, agricultural workers were hardly any better off.

The Labour government of 1974-79

The manifesto issued by the Labour Party prior to the October 1974 General Election contained a significant admission that previous Labour governments had failed to satisfy the interests of farmworkers in connection with the tied cottage issue. For, like many manifestos before it, it carried a promise to 'abolish the tied cottage system', thereby acknowledging how little had been done so far for tied cottage inhabitants. Observers could be forgiven for the cynicism with which they may have greeted this well-worn promise; but, on this occasion, their cynicism was arguably misplaced. For, although the Labour government of 1974–79 by no means 'abolished' the tied cottage system, it did tinker with it to an unprecedented extent.

The greater willingness and ability of the new Labour government to deal with the tied cottage issue, as compared to previous Labour governments, is attributable to three factors. (It should be noted that each of these factors emerged independently of any efforts which the NUAAW may have made to create a favourable climate for tied cottage reform.) Firstly, there was more housing available in Britain than there had been even ten years earlier. This gave the government greater flexibility for reforming the tied cottage system, as it provided them with the option of rehousing at least some tied cottage occupants.[46]

Secondly, the composition of the National Executive Committee (NEC) and the Parliamentary Labour Party (PLP) had changed over the years, such that by 1974 they held a more favourable attitude than previously to the repeated insistence of party Conference and the TUC that something be done to improve the agricultural tied cottage system.[47] In particular, two MPs with key positions were determined to see the passage of legislation which would improve the farmworkers' housing situation. The first was Joan Maynard, who joined the NEC in 1972 and became the MP for Sheffield, Brightside in October 1974. Although she had lost her post as NUAAW Vice-President in 1972 when the office was abolished as an 'economy measure', Maynard remained an active member of the union and she carried her support for it into Parliament where, as the NUAAW's sponsored MP, she devoted most of her maiden speech to the issue of tied cottage abolition.[48] The combination of Maynard's dedication to the issue and her key position in the party was crucial because it meant that she could ensure its safe passage from becoming a Conference resolution, into a manifesto commitment, into part of the Queen's Speech and finally an item for discussion and legislation in the House of Commons. Maynard was successful in guiding the issue through this complex process and Gavin Strang, MP, complemented her efforts with his own. Strang's particular contribution was his continuous drumming up of support for the government's tied cottage programme both within and beyond Parliament, and his careful steering of the Bill through the parliamentary process. In particular, Strang's position as Parliamentary Secretary to the Ministry of Agriculture, Fisheries and Food (MAFF) enabled him to fulfil his role as successfully as Maynard had fulfilled hers.

Thirdly, the new government's determination to reform the tied cottage system can be explained by its commitment to the Social Contract. This was a programme designed to promote mutual support and co-operation between the Labour government and the TUC, with the intention of serving the interests of both government and the unions. Although the spirit and the substance of the Social Contract had long dissolved by 1979, they had a beneficial effect upon the NUAAW's campaign for tied cottage reform in the government's earlier years. The government looked relatively favourably upon Maynard's and Strang's efforts because the question of tied cottage reform was framed in terms of the Social Contract in which the government placed so much hope; if the government helped the unions on issues such as housing, then it could expect in return the unions' co-operation over the otherwise conflictual issue of incomes policies. It was particularly significant that Anthony Crosland, the Secretary of State for the Environment in 1974 and 1975, viewed the tied cottage issue within the Social Contract framework, because he was to play an important role in promoting the tied cottage legislation (which was regarded partly as a 'housing' issue, rather than strictly as the concern of agricultural Ministers).

Labour's election manifesto committed the new government to enforcing the 'abolition' of the agricultural tied cottage system, but by the mid-1970s the concepts of tied cottage abolition and tied cottage reform were being used interchangeably by politicians and union officials alike. The manifesto promise was consequently interpreted by most people as a pledge to improve farmworkers' security of tenure *within* the tied cottage system, rather than to abolish the system as such. It is, therefore, surprising to find that in the government's early days discussions were held between some Labour MPs over the respective merits of abolition versus reform. One or two voices were raised in favour of total abolition, by MPs who proposed the municipalisation of farm cottages. However, the financial cost involved in the compulsory purchase of farmers' cottages by local authorities was regarded by the great majority of MPs as being far in excess of what was practical. Moreover, the panic and opposition that compulsory purchase was expected to generate made such a move politically undesirable. With the use of dominant values such as 'practicality' and 'pragmatism' Labour's MPs swiftly mobilised the option of wholesale tied cottage abolition off of the parliamentary agenda at an early stage in the government's period of office. However, to compensate for this exercise of power over the farmworkers the party turned its attention to finding a means by which it could promote farmworkers' more limited interests in gaining security of tenure within the tied cottage system.

The government was well-equipped to counter any possible accusations of having 'sold-out' the NUAAW by opting for reform instead of abolition. Most notably, it could point to the enthusiastic support given by the NUAAW leadership to the government for its proposals on tied cottage reform. When the government first put forward these proposals to the union's leaders, the latter accepted them without hesitation for, although they did not constitute abolition, 'they went 90% of the way'.[49] After waiting sixty years for a significant improvement in farmworkers' housing, the union leaders regarded the government's proposals as a giant step forward, however far they fell short of abolition.

The government's aim, then, was to provide tied cottage occupants with the same security of tenure which other *Rent Act* protected tenants enjoyed. This would mean that farmworkers could not be forced by their landlords to move out of their homes and, sometimes quite literally, onto the streets. In so far as this reform enabled the farmworker to retain control of the tied cottage after the termination of his employment, it represented a severe threat to the interests of farmers who insisted on their need to retain complete freedom in the use of the cottages as a means of attracting an adequate work-force. The more security of tenure the farmworker was given, the less leeway the farmer would be left with in the operation and use of his housing stock as an instrument of labour control. It was to be expected, therefore, that the NFU would oppose the government's proposed tied cottage reform in the hopes of preventing it from reaching the statute books.

The NFU's most extensively and skilfully used resource in its campaign against the government's proposed tied cottage reform was its ability to control and manipulate information.[50] Although the NFU used this resource to influence Labour MPs, it did this ultimately in order to exercise power over farmworkers rather than the Labour MPs as such, for it was the farmworkers', not Labour's, interests which were to be frustrated by the NFU's actions. The Labour MPs acted as intermediaries in this power relationship between the NFU and the farmworkers, for it was via the NFU's influence over the MPs that the NFU succeeded in preventing the proper promotion and defence of farmworkers' interests within the parliamentary arena.

Prior to the parliamentary passage of the new Rent (Agriculture) Bill, the government had set aside a period for consultation during which it invited the views of all interested parties on its proposed reforms. During this period, the NFU conducted an extensive lobbying campaign which involved issuing all MPs with written accounts of the chaos and impoverishment which would allegedly result in the agricultural industry (and beyond) if the government went ahead with its tied cottage plans. The NUAAW's General Secretary later described the NFU's campaign as being

> Total and complete. Every string was pulled. All MPs were circulated. [The NFU made out that] it was going to be a disaster from British agriculture. Every stop was pulled . . . they left no stone unturned.[51]

The information which the NFU distributed to MPs was essentially contained in their formal reply to the government's 'Consultative Document'.[52] In this the NFU made the following claims:

The provision of accommodation on the farm for farmworkers is essential if the full food-producing potential of agricultural land in the UK is to be achieved. The abolition of the system without the creation of an effective alternative will surely lead to a decline in the efficiency of all sections of farming and will have particularly harsh consequences in the livestock sector . . . If service houses are to cease to be available on farms the resulting disruption of agriculture will mean inevitably that food prices will need to be increased . . . any interference with the freedom of the worker to be housed on the farm, and hence with the chances of attracting the right type of labour, will be an added disincentive to expansion and will lead ultimately to reduced food production.[53]

The NFU thus resorted to its own most frequently invoked arguments in defence of the agricultural tied cottage, or 'service cottage' as the NFU prefers to call it. The first argument concerned the need among livestock farmers to have a man on the spot, and the second related to the necessity of providing housing in order to attract the 'right type of labour'.

The validity of the first of these two arguments was questionable. Giles and Cowie pointed out as early as 1960 that if it was, in fact, essential for a farmer to have a farmworker living in a particular house then one would expect that if the worker wished to move from the house into a non-tied house off the farm, the farmer would be compelled to replace the worker altogether. Giles and Cowie's survey showed, however, that only about one-quarter of farmers in their sample reacted in this way. The remainder allowed the ex-tied cottage dweller to remain in employment, despite living off of the farm; or else they considered each case on its own merit. Giles and Cowie concluded that

> Natural reaction as this may seem, it is not logical if the cottage is really essential. There is surely some suggestion here that the tied cottage may not always be as important in reality as some farmers think.[54]

A further counter argument to the 'man-on-the-spot' claim was raised by an alert Labour MP

> I am told that it will be quite impossible to run any kind of dairy undertaking without the agricultural tied cottage . . . I am told that the cottage is essential because the worker must be on the spot at all hours, day and night. One never knows, apparently, when a cow will have a calf or when a sheep will have a lamb. We are told that there will be dire consequences if the worker is not present. My

wife managed to have a son on a couple of occasions, once very
recently, and I found no need to employ a midwife in a tied cottage
anywhere near the house. This argument seems a little out of touch
with modern developments, particularly in transport.[55]

Conversely, in the context of the existing rural council
house shortage and the inflated prices of private sector
housing, the NFU's second argument in favour of retaining
the tied cottage system was a highly convincing one. The
NFU insisted that unless farmers were allowed to continue to
provide their workers with cheap housing, they would be
unable to attract the necessary quantity and quality of labour,
for where would such labour be housed? As plausible as this
argument was, it was firmly rooted in two tacit assumptions:
that the rural council house shortage and the low pay of
farmworkers were both immutable facts of life.

It is not surprising that the NFU built these assumptions
into its arguments, for to campaign in support of higher wages
for farmworkers or in favour of extensive council house
construction would have been contrary to their interests in
keeping their production costs (and their rates) low while
retaining maximum control over their workers. The NFU
was, therefore, behaving entirely rationally when it defended
the status quo against the perceived threats posed to it by
Labour's plans for tied cottage reform.

The most notable feature of the NFU's campaign was not
that it was aimed at satisfying farmers' legitimate interests in
profit maximisation and labour control: it was that in spite
of the inaccuracies and assumptions on which the campaign
was based, and despite Labour's professed commitment to
the farmworkers' cause, many Labour MPs were convinced
by the NFU that extensive tied cottage reform was
undesirable. It was by persuading Labour MPs that tied
cottage reform would be ill-advised that the NFU managed
to defend its interests in labour control, while rendering the
NUAAW powerless to promote, via the government, the
interests of farmworkers in housing security. Although the
MPs may not have wanted to frustrate farmworkers' interests,
their intermediary role in the NFU's exercise of power was
crucial to the success of that power exercise: in this respect
Labour shared (causal) responsibility with the NFU for the
continued thwarting of farmworkers' interests.[56]

The NFU's indirect exercise of power over the NUAAW
was made possible by the interplay of a number of factors.

Firstly, side-by-side with the party's promise to improve the lot of the farmworkers there was an overriding commitment among the majority of Labour MPs to support the agricultural industry, whose continued generation of wealth was regarded as a vital asset for the country's balance of payments. Any threat to the industry's output was viewed by MPs as an economic crisis which was to be pre-empted or overcome by whatever means necessary. If the industry's efficiency demanded a degree of sacrifice from the work-force, as the NFU suggested it did, this would have to be carried out in the interests of the nation as a whole. Since MPs did not contemplate restructuring the social basis of the agricultural industry so as to remove this division between capital ('efficiency') and labour's interests, farmworkers found that they could hope for tied cottage reform only in so far as it did not threaten the existing structure and levels of agricultural production. This constraint was made clear in the government's Consultative Document

> The focus should be on how to shape the legislation on lines that will enable farmers, farmworkers, local authorities and other interests concerned effectively to adapt themselves to the changing requirements of modern society *while maintaining the key contribution which this great industry can make to the national economy.*[57] [my emphasis]

In this respect there was a degree of tension, as there was in previous Labour governments, between the government's commitment to the irreconcilable interests of both agricultural capital and labour. The NFU promoted the interests of agricultural capital by highlighting at every available opportunity its economic importance in terms of the national economy. Conversely, by virtue of farmworkers' structural location in the economy, the NUAAW had no comparable economic resource with which to influence the political decision-makers. Nor did the farm work-force have significant electoral resources which it might have been able to use to compensate for its economic weakness. Hence, as on previous occasions, it was the government's commitment to capital that prevailed.[58]

The commitment of virtually all Labour MPs to the interests of agricultural capital does not in itself explain why they should be prepared to believe that extensive tied cottage reform would seriously damage agricualtural production. The reason for their adoption of this belief was that their commitment to agricultural efficiency combined with two other factors: the ignorance of many Labour MPs about agricultural affairs; and the excellent resources which the NFU had access to with which to exploit this ignorance.

The lack of knowledge about agriculture among Labour MPs was due above all to their predominantly urban origins, interests and political bases. The Labour MP for Lichfield and Tamworth noted that although he himself represented a constituency in which there was a considerable amount of agricultural activity, '. . . on the Labour side of the House it is increasingly rare to represent such a constituency, because the division between the parties is becoming increasingly one of urban and rural interests and seats'.[59] Not only has the Labour Party had historically little support or political representation among agricultural constituencies; its MPs have also had far less personal experience of the agricultural scene than their Conservative counterparts. In the parliament of 1975-76 there was a total of seventy-eight MPs who declared themselves to have private interests in agriculture: sixty-five of these were Conservative, whereas only seven were on the Labour benches, with the remainder being shared out between four other parties.[60]

In the context of Labour's relative inexperience in agricultural matters, the NFU was encouraged to use its organisational and economic resources to their full capacity, putting forward to MPs at every available opportunity the notion of impending agricultural disaster if the government's plans were implemented without first being modified.[61] The NFU's superior knowledge of agricultural matters, coupled with the economic importance of agricultural capital which Labour politicians did not question, provided the NFU with a certain authority to pronounce upon the needs of the industry as a whole. Thus, when the NFU claimed that the profitability of agriculture would suffer if extensive tied cottage reform were instituted, Labour politicians tended to believe the argument rather than to challenge it, for they wished to avoid any risk of damaging the efficient production of food. At the same time, the NFU's tradition of 'political neutrality' proved to be of great value, for it meant that the NFU had channels of communication not only with its 'natural allies' (the Conservative and farming MPs) but also with Labour MPs whose ignorance over farming issues meant that they would be relatively open to the NFU's views on tied cottage reform. In this sense the NFU's organisational, economic and information resources were mutually reinforcing, with the result that the NFU encountered few difficulties in persuading the Labour government not to promote farmworkers' interests in gaining full security of tenure.

Nor was the NFU hindered in its lobbying by the NUAAW's counterlobbying. Indeed, one could hardly speak of a competition in this sphere between the two organisations because of the tremendous inequality of their organisational and financial resources. For example, while the NUAAW was struggling with debts which forced it only a few years later to merge with the TGWU, the NFU had a healthy financial balance with which to pay for a political campaign. Its budget for 1976–77 was as follows:

Table 2 NFU budget 1976-77

Expenditure	Amount
	£
County branch	1 562 521
Headquarters	2 412 677
Overall (including provision for contingencies)	4 075 198

The NFU's income for that year from subscriptions alone was £4·2 million, on top of which it earned an undisclosed income from its numerous financial investments. Compared to this wealth, the NUAAW claimed an income in 1977 of £869,545 and a total expenditure of £830,355.[62]

Moreover, the NFU had to its advantage many years' experience of parliamentary lobbying, with the result that its methods were by the 1970s highly sophisticated and effective. Traditionally, the NFU had relied on lobbying MPs directly in the House of Commons, either orally or by circulating them with written information sheets. The great success of this approach led other pressure groups to adopt similar tactics, with the result that by the 1970s, the NFU found the halls of Westminster to be 'packed with lobbyists'. Consequently, the NFU complemented its traditional lobbying practices with the more subtle approach of 'taking MPs out to lunch or dinner' and discussing the issues with them in a more relaxed and congenial atmosphere.[63]

By contrast, the NUAAW held purely formal meetings with Labour MPs and with a few Liberal MPs whose support in the tied cottage campaign was regarded as crucial, given

Labour's tiny and unreliable overall majority of three in the House of Commons in 1975. In spite of this precarious parliamentary situation, the union never met with any Conservative MPs to discuss the tied cottage campaign because the NUAAW anticipated their opposition to the campaign, regardless of anything the NUAAW might say or do.[64] Given Labour's small majority, this difference of approach between the NFU and the NUAAW (in which the former confronted MPs of all parties, while the latter devoted its energies largely to negotiating with its known allies) was vitally important. If more Labour MPs became convinced of the NFU's case than Liberal MPs were of the NUAAW's, the union would lose the opportunity of achieving any tied cottage reform at all, and this eventuality appeared highly likely.

In an attempt to compare more systematically the strength of the ties that exist between the NFU and MPs on the one hand, and the farmworkers' union and MPs on the other, I carried out a postal questionnaire in January 1985. The survey was relatively simple so as to ensure maximum returns from the respondents. Copies of the questionnaire were sent to the NFU's thirty-seven county secretaries in England, and the Agricultural and Allied Workers' National Trade Group's (AAWNTG-TGWU) thirty-seven district officers in England. The response rate was eighteen out of thirty-seven from the NFU and twenty-seven out of thirty-seven from the AAWNTG. The results of the survey are set out in Table 3.

Table 3 Relationships with local MPs among officers of the NFU and the AAWNTG, 1985

Question	NFU	AAWNTG
	%	%
1. Is consultation with local MPs a significant part of your work?		
Yes	95	7
No	5	93
2. How often do you meet with MPs to discuss NFU/AAWNTG business?		
Weekly	0	0
Every 2 weeks	0	0
Monthly	17	0

Table 3 *continued*

Every 2 months	50	4
Every 6 months	11	11
Other	22	52 rarely/never
		23 as need arises
		11 other

3. How successful is your consultation with MPs?

Not very	0	40
Fairly	66	11
Very	17	4
Other	17	33 na
		11 other

4. Does the success of the consultation depend significantly on the MP's party affiliation?

Yes	17	52
No	83	7
		41 na

5. Which party is generally most co-operative?

Conservative	22	0
SDP/Lib Alliance	22	0
Labour	5	60
*Mainly/only Conservative MPs in the area**	61	7
	17 * whoever is in opposition	33 na*
	N = 18	N = 27

*   This response was not offered as an option in the questionnaire, but was given without prompting by respondents.

Notes
1. Figures are rounded to add up to 100 per cent.
2. NFU responses to question 5 add up to over 100 per cent because a number of respondents gave more than one answer.
3. na   not applicable.

Several conclusions concerning the political resources of the two organisations can be drawn from the survey. First of all, unlike the farmworkers' head office in London's Grays Inn Road, the NFU's Knightsbridge headquarters can depend on their regional officers to back up direct contacts with Westminster through extensive consultation with MPs at the constituency level. Second, to the extent that lobbying is carried out in the constituencies, that which the NFU's county secretaries have undertaken has not only been more consistent but also more successful than that performed by the AAWNTG's district officers. Third, the NFU's county secretaries replicate the practice of headquarters officials by negotiating successfully with MPs of *all* parties. Conversely, to the limited extent that the farmworkers' district officers consult their local MPs, they claim to have achieved success only with Labour MPs. Given the predominance of Conservative MPs in rural areas, which numerous respondents commented on without prompting, the overall lack of lobbying by the district officers can be attributed at least partly to their anticipation of failure were they to contact their local (Conservative) MPs on union business. By contrast, 63 per cent of NFU respondents who noted the prevalence of Conservative MPs in their areas also pointed out that where local MPs have been in the past Labour, or where one or two Labour MPs exist among a majority of Conservative MPs in a given county, these Labour politicians have proved to be as co-operative as those from the Conservative Party. This record of cross-party success encourages the NFU's county secretaries to maintain their consultation with local MPs as a significant part of their work.

The NFU's programme of opposition to extensive tied cottage reform highlighted its ability to draw upon a relatively abundant supply of capital and parliamentary contacts for use in a campaign directed against a measure which it regarded, and portrayed, as prejudicial to the interests of farmers and farm production. By contrast, the farmworkers' poor economic and organisational resources, plus their electoral weakness and lack of parliamentary allies, were such that they depended overwhelmingly on the efforts of the NUAAW's sponsored MP, Joan Maynard, and her parliamentary colleague, Gavin Strang, for the promotion and protection of even their very limited interests.

The superiority and apparently cumulative nature of the NFU's campaigning resources became evident during the consultative period which preceded the parliamentary stage of enacting tied cottage reform. It was during this period that the NFU mobilised its resources and succeeded in convincing at least some Labour MPs that any far-reaching reform of the tied cottage system would have detrimental effects upon levels of farm production. When I spoke with Gavin Strang about this, he commented that the NFU even had some influence on Labour Ministers, 'who reckoned that [tied cottage reform] would damage agriculture'. The

NFU achieved its influence among Labour backbenchers and Ministers chiefly by 'lobbying MPs and creating a climate of opinion whereby people were receptive to the idea that the dairy industry, for example, could not go a long way without tied cottages . . .'.

Strang attempted initially to counter this notion by travelling up and down the country in an effort to explain to a variety of agricultural and non-agricultural audiences that there were potential benefits to be derived from the Government's plans for tied cottage reform. According to Strang, a 'hard line' approach was adopted at first, in which he refused to bow to the NFU's threats, attempting instead to point out the alleged spuriousness of some of the NFU's arguments. However, the NFU held out its campaign against the government's proposals and managed to sustain its influence over Labour politicians. The result was that Strang was eventually compelled to moderate his 'hard line' through the introduction of a concessionary measure into the government's guidelines for the forthcoming legislation.

The government's eventual revision of its original plans for tied cottage reform constituted an effective exercise of power over farmworkers in so far as it once again rendered farmworkers powerless to promote their interests in gaining complete (*Rent Act*) housing security through the parliamentary channels of policy-making. However, the government's exercise of power was far from straightforward. It was compelled to renege on its original commitments, and to exercise power over the farmworkers because of external pressures which were acting upon the government at the time.

Firstly, the country faced a creeping 'balance of payments crisis' which, unless halted and reversed, spelt doom for the government and (allegedly) the country as a whole. This economic crisis shaped the government's entire political agenda, including its policy on tied cottage reform. The government regarded agricultural capital as a useful asset in forestalling the impending crisis and for this reason it sought to appease and satisfy the interests of the representatives of agricultural capital. One way of doing this was to retreat from its original proposals for tied cottage reform and to move towards sufficient moderation for agricultural efficiency not to be threatened.

Secondly, the government's compulsion towards moderation is explicable by Labour's small majority in the House of Commons at the time of the tied cottage debate. The parliamentary 'rules of the game' were such that if the government could not carry the entire PLP as well as some Liberals on the tied cottage issue, then the Bill would be lost altogether. The only perceived means of avoiding such a defeat was by moderating the government's original tied cottage reform plans so as to quell the NFU's opposition, which, in turn, would guarantee the PLP's and Liberals' support for the forthcoming legislation.[65]

The Labour government's exercise of power appears to have been both reluctant and yet unavoidable; above all, however, it was highly effective, for it cemented the farmworkers' powerlessness to promote their interests in achieving extensive tied cottage reform. Labour, along with the NFU, must be held causally responsible for this setback; however, to refer to 'moral' responsibility in this context would be wholly inappropriate.[66]

The concession introduced by the government involved the proposal to establish Agricultural Dwelling House Advisory Committees (ADHACs) whose composition will be considered in Section III of this chapter. The broad effect of the ADHAC measure was to enable agricultural employers to evict ex-employees from their cottages as long as two conditions were satisfied. Firstly, the farmer had to prove to the satisfaction of the ADHAC that the tied cottage in question was essential for an incoming worker to move into; and secondly, the local housing authorities had to be able to provide the ex-worker with suitable alternative accommodation. The proposed procedure was that once the farmer had convinced the ADHAC that the cottage was needed for a new worker, the ADHAC would advise the local authority on the urgency of the case in question. In its turn, the local authority would act on the basis of this advice, using its 'best endeavours' to find suitable alternative accommodation for the ex-farmworker to move into within the time advised by the ADHAC.

The ADHAC provision was agreed in principle during the consultation period prior to the Bill's parliamentary passage, at a meeting held between Ministers, civil servants and representatives of the NFU and NUAAW. When the NUAAW first heard about the ADHAC measure it opposed it on the grounds that the measure threatened to dilute farmworkers' long-awaited security of tenure. However, having already compromised their interests in tied cottage abolition, the workers' leaders were now compelled to compromise yet again, this time on the ADHAC measure, for they feared that their failure to do so would jeopardise the satisfaction of even their limited interests in acquiring a degree of housing security. Consequently, the NUAAW representatives finally agreed to the concession (in spite of opposition to this move by the union's left wing which significantly was excluded from the decisive consultative meetings).

Once the ADHAC provision was agreed in principle (its precise form was not thrashed out for some months), the NFU's greatest fears over the government's reform plans dissolved. It no longer opposed the Rent (Agriculture) Bill to the extent which it previously had done, resigning itself instead to the forthcoming legislation. There were a few final attempts to prevent the legislation from going through, such as the move within MAFF to publish a White Paper instead of a Bill, thus leaving the publication of a Tied Cottage Reform Bill for a later date. Gavin Strang was aware that such procrastination would probably destroy altogether the existing opportunity to pass tied cottage legislation. He therefore convinced the Minister of Agriculture, Fred Peart, to go ahead with the planned Rent (Agriculture) Bill.

Similarly, the NFU rallied opposition to the Bill among its political allies in the House of Lords who (many of them being farmers and landowners) took a hostile view of the Rent (Agriculture) Bill. The Lords introduced amendments to the Bill which, if passed, would have left the Act with scarcely more bite than that of previous tied cottage reform Acts. Among other amendments, the Lords proposed: the exclusion of livestock and forestry workers from the Bill; the replacement of the 'best endeavours' clause with one which placed an absolute duty upon local authorities to provide alternative accommodation within three months; the enablement of authorities to house farmworkers in caravans and other temporary accommodation if no alternative accommodation were available; and the annulment of all provisions where the worker had been dismissed from his job for 'misconduct'.[67] As the NUAAW's General Secretary put it, the Lords '. . . emasculated the Bill beyond recognition, and returned to the Commons an instrument that was virtually meaningless as far as both the Government and the Union were concerned'.

However, Bottini reported to his members that '. . . the Government again stood firm and reversed the Lords' amendments by use of the guillotine procedure. On its return to the House of Lords, the Bill was accepted and re-amended'.[68]

The *Rent (Agriculture) Act* was passed in 1976 and came into effect on 1 January 1977. The NUAAW heralded the Act as 'the most significant development in the Union's history'[69] and breathed an almost audible sigh of relief and achievement, having finally reached its seventy-year old goal. Many Labour MPs and Ministers also showed signs of satisfaction with their work, in the apparent belief that the *Rent (Agriculture) Act* fulfilled the party's promise to 'disengage farmworkers' conditions of employment from the circumstances in which they are housed'.[70]

In so far as the *Rent (Agriculture) Act* 1976 did mark a 'significant development' in the union's history, it was an accomplishment which owed a great deal to the fortuitous presence in the House of Commons of two sympathetic MPs, Gavin Strang and Joan Maynard, whose efforts to overcome some of the obstacles to tied cottage reform proved to be successful.

The achievement of tied cottage reform owed something also to the fact that the NFU was not seriously opposed to it. Once the NFU had secured the ADHAC concession from the government, the only serious opposition to reform came from the NFU county secretaries who in certain cases voiced local hostility to the Bill. At NFU headquarters, however, there was a general recognition that with the inclusion of the ADHAC provision the Bill did not in practice present a threat to farmers' interests. Therefore, apart from a posture of opposition which they adopted chiefly for the benefit of the county secretaries, the NFU's national officers co-operated with the government in most respects, hoping in this way to win for farmers the best possible terms in the final drafting of the Bill.

The NFU's broad assent to the Rent (Agriculture) Bill following the introduction of the ADHAC proviso and throughout the Bill's parliamentary passage should not be interpreted as a sign of the NFU's powerlessness or defeat. On the contrary, it signifies that the NFU had already won its battle, a battle which had been fought *prior* to the Bill's parliamentary passage and on battlegrounds *other* than the formal parliamentary arena. Its chief outcome—the introduction of the ADHAC measure—had been such that the NFU could afford to remain relatively silent when the Bill was discussed formally and publicly in Parliament.[71]

The NFU's experience suggests that certain notions central

to the pluralist approach to power are mistaken. Political power is not exercised simply in the formal arena of decision-making, nor can power be measured by locating 'who prevails' in the formal decision-making process.[72] Rather, the NFU exercised its power *before* the Bill was even discussed (let alone decided upon) in Parliament. Moreover, the apparent victory of the Labour–NUAAW alliance in pushing the *Rent (Agriculture) Act* through Parliament disguised the actual victory of the NFU in protecting the interests of farmers at the cost of those of the farmworkers. The NFU congratulated itself justifiably on its success, recognising that 'the Bill to abolish the agricultural service house system is very far removed from what most farmers had feared and it provides yet more testimony to the NFU's moderating role in safeguarding farmers' interests'.[73]

The ADHAC provision satisfied the NFU, as a result of which it ceased exercising power over farmworkers through the pressure it had been applying on Labour MPs. In turn, these MPs were able to give their necessary support to the much diluted Bill during its parliamentary passage without worrying about its possible damage to agricultural production levels. In this way, the Rent (Agriculture) Bill became an Act in 1976.

III THE PROMOTION OF FARM-WORKERS' INTERESTS? *RENT (AGRICULTURE) ACT* 1976

The chief regret expressed by the NUAAW's General Secretary, Reg Bottini, in connection with the *Rent (Agriculture) Act* was that he was prevented by ill health from attending the union's celebrations when the Act received Royal Assent in 1976. Apart from this, the NUAAW leadership and the Labour Party were openly pleased with the Act, and they congratulated one another on what seemed to represent a major step forward in the promotion of farmworkers' occupational interests. How well-founded was this interpretation of the Act's provisions?

The terms of the *Rent (Agriculture) Act* have been summarised as follows

The main purpose of the Act is to give a form of security of tenure to agricultural workers living in housing provided by the farmers who employ them. This security is not security of tenure in the full Rent Act sense. When the employment comes to an end, the farmers may require the local authorities to rehouse such workers, if it can be shown that the cottages are urgently required for incoming workers in the interests of agricultural efficiency. The local authorities have a statutory duty to provide alternative accommodation in such circumstances and the outgoing workers to accept it or have no home. Thus farmworkers are given guaranteed housing rather than security in their own home.[74]

To what extent do these provisions serve the interests of the tied cottage dweller? Contrary to the claim of the Labour Party, the *Rent (Agriculture) Act* did not 'effectively abolish[ed] the tied cottage system, whereby a man's home was tied to his employment'.[75] Instead, home and job remain closely entwined for the tied cottage dweller, despite the introduction of the Act.

The government's main contribution to tied cottage reform was to provide farmworkers with 'housing security', explained to farmworkers as follows

'housing security' means that you will not be called upon to leave your cottage unless and until suitable alternative accommodation is available, or unless certain limited grounds for possession apply (e.g. if you fail to pay any rent that was due . . .).[76]

The main benefit to farmworkers, then, is that they no longer fear homelessness as a result of losing their job, whether through injury, illness, retirement, redundancy or dismissal. If the farmer wishes to repossess the cottage, the farmworker must first be given somewhere suitable to live. Nor is the process of eviction as traumatic as it was prior to 1976. The experience of being dragged through the county courts by an ex-employer has been replaced by the more civilised ADHAC procedure. This change has removed the farmworker's sense of degradation and has also spared the union the considerable expense of defending hundreds of members in the courts each year.[77]

The improvement in farmworkers' working conditions brought about by the Act was warmly welcomed by the NUAAW's leaders who proclaimed in 1976 that it would be regarded by many as 'the most notable and far-reaching achievement in the Union's history'. To some extent this joyous reception of the Act was well-founded.[78] The tied cottage inhabitants with whom I spoke during the summer of

1984 were all very aware of the improvement in their conditions which had taken place over the past ten years. Few of them knew the precise details of the improvement, for example, that it had been the legacy of the last Labour Government, or how it had been worked out in the corridors of Whitehall and Westminster. Nevertheless, the tied cottage dwellers spoke with a distinct sense of pride about the fact that they were safe in their homes, and that if for any reason they were required to move out, it was the duty of someone else to find them a new home. When they spoke of this relatively novel security there was a sense of defiance in their words; the farmer could try as hard as he liked to intimidate the workers, but the workers were protected against eviction and the pain that once accompanied it.

The introduction of this new element of security in the tied cottage dwellers' lives suggests that they might be able to bargain more freely than previously for higher wages and better conditions. This is not, however, the case, for farmers still wield considerable power over their workers by threatening them with dismissal, as the 1984 Overtime Ban illustrated. Moreover, there remain the problems which are related to tied accommodation which the *Rent (Agriculture) Act* did not tackle. Tied cottage dwellers remain isolated in many cases from the neighbouring village community and they often have to travel long distances to reach important amenities and services. Many are still expected to fulfil a twenty-four hour duty on the farm, in the sense that they can be called out at any time of day or night to attend to 'emergency situations'. Tied cottage dwellers also continue to suffer occupational immobility in so far as they are able to accept new jobs only where they provide further tied accommodation: in many cases this restricts their mobility to within the agricultural industry. Furthermore, Labour's *Rent (Agriculture) Act*

> has not really modified the system of labour control that tied housing represents. Farmers are still free to use the lure of a tied cottage to attract workers. Due to the overall shortage of rural housing many agricultural workers have no choice but to accept such an offer. They are still then dependent on the farmer for housing, even if they have security.[79]

In other words, in spite of the Act, the tied cottage continues to be dangled in front of farmworkers as 'the carrot' which entices them to accept a low wage. Moreover, the tied cottage is still used in the AWB where farmers' representatives continue to insist that farmworkers' 'free housing' justifies the payment of a relatively low wage. The union's sponsored MP, Joan Maynard, was one of the few people to point out that as long as tied cottage inhabitants continued to pay the 'privileged rent' set by the AWB, there would remain a crucial and oppressive bond between the workers' homes and jobs.[80] Her proposed solution to these problems was for farmers to charge tied cottage inhabitants the market rent for the tenancy of the cottages. This, she alleged, would be beneficial to farmworkers in the long run because it would force farmers to pay their workers adequate wages so that, in turn, the workers could pay their rents. This development would lead to the farmworker being given the option of moving out of the tied cottage, as he would be able to pay for non-tied housing. However, Maynard's proposal was rejected by other MPs on the grounds that it was wholly impractical. Not only did it rest upon the dubious assumption that farmers *would* increase wages sufficiently for farmworkers to afford market rents; it also depended essentially upon the construction of a great deal more cheap non-tied rural housing for farmworkers to move into. Until these two hurdles were overcome, long-term solutions to the tied cottage problem such as Maynard's would continue to be seen as unrealistic.[81]

The remaining problems attached to agricultural tied housing suggest that, contrary to the Labour Party's claims, the tied cottage system had not been 'abolished'; nor did the *Rent (Agriculture) Act* satisfy many of the farmworkers' more limited interests which might have been served by more thorough-going tied cottage reform. The discrepancy between the government's original plan to disengage farmworkers' conditions of employment from their housing, and what it eventually carried through, must be related at least partly to the NUAAW's actions and inaction.

The NUAAW's leaders did not press the government for full-scale abolition at any time during the two-year prelude to the passage of the *Rent (Agriculture) Act* 1976. Instead of emphasising the tied cottage problems which would persist if abolition or extensive reform were not introduced, the leadership accepted the government's offer of security of tenure because 'it went 90% of the way'. Moreover, when the government diluted its original notion of security of tenure by adding the ADHAC measure to the proposed reform, the union refrained from opposing this further step away from farmworkers' interests, so as to see at least *some* reform passed.

The union's rank and file appeared to accept without criticism the leadership's compromising line, apart from a few notable exceptions, such as this

> In my estimation, the blackest day in our Union's history was the day the [Conference] delegates rolled over on their backs to have their tummies tickled by the Government's and the Union's top brass, and accepted their own practical version of what we all thought was going to mean the abolition of the agricultural tied cottage, and with it the disengagement we have been promised in the Labour Party's manifesto and the Government's Consultative Document.[82]

It is significant that the writer of this letter to the *Land-worker* blamed not only the government's but also the union's 'top brass' for the perceived shortcomings of the *Rent (Agriculture) Act*. The NUAAW leaders received from the government that which they had argued for: security of farmworkers' housing, which was in no way comparable to tied cottage abolition or 'disengagement'. The important question is: what reforms would have been achieved if the union leaders *had* applied pressure on the government for full-scale abolition?

The experience of Joan Maynard is enlightening in this context. When the tied cottage issue was first debated by the Labour Party during its 1974–79 period of government, Maynard supported the suggestion of Gerald Kaufman, MP that local authorities should purchase all tied cottages from farmers and then rent them out to farmworkers. Both Maynard and Kaufman recognised that only a drastic move such as this would enable the government to fulfil its pledge to 'disengage farmworkers' conditions of employment from the circumstances in which they are housed'. The suggestion was immediately opposed, however, by the great majority of Labour MPs on the grounds of excessive cost, both in financial and political terms. Maynard and Kaufman were consequently obliged to shelve their proposal. As a second-best measure, Maynard then suggested an amendment to the proposed legislation which would make market rents payable for tied houses, instead of the AWB-determined privileged rents. This reform would serve to untie houses from jobs and allegedly would give rise to an improvement in agricultural wages and conditions. This second proposal was similarly blocked by Maynard's parliamentary colleagues, who argued that it would jeopardise the entire Bill. Maynard regarded such arguments as spurious, but she was obliged to bow to the pressure of the great majority of Labour MPs in order to get at least some reform through parliament before its dissolution.[83]

The NUAAW recognised that prevailing attitudes in Parliament, and the NFU's proven ability to mobilise and exploit these attitudes, were such that abolition would have been construed almost automatically as an unrealistic and unacceptable demand. In this sense, the NUAAW can be said to have achieved success in its tied cottage campaign chiefly because it defined its goals according to what it anticipated it could achieve.[84]   The NUAAW thus heralded the *Rent (Agriculture) Act* as a major breakthrough for farmworkers in a spirit of 'realism' which had been shaped by successive nondecisions carried out by the NFU, the PLP and Parliament as a whole.

The main service brought to farmworkers' interests by the *Rent (Agriculture) Act* was the provision of a new housing security which liberated the tied cottage dweller from his earlier fears of eviction and homelessness at the whim of his employers. Apart from this, the Act failed to satisfy many of the farmworkers' occuaptional interests, which consequently continue to be frustrated by the tied cottage system. The tied cottage dweller is still often obliged to accept low wages, to work long hours, live in isolation from the village community and remain tied to agricultural employment. By contrast, the agricultural employer's interests continue to be served by the tied cottage system; indeed, the Act has in certain respects enhanced the tied housing system from the employer's point of view.

The gains which accure to farmers from the Act derive almost exclusively from its ADHAC provision. The ADHAC consists of three members: an 'independent' chair (selected by local MAFF officers in consultation with the Chair of the local Agricultural Wages Committee); one representative for the farmer; and one for the farmworker, each being drawn from their respective union organisations, even where the farmer and/or farmworker is not a member of their union. The farmer concerned always appears at the ADHAC, so as to put forward his case; the worker has the opportunity to attend, too, but in practice does so less frequently than the farmer.

An ADHAC meets each time a farmer applies to have an ex-employee removed from his cottage. If the farmer proves to the ADHAC that it is in the interests of agricultural efficiency for a new worker to move into the house, then the ADHAC will advise the local authority to find the ex-worker a new home. The local authority reacts to this advice by placing the farmworker's name at or near the top of the council waiting list so that the continued shortage of council houses does not obstruct the ADHAC's operation.

Every time the ADHAC agrees to make such an application to the local authority on the farmer's behalf, it is doing the farmer a great service, for it enables the farmer to remove unwanted workers from their homes without resort to conflictual and bitter court procedures. In many (but not all) cases, such action by the ADHAC is welcomed by the farm-worker, too, as he often desires to move from the farm cottage into a council house in a nearby village or town.

When it meets, the ADHAC is not expected to make decisions about 'eviction' and 'homelessness' which were the issues which the courts had to deal with prior to the Act. Rather, the ADHAC is concerned with the more straight-forward questions of whether it is agriculturally necessary for a given farmer to gain possession over his cottage and whether the worker should, therefore, be provided with alternative housing. The ADHAC meetings are consequently relatively unemotional and non-conflictual, their main topic for discussion being the technical one of whether it is in the interests of 'agricultural efficiency' for a new worker to move into the cottage in question. In the six ADHACs which I attended as an observer, discussion between the ADHAC members and the farmer and worker concerned (when they attended) was always cordial, consensual and businesslike.[85] Nobody concerned themselves with emotive issues such as insecurity, independence or justice: courtroom dramas have been replaced by technical evaluations of the 'agricultural need' for particular cottages. Thus, the ADHAC has made it unnecessary for farmers to engage in the messy business of tied cottage eviction.

In an effort to ensure the 'independence' of ADHAC chairs, MAFF's policy dictates that the Chairs, '. . . whilst having a sympathetic understanding of the rural scene, should have no direct agricultural or local authority housing interest . . .'.[86] Many commentators have pointed to this lack of agricultural experience among ADHAC chairs to explain why ADHACs so often find it 'agriculturally necessary' for farmworkers to vacate their homes in order that a new worker can move in.

Table 4   ADHACs: statistical summary (national figures)

Item	1981	1982	1983
Cases brought forward	35	34	33
Cases received	639	644	620
Cases withdrawn	106	107	88
Cases heard	534	538	522
Agricultural need established	459	469	448
No agricultural need established	75	69	74
Cases carried forward	34	33	41

Source: MAFF

From the farmers' point of view, this trend of finding 'agricultural need' in the great majority of cases is an unqualified benefit. It means that they can remain confident about removing ex-workers from their cottages, without having to engage in the conflict and bitterness attached to such action in earlier years. The advantages that the ADHAC brings for the farmworkers are less clear-cut. It is true that in many cases, the farmworker hopes that the ADHAC will find 'agricultural need' because this enables him to move to council housing which is often situated nearer to friends, relatives, amenities, and the worker's new place of work. However, in other instances, farmworkers do *not* wish to be uprooted from their homes of many years or decades. In spite of this, the ADHAC's priority is always 'agricultural requirements'—the *Rent (Agriculture) Act* makes no provision for the requirements of farmworkers and their families in cases where they wish to remain in their homes. The number of such cases is unknown, but clearly some do exist.[87] Moreover, the contracting stock of council houses (due to the increased sale of such houses) and the concomitant council house rent increases, will almost certainly mean that more farmworkers will in future prefer to remain in their farm cottages.[88]

Overall, the conclusion must be that, far from representing the clear-cut promotion of farmworkers' interests, the *Rent (Agriculture) Act* satisfies the interests of agricultural employers to a large degree and those of tied cottage dwellers to a lesser extent. The single most important feature of the Act is that, through the introduction of the ADHAC mechanism, it has ensured the future smooth running of the tied cottage system. Tied cottage conflict has been replaced by what is usually the orderly rehousing of ex-employees—a development which has provided the agricultural tied cottage system with at least a semblance of harmony and efficiency. This image has, in turn, guaranteed the perpetuation of the tied cottage system, for, who would wish to tamper with such an efficient system?

It is the agricultural employer who benefits most from this situation. As long as the rural council house shortage continues, he will be able to use the tied cottage as a means of attracting skilled labour for low wages. At the same time, he can continue to force ex-employees out of their homes while avoiding the disruption to labour relations which tied cottage evictions gave rise to so often in the past. Conversely, the tied cottage dweller's newly found security of housing must be set against the significant disbenefits brought about by the Act. Not only can the tied cottage inhabitant be made to leave his home in what is made to appear a humane manner; but also (and more importantly) the tied cottage related problems which the Act left intact will be lasting ones, given the tied cottage system's new lease of life provided by the *Rent (Agriculture) Act*.

NOTES

1 G. M. Trevelyan, quoted in, Jones, A. (1975), *Rural Housing: the Agricultural Tied Cottage*, Occasional Papers on Social Administration, No. 56, York, p. 13.
2 Jones, *Rural Housing*, pp. 13–16.
3 Newby, H. (1977), 'Tied cottage reform', *BJLS*, 4.
4 Clark, D. (1982), 'Rural housing: problems and solutions', in *Rural Housing: Problems and Solutions—A Seminar Report*, Peak National Park Study Centre, NCVO and the Development Commission; Phillips, D. (1981) and Williams, A., 'Council house sales and village life', *New Society*, 28 November; Rogers, A. (1976), 'Rural housing' in G. Cherry (ed.), *Rural Planning Problems*, Leonard Hill, London.
5 Newby, H., Bell, C., Rose, D. and Saunders, P. (1978), *Property, Paternalism and Power*, Hutchinson, London; Phillips D. and Williams, A. (1984), *Rural Britain*, Blackwell, Oxford, Chapter 5; Larkin, A. (1979), 'Rural housing and housing needs', in J. Martin Shaw (ed.), *Rural Deprivation and Planning*, Geo Abstracts, Norwich.
6 Newby *et al.*, *op. cit.*, p. 252; Clark, *op. cit.*

7 Shelter, (1979), *The Forgotten Problem: a Study of Tied Accommodation and the Cycle of Insecurity*, Shelter, London, p. 14.
8 Irving, B. and Hilgendorf, L. (1975), *Tied Cottages in British Agriculture*, Working Paper No. 1, Tavistock Institute, London.
9 Shelter, *Forgotten Problem*, p. 14.
10 Irving and Hilgendorf, *op. cit.*, p. 48.
11 Giles, A. K. and Cowie, W. J. G. (1960), 'Some social and economic aspects of agricultural workers' accommodation', *JAE*, 14 (2), p. 148.
12 Shelter, (1974), *Report on Tied Accommodation*, Shelter, London, p. 10; Clark, G. (1982), *Housing and Planning in the Countryside*, Research Studies Press, Chichester, p. 35.
13 Gasson, R. (1975), *Provision of Tied Cottages*, University of Cambridge, Department of Land Economy, Occasional Paper No. 4, p. 84.
14 See Shelter, *The Forgotten Problem*, Chapter 2 for a depiction of this tied housing trap.
15 E.g. *Landworker*, September 1946, March 1949, August 1960, December 1972.
16 *Landworker*, August 1960.
17 Shelter, *The Forgotten Problem*, p. 15; Newby, *Tied Cottage Reform*, p. 97.
18 Hansard, Volume 910, 4 May 1976, Col. 1092.
19 Giles and Cowie, *op. cit.*, p. 155.
20 Gasson, *op. cit.*, p. 79.
21 *Landworker* July 1966 provides an illustration of this phenomenon. It relates the case of 'a sixty-nin-year old colleague who had been working with cutting cabbages in the pouring rain. When asked why he was doing it he replied: "You know how it is. I am living in a house. If I do not do it, he will want it for someone else".'
22 Giles and Cowie, *op. cit.*, p. 156.
23 For example, Mingay, G. E. (1972), 'The transformation of agriculture', in R. Hartwell, G. Mingay, R. Boyson, N. McCord, C. Hanson, A. W. Coats, W. Chaloner, W. O. Henderson and M. Jefferson, (1972), *The Long Debate on Poverty*, Institute of Economic Affairs, pp. 51-2; Groves, R. (1981), *Sharpen the Sickle!*, Merlin Press, London; Fussell, G. E. (1948), *From Tolpuddle to T.U.C.*, Windsor Press, Slough: Chapter 5.
24 Joan Maynard quoted in the *Landworker*, June 1975.
25 Newby, *op. cit.*, p. 97.
26 Rossi, H. (1977), *Shaw's Guide to the Rent (Agriculture) Act 1976*, Shaw & Sons Ltd., London, p. 4; Gasson, *op. cit.*, p. 81.
27 Shelter, *Report on Tied Accommodation*, p. 9.
28 Newby, H. (1979), *The Deferential Worker*, Penguin, Harmondsworth, p. 190; Giles and Cowie, *op. cit.*, p. 155.
29 Cf. Hansard, Volume 910, 4 May 1976, Col. 1092.
30 Newby, *op. cit.*, p. 184.
31 Gasson, *op. cit.*, p. 1; Jones, *op. cit.*, p. 52; Clark, *op. cit.*, p. 1.
32 Newby, *Tied Cottage Reform*, p. 98.
33 Newby, *Deferential Worker*, pp. 421-2.
34 Quoted in Jones, *op. cit.*, p. 16.
35 *Landworker*, January 1957.

36 Self, P. and Storing, H. (1962), *The State and the Farmer*, Allen & Unwin, London, pp. 175-6.
37 For example, *Landworker*, August 1921, July 1942, December 1946, July 1952.
38 Cf. Bachrach, P. and Baratz, M. (1970), *Power and Poverty*, Oxford University Press, New York, p. 44 '. . . nondecision-making is a means by which demands for change in the existing allocation of benefits and privileges in the community can be suffocated before they are even voiced'.
39 *Ibid.*, p. 45.
40 Jones, *op. cit.*, p. 16.
41 From a speech by George Brown MP at Swaffham during Labour's 1964 General Election campaign.
42 *Landworker*, July 1947.
43 Self and Storing, *op. cit.*, p. 147.
44 *Landworker*, January 1965.
45 Hansard, Volume 702, 16 November 1964, Col. 1569.
46 Clark, *op. cit.*, p. 39.
47 For detailed comparisons of the NEC's changing composition between the 1960s and the 1970s, and the significance this had for tied cottage reform, see Michael Darke's forthcoming book on the *Rent (Agriculture) Act* 1976.
48 *Landworker*, June 1975.
49 This was explained to me during an interview with Reg Bottini (on 30 November 1984), who was the NUAAW's General Secretary 1970-77.
50 Cf. Dahl, R. (1961), *Who Governs?*, Yale University, New Haven, Chapter 23.
51 Reg Bottini during interview, see Note 49.
52 Department of the Environment (DOE) and MAFF (1975), *Abolition of the Tied Cottage System in Agriculture: Consultative Document*.
53 NFU Paper Cyclo 1633/75 Parl. 201, 29 September 1975.
54 Giles and Cowie, *op. cit.*, p. 151.
55 Hansard, Volume 910, 4 May 1976, Col. 1137.
56 Saunders, P. (1970), *Urban Politics*, Hutchinson, London, pp. 49-59; Gaventa, J. (1982), *Power and Powerlessness*, University of Illinois, Chicago, p. 67.
57 DOE and MAFF, *Consultative Document*, Preface, my italics.
58 Miliband, R. (1973), 'The power of labour and the capitalist enterprise', in J. Urry and J. Wakeford, *Power in Britain*, Heinemann, London, p. 136; McEachern, D. (1980), *A Class Against Itself*, Cambridge University Press, p. 100; Dahl, *op. cit.*, pp. 228 and 163-5.
59 Hansard, Volume 910, 4 May 1976, Col. 1135.
60 Roth, A. (1975), *The Business Background of MPs: 1975-1976*, Parliamentary Profiles, London.
61 See the NUAAW *Annual Report* 1974.
62 NFU *Annual Report* 1977; NUAAW *Annual Report* 1980-81.
63 Explained to me during an interview with Michael Darke (26 February 1985) who was the NFU's Parliamentary Secretary at the time when the Rent (Agriculture) Bill was being discussed in and outside of Parliament. Mr Darke was responsible for NFU

contacts with MPs at Westminster.
64 Explained to me by Reg Bottini, see Note 49.
65 Coates, D. (1980), *Labour in Power?*, Longman, London, pp. 94–6 and 150–1.
66 Lukes, S. (1974), *Power: a Radical View*, Macmillan, London, pp. 55–6; Connolly, W. E. (1983), *The Terms of Political Discourse*, second edition, Martin Robertson, Oxford, pp. 94–101, 131; Saunders, *op. cit.*, pp. 49–59; Parenti, M (1978), *Power and the Powerless*, St. Martins, New York, p. 5; Therborn, G. (1982), 'What does the ruling class do when it rules?', in Giddens and Held (eds), *Classes, Power and Conflict*, Macmillan, Basingstoke, pp. 231–2.
67 Newby, *Tied Cottage Reform*, p. 107.
68 *Landworker*, January 1977.
69 *Ibid.*
70 DOE and MAFF, *Consultative Document*, p. 2. This is seen in certain Labour Party documents which have been published since 1977. For example, the Labour Party's *Campaign Handbook for Agriculture* (printed in 1978) says that the *Rent (Agriculture) Act* 'effectively abolished the tied cottage system'. A similar line is taken in private correspondence from John Silkin (Minister of Agriculture in 1978) and from Ernest Armstrong (Parliamentary Under-Secretary in the Department of the Environment in 1977) addressed to Reg Bottini.
71 Clark, *op. cit.*, p. 38; Bachrach, P. and Baratz, M. (1962), 'The two faces of power', *APSR*, 56, p. 948.
72 Polsby, N. (1980), *Community Power and Political Theory*, second edition; Yale University, London, pp. 3–5 and 189–218; Bachrach and Baratz, *op. cit.*
73 *British Farmer and Stockbreeder*, 24 April 1976.
74 Rossi, *op. cit.*, p. 1; *Note* the 'statutory duty' placed upon local authorities by the Act is to use their 'best endeavours' to rehouse agricultural workers.
75 Labour Party, (1978), *Campaign Handbook on Agriculture*, The Labour Party, London, p. 18.
76 DOE and MAFF, Welsh Office (1977), *Some Questions and Answers about the Rent (Agriculture) Act 1976.*
77 See the NUAAW's *Annual Reports* for details of this expense. Also *Landworker*, July 1966 and May 1974.
78 NUAAW *Annual Report* 1976; NUAAW (1976), *Outlook for Agriculture*, NUAAW Policy Document, London; *Landworker*, January 1977, March 1977, November 1977 and February 1978.
79 Shelter, *The Forgotten Problem*, p. 16.
80 Hansard, Volume 910, 4 May 1976, Cols. 1097–8.
81 Phillips and Williams, *Rural Britain*, p. 124; Gasson, *Provision of Tied Cottages*, p. 119; Shelter, *op. cit.*, p. 16; *Times*, 14 March 1975, 'Can the Government Ever Settle the "Feudal Relic" of tied cottages?'; Royal Institute of Chartered Surveyors (1975), *The Agricultural Tied Cottage—Discussion Papers*, London, p. 5.
82 Letter to *Landworker*, December 1978.
83 Explained to me in an interview with Joan Maynard, MP (8 November 1984); Cf. Westergaard, J. and Ressler, H. (1975), *Class in a Capitalist Society*, Heinemann, London, pp. 146–7.

84 Bachrach and Baratz, *Power and Poverty*, p. 46; '. . . situations where B, confronted by A who has greater power resources, decides not to make a demand upon A for fear that the latter will invoke sanctions against him'.
85 By kind permission of MAFF in Oxfordshire and in Suffolk.
86 Taken from a private explanatory letter sent by MAFF in reply to my request for information.
87 *Landworker*, July 1982.
88 HMSO (1984), *Social Trends 1984*, p. 120 for details.

Chapter 6

'Whitewash is no antidote to poison': the farmworkers' campaign to ban 2,4,5-T

This chapter continues the analysis of powerlessness, by evaluating the NUAAW's efforts to promote and defend farmworkers' interests in maintaining a reasonable standard of occupational health and safety. In particular, it concentrates on the union's attempts to promote its members' interests by securing a ban on the controversial weedkiller known as 2,4,5-T. Evidence from this campaign confirms the arguments of Chapters 4 and 5, that an appreciation of the 'second face' of power is crucial to an understanding of political powerlessness. More interestingly, perhaps, this case study highlights certain limitations in the 'second face' approach as it has been put forward by Peter Bachrach and Morton Baratz.

In particular, this chapter challenges Bachrach and Baratz's refusal to include unobservable phenomena, such as objective interests, in a study of power and powerlessness. What this chapter shows is that a conception of Q's objective interests is imperative if one is to locate some of the more insidious ways in which power is exercised, such that Q is unaware of its exercise and consequently unable to 'inform' the observer in any behavioural fashion that it is being exercised. The only way that the observer can recognise that power is being exercised in such a case is by beginning with a conception of Q's interests which exists independently of Q's subjective desires.

This is not to deny that considerable methodological difficulties might be involved in identifying those power exercises of which Q is unaware. In this chapter these difficulties are overcome by adopting the approach set out in Chapter 1; that is, by combining a prior conception of Q's objective interests with historical analysis.

Beginning with the heuristic proposition that it is in farmworkers' objective interests not to use 2,4,5-T until its safety is guaranteed, the study inquires into farmworkers' apparent harming of their own interests through their use of the herbicide without the benefit of such a safety guarantee.

Research reveals that farmworkers acted against their objective interests for many years primarily because, through the control of information, they were kept ignorant of the possible harm which the use of 2,4,5-T might entail. The identification of this power exercise is reached through the study of the changes in farmworkers' behaviour before and after information was released concerning the weedkiller's possible dangers. Once information was released, farmworkers began to act upon their objective interests by refusing to use the chemical. It is by commencing with a heuristic conception of farmworkers' objective interests, and a definition of power which includes all those (in)actions which contribute significantly to the harming of Q's interests, that this exercise of power through the control of information can be located.

This chapter also continues the theme of the distribution of power resources which was raised in Chapter 4 and then studied in greater empirical detail in Chapter 5. The present chapter finds that the single greatest resource available to farmworkers is solidarity with occupational groups whose interests are similar to their own. In the case of the 2,4,5-T campaign, the NUAAW's skilled use of this resource led to what some regard as an unprecedented success by the union.

However, the chapter also notes the limits to this success— limits which are attributed above all to the union's lack of access to any other significant power resources. It is this lack of power resources, in particular the resources which Dahl refers to as legality and social standing, which is shown to have prevented the NUAAW from withstanding the 'second face' of power. The government and its Advisory Committee on Pesiticides (ACP) are found to have resorted successfully to the mobilisation of dominant values, the use of silence, the use of membership bias in decision-making institutions, and other techniques noted in Chapter 1 in their efforts to invalidate the union's demands for a ban on 2,4,5-T and for workers' representation on pesticide safety decision-making bodies.

In finding that power is exercised over the NUAAW by the government and ACP in these ways, this chapter also confirms the proposition in Chapter 1 that, although it may be useful to begin with an idea of which group's objective interests conflict with those of Q, it would be mistaken to assume that this group is necessarily responsible for the frustration of Q's interests. Although such an assumption proves to be warranted in Chapters 4 and 5, in this chapter the conflict of interests over pesticide use which exists between agricultural employers and workers *cannot* be taken to imply that the former is responsible for the frustration of the latter's interests in the chosen case study. Empirical investigation reveals instead that farmworkers' interests *vis-à-vis* 2,4,5-T are harmed above all by the (in)action of the ACP.

At an empirical level, this chapter is concerned with farmworkers' interests in maintaining an adequate standard of occupational health and safety as a basic requisite to satisfying their interests in economic maximisation. It therefore begins with a general review of the health and safety problems which characterise the contemporary agricultural industry.

In Section II the extent of pesticide use in British agriculture is outlined, and the conflict which exists between agricultural employers and workers over its use is discussed.

Section III examines the NUAAW's powerlessness to reverse the official clearance of 2,4,5-T, using the concepts of information control, the mobilisation of bias, the use of silence and the distribution of power resources to explain the nature of this powerlessness.

Then, in Section IV the union's response to its powerlessness in the 2,4,5-T campaign is considered. The union's successful use of the power resource referred to as 'solidarity' is considered, as is the union's overall failure to enforce an official ban on the herbicide. This failure signifies the union's wider powerlessness to assert its claimed right to participate in pesticide safety decision-making at all levels of the decision-making process. The provisions of the *Food and Environment Protection Act* 1985 confirm the government's persistent refusal to recognise such a right. As a result, the union is shown to remain relatively powerless to regulate the standard of its members' occupational health and safety.

I HEALTH AND SAFETY IN THE CONTEMPORARY AGRICULTURAL INDUSTRY

The key to the post-war boom in agricultural output which was outlined in Chapter 2 has undoubtedly been the introduction of heavy machinery and of numerous new chemicals into the agricultural production process. However, the infusion of science and technology into the farming industry, financed through state subsidies, has not simply given rise to enormously increased production levels, it has also profoundly changed the nature of agricultural work.

A major aspect of this change has been in the area of occupational health and safety. Agriculture has always been a dangerous industry in which to work, but whereas once farmworkers faced dangers relating primarily to their work with animals and their immensely long hours of work, today they confront new dangers deriving from their use of complicated machines, and new and potentially toxic chemicals. The seriousness and prevalence of contemporary farmworkers' health and safety problems helps to explain the rising devotion of their union's resources to campaigns relating to farmworkers' interests in securing the best occupational health and safety standards possible.

Farmworkers are marked by the undesirable distinction of working in the country's third most dangerous industry, after mining and construction. Between 1976 and 1981 nearly 200 work-related deaths among farmworkers were reported, and during that period a rough average of 4,000 non-fatal accidents were reported *each year*. However, these figures do not reveal the true extent of agricultural health hazards, for the Health and Safety Executive (HSE) acquires its statistics from the Department of Health and Social Security (DHSS) and not all work-related accidents are reported to the DHSS. The causes of this non-reporting of accidents are varied; what is significant is that according to the Robens Committee (whose report led to the *Health and Safety at Work Act* 1974), for every reportable accident at work a further thirty are not reported. On this basis, it can be argued that non-fatal accidents among farmworkers occur at a rate of 120,000 per annum, leaving farmworkers with a one-in-three chance of being injured at work each year.[1]

Death and injury are caused in agriculture by a host of different elements and circumstances. These have included accidents with stationary, self-propelled and other field machinery; disease; poisoning; asphyxiation; electrocution; drowning (in liquid and in grain); and collisions with falling and swinging objects.

Until relatively recently the greatest single recorded cause of farm deaths was the overturning tractor.[2] When a tractor overturned the driver would invariably fall out and, in almost all cases, would sustain serious, if not fatal, injuries.

The frequency with which tractors overturn has meant that for many years farmers and farmworkers were being injured or killed by the very same machine which had so dramatically revolutionised their industry.[3] It was not until 1974 that legislation was passed which required new agricultural tractors to be fitted with approved protective safety cabs and frames, and only in 1977 was the legislation extended to cover *all* tractors driven by employees. Although the swift drop in the number of farm deaths relating to overturning tractors after 1977 was a welcomed development, many people regretted the relatively late introduction of the safety legislation which had led to this improvement.

While the overturning tractor is no longer as great a cause for concern among hired farmworkers as it once was, the continuing prevalence of occupational hazards in agriculture continues to bear down upon the farm work-force. The HSE lists each year the causes of work-related deaths among farmworkers and farmers. Its lists for one year included, among other items, the following

(i)   an employee was killed when attempting to pull free a bogged tractor. He attached a wire rope to the top link of his tractor causing it to overturn on top of him;

(ii)   an employee entered a tower silo to dislodge grain that had bridged and was overcome by carbon dioxide;

(iii) an employee was killed when his clothing caught in the un-guarded shaft of a slurry tanker;

(iv)   a worker was killed when he fell and was run over by a flat bottomed trainer.[4]

This diversity of farm-related accidents suggests that, regardless of how skilled and careful a worker might be, the nature of his work is such that unforeseeable accidents are always just around the corner.

The high number of occupational deaths and injuries in agriculture has led the farmworkers' union to adopt the issue of occupational health and safety as one of its major concerns. Indeed, in recent years health and safety issues have assumed a prominence which is arguably equal to that of the wages and tied cottage issues. The importance which is attached to health and safety issues by the union is shown most clearly by its dedication of scarce resources to the running of a separate Legal/Health and Safety Department, by the space in *Landworker* devoted each month to health and safety matters, and by the rising number of health and safety

related motions put forward at the uinion's Annual Con-
ferences. Equally telling is the union's continuous campaigning over a number of different health and safety issues.

The NUAAW was a major force behind the introduction
of the tractor cabs legislation, and it has been fighting with
vigour for the right to appoint its own work-place health
and safety representatives. Another issue over which it has
fought (without success) has been the fall in the number of
Agricultural Inspectors—from 198 in 1979 to 155 in 1983.
This drop has meant that 'labour holding farms' are inspected
once every six years which, according to the union, has led
to a situation 'whereby the most consistently productive,
most consistently underpaid workers are also becoming the
least protected in terms of health and safety at work'.[5]
However, the most vociferous of the union's campaigns has
been over pesticide use and its related dangers: it is with
this area of health and safety campaigning that the rest of
this chapter is concerned.

II PESTICIDE USE AND PESTICIDE SAFETY: A CONFLICT OF INTERESTS

Pesticides are materials which control pests by killing them.
Applied in agriculture, they allow crops to grow without
being impaired by weeds (which are killed by herbicides),
insects (killed by insecticides), or fungi (killed by fungicides).[6]

Since the 1940s the British pesticides market has become
increasingly sophisticated, with a growing number of products
becoming available annually. In 1944 there were sixty-five
approved pesticide products on the market, based on a few
simple active ingredients; by 1980 there were over 800
approved products to choose from, containing some 200
different and mostly complex, synthetic ingredients.[7]

The figures in Table 1 suggest quite clearly that the British
pesticides industry has achieved a striking success in terms of
the sale of its products. By 1982 total agrochemical sales in
Britain were estimated at £542 million, and a leading stock-
broker predicted a 'favourable outlook' for the industry in
the coming years.[8] This prediction has been borne out, with
the result that pesticide companies have concentrated in the
1980s on the manufacture of more and more new products.

Table 1 Sales of formulated pesticides by British manufacturers

Pesticide	1974	1975	1976	1977	1978
	£'000	£'000	£'000	£'000	£'000
Herbicides	49 719	76 156	81 422	96 894	93 453
Insecticides	16 330	27 134	35 434	45 858	47 830
Fungicides	9 915	14 272	14 028	17 061	21 560

Source: Keynote Publications Ltd, 1981.

For example, ICI, one of the world's largest pesticide producers, announced plans in 1985 to invest a further £20 million in research and development alone, with the aim of doubling its sales figures of £635 million worldwide by the early 1990s.[9]

This outstanding growth of the pesticide industry is closely bound up with the 'high input–maximum output' cycle which has come to characterise modern British agriculture, particularly since 1973 when Britain joined the EEC (see Chapter 2). As agricultural grants from the EEC's Common Agricultural Policy (CAP) have risen in value and been weighted in favour of the largest producers, so farmers have invested more and more of their capital in materials which promise to stimulate crop production in the hopes of claiming even larger grants and subsidies from the CAP. The CAP capital which they then receive is used (at least partially) for the purchase of still more agrochemicals, with the aim of increasing output yet further and thus securing the farmer's eligibility for even greater financial support. This high input–high output cycle entails clear benefits for the agrochemical companies, who were active 'pro-Marketeers' when Britain's EEC membership was being debated in the early 1970s,[10] in so far as it ensures the continued large-scale purchase of their products. It is chiefly because of the capital intensity of EEC farm policies that the value of pesticides sprayed in Britain has lept from £40 million in 1972 to £329 million in 1985. Even allowing for inflation, this represents a 400 per cent increase in chemicals sprayed per square inch in Britain.[11]

Although the pesticide industry, together with many of the country's large farmers, have vested interests in the current boom in pesticide production and application, not all groups share their enthusiasm for pesticide use. As well as being seen by many as an 'irrevocable assault on the environment' and a terrible threat to wildlife,[12] pesticides are regarded by some people as a potential, and sometimes actual, danger to the health and safety of human beings. The chemicals used in pesticides designed to kill fungi, insects and plants, are often suspected of being sufficiently toxic to harm, if not kill, those people who come into contact with them. Workers involved in the manufacture of pesticides form one group of possible victims of pesticide poisoning; the people who apply pesticides form another.

Pesticides can thus be found at the centre of a conflict of interests between agricultural employers and workers, where the former demands that the latter apply a potentially dangerous pesticide with a view to increasing crop production. This conflict is not a simple one. Sometimes the conflict remains latent when the farmworker and often the employer are unaware of the harm that a given pesticide can cause to the farmworker who applies it. Moreover, pesticides do not in themselves necessarily give rise to conflict. Just as most employers are concerned to ensure an adequate standard of safety for their employees, so too many farmworkers would agree that at least certain pesticides can be used without danger to themselves in the interests of lucrative farming. Conflict becomes actual and overt when the two sides seek to defend their respective interests at the cost of the other's: that is, when the farmer attempts to compromise his employee's health and safety in the interests of increasing production levels, and when the worker threatens those production levels by refusing to apply an effective pesticide to crops on the grounds that it may be dangerous to his health.

When overt conflict of this nature arises, the employer can often strengthen his case by pointing to the official safety clearance of the given pesticide by the government's appointed safety regulators. In response to this, the worker often concedes to his employer's demands, for the official safety regulators are usually seen as too remote to be approached and challenged on their decisions as to the safety of the given pesticide.[13] Not only are the safety officers based in far-away London but they are shrouded in an aura of expertise and officialdom which does not invite the layman's challenge.

The safety of pesticides is under the control of the Ministry of Agriculture, Fisheries, and Food (MAFF)'s Pesticides Safety Precautions Scheme (PSPS) which was set up in 1957. The PSPS was, until 1985, a non-statutory scheme, in the sense that no individual firm was compelled by law to join it.[14] In practice, however, most firms were voluntary members of the PSPS, and this membership committed them to abide by all government regulations relating to pesticide safety. In return for their compliance, the member firms gained a certain legitimacy, derived from the official safety clearance of their products, which, in turn, helped to improve their sales figures.

The PSPS functions through the Advisory Committee on Pesticides (ACP), a body of ten academics and civil servants who are trained in pharmacology, clinical toxicology, biology, agricultural science and other related disciplines. The chemical companies which participate in the PSPS submit to the ACP confidential results of safety tests which they themselves have carried out on their products, which the ACP then scrutinises, sometimes asking for further tests to be done before clearing or rejecting the product for safe use. The ACP is serviced by a Scientific Sub-Committee (which is also drawn from academic and government circles) whose specialist knowledge is drawn upon before the ACP passes judgement on the safety of pesticide products.

The safety element in MAFF's duties has been reinforced to some extent by the British Agrochemical Supply Industry Scheme (BASIS), which involves a commitment by agricultural merchants to sell only those products cleared by PSPS. The force of BASIS rests upon the undertaking of the British Agrochemicals Association (BAA) (a trade association representing most firms in the industry) that its member firms will only supply PSPS-cleared pesticides to registered distributors.

It should be noted that MAFF is also responsible for the approval of pesticides in terms of their efficacy. This task is carried out through the Agricultural Chemicals Approval Scheme (ACAS) which grants approval as to the efficacy of those products which have first been cleared for safety under the PSPS. According to MAFF, 'This arrangement enables users to select, and advisers to recommend, efficient and appropriate proprietary brands of agricultural chemicals; and discourages the use of unsatisfactory products.'[15]

The complicated network of safety regulation and the predominance of academic and governmental experts within that network have tended to deflect potential challenges by farmworkers over the alleged safety of particular pesticides. On one occasion, however, the farmworkers' union decided to pursue such a challenge because of the very strongly expressed doubts among its members, and by the community at large, over the safety of the herbicide 2,4,5-T. Although farmworkers' interests have been shown to conflict at times with their employers' in the sphere of pesticide use, the exercises of power which the union encountered when it sought a ban on 2,4,5-T were in fact the work of groups other than agricultural employers whose objective interests, like those of the employers, conflicted with those of farmworkers and their union.

III   THE NUAAW'S CAMPAIGN TO BAN 2,4,5-T

Background to the 2,4,5-T conflict

The chemical 2,4,5-trichlorophenoxyacetic (2,4,5-T) is an effective herbicide which has been produced and used since the 1940s. It is manufactured in a series of chemical reactions from trichlorophenol, during which process a toxic contaminant known as dioxin is almost invariably produced. There are about seventy dioxins in existence, and the one which is found in 2,4,5-T is known as TCDD. TCDD is widely regarded as one of the most toxic synthetic chemicals known to man, being one of the most potent known carcinogens (a substance causing cancer) and teratogens (a substance causing birth deformities).[16]

Although 2,4,5-T is surrounded by international controversy, there are a few points relating to the weedkiller which many people agree upon. Firstly, there is little question that contact with the TCDD contaminant can be disastrous, if not fatal, causing a disfiguring skin disease known as chloracne, muscular weakness, pains in limbs and joints, increase in blood lipids, poryphoria, behavioural abnormalities, and a rare and fatal form of cancer known as soft-tissue sarcomas.[17] Secondly, there is wide agreement (although by no means universal) that contact with pure 2,4,5-T (i.e. without its TCDD contaminant) can in at least some cases cause birth defects. Thirdly, and least controversially, there is a broad consensus that 2,4,5-T operates highly effectively as a weedkiller, killing weeds by artificially stimulating their growth so that they eventually collapse and die under their own weight. It has been particularly useful in forestry work, but has also been used widely in agriculture, in gardening and in other sectors such as the railways where it is used to clear train tracks of potentially obstructive weeds.

The herbicide 2,4,5-T is best known for the conflict rather than the consensus which it generates. For, while there is little question that TCDD *can* be dangerous, there is fierce disagreement over whether there is a level of TCDD content in 2,4,5-T which is sufficiently low to be considered safe and, if so, what that level is.[18] Similarly, although pure 2,4,5-T is generally recognised to have teratogenic potential, there is some debate as to whether it acts as a teratogen in humans, as opposed to laboratory animals, and, if so, whether the chemical can be handled in such a way as to avoid its teratogenic effects. Finally, there is the question of whether it is worth taking allegedly minor health risks by using 2,4,5-T, given the weedkiller's efficacy.

The debate in Britain over whether or not 2,4,5-T is, or can be, a 'safe' weedkiller has been fuelled by well-publicised events at home and abroad. In 1968 an explosion took place at a Coalite factory in Bolsover, Derbyshire which was producing trichlorophenol, for, among other things, 2,4,5-T. As a consequence of their exposure to the chemical during the explosion, seventy-nine workers developed chloracne, while others died from liver damage. The persistence of heavy dioxin contamination within the factory led to the removal of its equipment which was then buried 150 feet down a disused coal mine.

Eight years later, in July 1976, there was another explosion, this time in a chemical factory in Seveso, near Milan in Italy. One of the vapours which was released into the atmosphere was TCDD. In spite of the company's attempts to suppress information on the nature of its products, and on the explosion itself, there were certain consequences which followed from the explosion which could not be kept secret. Crops and animals in the area began to die almost immediately, and human illness, including kidney and liver problems, diarrhoea and vomiting, broke out. When pregnant women began to miscarry and give birth to deformed babies, the public had its worst fears confirmed— that the explosion had been highly toxic, in spite of the company's earlier assurances to the contrary.

Less 'sensational' but nonetheless tragic events have occurred in 2,4,5-T manufacturing plants in West Germany,

Holland and Czechoslovakia.[19] However, 2,4,5-T did not receive widespread public attention and notoriety until the late 1970s, when certain events which had occurred during the Vietnam War became known. Between 1962 and 1970 the US Air Force sprayed a herbicide mixture known as 'Agent Orange' in South Vietnam, the purpose being to defoliate jungle growth and to destroy enemy crops. Agent Orange was a herbicide 'cocktail', based on 2,4,5-T and a related herbicide known as 2,4-D, whose effectiveness from the point of view of the US Air Force was indisputable. In spite of this, in April 1970, the American government ceased using Agent Orange because, it said, 2,4,5-T had been shown to cause disturbing birth defects in animals.

Since 1977 many veterans of the Vietnam War have attributed numerous illnesses, including cancer, skin disease, fatigue, nervous disorders and birth defects, to their earlier exposure to Agent Orange. Yet the majority of veterans who sought compensation for these problems from the Veterans' Association (VA) were unsuccessful because they failed to meet the VA's requirements for eligibility for compensation. Firstly, their illnesses had not arisen during military service or within one year of discharge from service and, secondly, there was 'inconclusive' scientific evidence establishing a relationship between Agent Orange and the veterans' health problems. Of the 20,728 disability claims linked to Agent Orange which were filed against the VA by July 1984, only 1,708 claimants had been granted disability compensation; the rest were refused, either because their disability had not been acknowledged by the VA, or because they did not meet the VA's 'service connection' criteria.[20]

It was largely because of the VA's position on Agent Orange disability claims that in January 1979 a group of veterans filed a class-action law suit against seven chemical companies which had manufactured Agent Orange under government contract. Their suit was a long and drawn-out affair which attracted considerable publicity, both nationally and internationally. Its connection with the Vietnam War made it a particularly 'media worthy' case to publicise, as did the visual nature of the veterans' complaints. After years of legal action, on 7 May 1984 the parties to the suit finally reached an out-of-court settlement in which the chemical companies agreed to pay $180 million to a fund which would be used for the veterans' compensation. This sum is believed to be the largest monetary award ever won in a product liability case, a factor which has added to the already established sensationalism of the lawsuit. Under the settlement the companies denied any liability for the veterans' health problems, insisting instead that they had agreed to the payment as a 'compassionate, expedient and productive means' of meeting the needs of all parties. Conversely, the veterans' lawyers have insisted that the $180 million payment amounted to an admission of responsibility for the veterans' suffering.[21]

A combination of factors has led to the banning of 2,4,5-T production and use in a growing number of countries. (At present its use is prohibited in eleven countries.) The widely publicised and highly emotive Agent Orange case in the USA has contributed to this trend, as has the international spread of disasters in and around industrial plants involved in the production of 2,4,5-T or dioxin. Equally important has been the role of the media, which has focused on the physical suffering which resulted from human contact with 2,4,5-T or its dioxin contaminant. Britain ceased to manufacture 2,4,5-T in 1976 when the Seveso tragedy confirmed the lesson of Bolsover: namely, that the production of 2,4,5-T entailed enormous and horrifying risks to the workers involved in the production process. However, although Britain no longer makes 2,4,5-T, it has not banned the use of the weedkiller which it obtains through imports from New Zealand, which is at present the only country still manufacturing 2,4,5-T.

The campaign by the NUAAW against the continued use of 2,4,5-T in Britain started in 1979, although preliminary discussion and intermittent action had taken place throughout the 1970s. The union's headquarters had been alerted to the possible hazards involved in the use of 2,4,5-T as early as 1970 by the growing number of complaints of skin rashes and boils which it had received from forestry worker members who had used 2,4,5-T. In response to the union's objections to the continued use of the weedkiller, the Forestry Commission, which was by far the largest employer of forestry workers, agreed to a temporary suspension of 2,4,5-T useage, pending an inquiry into its safety by the Advisory Committee on Pesticides (ACP). In 1971 the ACP announced that, on the basis of existing information, a ban on the use of 2,4,5-T on grounds of health hazards would be unwarranted. Thereupon the Forestry Commission lifted its suspension, since which time 2,4,5-T has continued to be used in forestry and farming in Britain.

The workers' objections to using 2,4,5-T coalesced into a formal and concerted campaign for a total ban on 2,4,5-T at the end of the decade. By 1979 the forestry workers' concern about the herbicide's possible ill-effects compelled their union leaders to speak out once again against the use of 2,4,5-T. By this time the union's case had been strengthened by the Agent Orange affair, which had led to a considerable restriction in the USA on domestic uses of 2,4,5-T. Equally, the NUAAW could draw on the Seveso and Coalite explosions, and reports of 2,4,5-T poisoning in Wales, Somerset as well as in Oregon. All of which had suggested that there was a connection between contact with 2,4,5-T and miscarriages and birth deformities. Incidents such as these gave the union a stronger voice on the issue than it had had in 1970. By 1979 there was sufficient data, as well as concern and anxiety among 2,4,5-T users, for the NUAAW to embark on a high-profile campaign against 2,4,5-T use in Britain.[22]

The conflict between the NUAAW and the ACP

By 1979 the NUAAW believed, on the basis of members' reports and international events, that there was sufficient evidence that 2,4,5-T was harmful to its users for the weed-killer to be withdrawn from the market, pending the production of 'substantial' evidence of its alleged safety. However, 1979 also saw the publication of the ACP's Eighth Review of 2,4,5-T which, like the previous seven reviews, declared that 2,4,5-T was safe, provided that it was used 'in the recommended way'.[23] The ensuing debate between the NUAAW and the ACP centred on two questions: is there a safe level of dioxin in 2,4,5-T? and is pure 2,4,5-T to be regarded as a teratogen?

The union's answers to these questions were that the only safe level of dioxin was zero, and that pure 2,4,5-T (which was alleged to be virtually impossible to produce) was almost certainly a teratogen. Conversely, the ACP disputed both of these claims.[24] Their disagreement over these issues was tied closely to the two sides' conflicting views on how much and what sort of evidence was necessary to establish the safety (or danger) of a substance, with their conflicting views on these issues being related to their different social values and priorities. Moreover, once the two sides were locked in battle over these matters, they found that an even more fundamental disagreement divided them. This concerned the question of who should be authorised to pronounce on the safety of 2,4,5-T, and on the safety of all of the pesticides which were being used in Britain. While the ACP defended its established sole right to pass judgement on the safety of pesticides, the NUAAW was inspired by the 2,4,5-T campaign to challenge this exclusive right and to demand a voice in the pesticide safety clearance system.

The disagreement between the NUAAW and the ACP over the toxicity of 2,4,5-T was not so much due to their use of different studies to back their respective claims as to their divergent interpretations of what were often the same reports and studies. For example, the two sides differed in their willingness to link suspected cause (contact with 2,4,5-T) with alleged effect (miscarriage, birth deformity or cancer). While the NUAAW believed that certain incidences of miscarriage and birth defects which had been reported by its members could be plausibly linked to the victims' exposure to 2,4,5-T, the ACP refuted this linkage. The ACP argued instead that since miscarriages and birth deformities were relatively common occurrences, regardless of whether 2,4,5-T had been used, a stronger cause–effect relationship would have to be demonstrated before 2,4,5-T could be declared firmly a human teratogen.

A similar difference in approach could be found in the two sides' conflicting evaluations of the various scientific experiments which had been carried out on 2,4,5-T. There are at least three different ways of studying the toxicity of a chemical, each of which has certain advantages over the others, as Irwin and Green note

> *Epidemiology* has the advantage of being based on human data but it must wait until *after* undesired physical effects have demonstrated themselves before it can even make the first steps towards detecting the responsible chemical agent . . . *animal testing* avoids this problem by allowing testing *before* human exposure, but the problem for regulatory authorities is that of linking animal results to human responses. Various *short-term tests* are available . . . these are cheap and relatively speedy but, again, there is the problem of drawing satisfactory conclusions for human reactions.[25]

While the NUAAW was prepared to accept evidence from

animal tests on 2,4,5-T and the limited evidence available from the few epidemiological studies which had been carried out, the ACP regarded such evidence as inconclusive and inadequate. The ACP insisted that it required absolute proof of 2,4,5-T's toxicity as derived from further epidemiological studies before it would be prepared to recommend a ban on the weedkiller's use in Britain.

As these disagreements suggest, the dispute over whether 2,4,5-T was safe to use was not a purely 'technical' one. On the contrary, the conflict between the NUAAW and the ACP was above all a social one, being based on the question of how much evidence was deemed necessary for establishing that 2,4,5-T was dangerous, and the related question concerning what level of human risk (if any) would be socially acceptable. The manner in which each side addressed these questions was shaped by their respective social and economic priorities.

The NUAAW used anecdotal evidence relating to its members' experiences and scientific evidence provided by animal tests conducted abroad to argue that 2,4,5-T was probably, although not definitely, a carcinogen and a teratogen. According to the union, the existing body of evidence suggested that it was more likely than not that 2,4,5-T was dangerous, on which grounds the union felt itself justified in calling for a ban on the weedkiller. The NUAAW recognised that placing a ban on 2,4,5-T on the strength of the existing inconclusive evidence carried a risk of banning what was in fact a non-harmful and highly effective weedkiller. Yet, because the union's overriding concern was the defence of its members' interests in good occupational health and safety, it declared itself willing to take the risk of sacrificing agricultural efficiency unnecessarily.[26]

On the other hand, the ACP argued for conclusive proof from epidemiological studies that 2,4,5-T was carcinogenic and/or teratogenic in humans before it would prescribe a ban on the herbicide. This stance could place the workers' health and safety at risk: but the ACP saw little likelihood of any danger occurring, provided that the workers used 2,4,5-T in the recommended way.[27] Moreover, the ACP balanced against what it perceived as a very slight risk to workers' health the certain benefits involved in 2,4,5-T's continued use in terms of agricultural production levels and concluded that the case for 2,4,5-T was stronger than the case against it.[28]

It should be noted that there is no evidence to suggest that the ACP's refusal to recommend a ban on 2,4,5-T was in any sense a 'malicious' attempt to place farmworkers' health at risk, nor did the NUAAW generally regard it as such.[29] The ACP's attitude can be understood at least partially in terms of its 'lack of imagination'. As Dr Jerry Ravetz has noted, there are three sides to any industrial hazard: those who create it (the chemical manufacturers), those who experience it (the workers) and those who regulate it (in this case, the ACP). Ravetz then explains

> Since risks are so difficult to study objectively or even to imagine, it is only natural that the way each 'side' sees a hazard depends strongly on the values and expectations of its role, and that this perception will be very different from that of another side. Hence a manager (or regulator) need not be callous or inhumane to allow a hazard to persist, even when warned about it: he just doesn't necessarily see it in the same way as others.[30]

A further explanation for the ACP's continued insistence that 2,4,5-T was safe lay in the very fact that the Committee had published numerous reviews on the weedkiller, each of which had cleared it for safety. To announce in the Eighth or Ninth Review that 2,4,5-T was *not* safe could call into question the credibility and alleged expertise of the Committee as a whole, and of its individual members.

The ACP's balancing of priorities—the usefulness of 2,4,5-T as a herbicide as against the possible risk it presented to human health—was a necessary process, given that the ACP's parent body, MAFF, was responsible for both occupational health and safety *and* the efficacy of agricultural production methods. The NUAAW argued that there was a potentially dangerous conflict of interests in this dual responsibility, a situation which the union found wholly unacceptable. The NUAAW claimed that where the safety of a particularly effective pesticide (such as 2,4,5-T) was in question, there might be a temptation on the part of MAFF's ACP to allow for greater health risk by clearing the pesticide than might be allowed for by a body concerned exclusively with matters of health and safety, such as the Health and Safety Executive (HSE). Consequently, in the course of the 2,4,5-T campaign, the union began to demand a transfer of responsibility for pesticide safety from MAFF to the HSE.

A second issue raised by the ACP's refusal to recommend

a ban on 2,4,5-T concerned the non-statutory status of the Pesticides Safety Precautions Scheme (PSPS). According to the NUAAW, the voluntary nature of the PSPS offered scope for informal links to develop between PSPS officials and the agrochemical companies, links through which the former could informally advise the latter as to what tests and information would be required of a given product for it to be cleared by the ACP. Any criticism of a chemical which was subsequently cleared could be taken as an implied criticism of the PSPS officials themselves, since they had previously advised on and approved the chemical, albeit informally. Consequently, these officials would be drawn to defend the chemical, on which their reputations seemed to depend.[31] The voluntary nature of the PSPS, along with MAFF's alleged conflict of interests, became central issues in the NUAAW's campaign to have the pesticide clearance system reformed.

The furthest-reaching criticism of the PSPS which the NUAAW began to voice as a result of the 2,4,5-T controversy concerned the ACP's monopoly in the field of pesticide safety decision-making. The union argued that although scientific experts had an important role to play in any pesticide safety clearance system, they were not the only group with relevant expertise. According to the NUAAW the pesticide user also had a valuable contribution to make to agenda-setting and decision-making on pesticide safety, which derived from his expertise in pesticide application. The union's demand for workers' representation in the pesticide safety decision-making process was an extremely ambitious one. Not only did the union have to contend with specific forms of opposition to this demand from the ACP and its allies but also, in making the demand, the union was challenging dominant and fairly widespread views as to the proper roles of scientific experts and of 'ordinary workers'. The union leaders were evidently aware of the problems they faced in their dissent from the prevailing view that workers (and especially manual workers) were not qualified to pass scientific judgements and that such judgements were best left to the 'experts'. The leaders' recognition of their difficult situation is suggested by the manner in which they raised the issue of workers' representation onto a philosophical platform, arguing that it was 'fundamentally undemocratic' to exclude workers from a decision-making process the results of which would have serious implications for the lives of the very workers who were excluded.[32]

MAFF responded to this latter argument by ignoring it, so that in effect the alleged 'democratic right' of the union to be represented in pesticide safety decision-making never became an issue for debate and resolution.[33] MAFF devoted its energies instead to reasserting the independence, specialist knowledge and above all the unquestionable suitability of the ACP to decide on issues concerning pesticide safety. The means by which dominant values were mobilised in the ACP's defence, and specifically in defence of its decision-making role, will be studied in greater detail in a later section of the chapter. Here it is important to note the wider ramifications of this dispute over who should participate in the decision-making process.

The ACP did not defend its privileged role simply by referring continuously to its independence and implied superiority over the NUAAW in matters relating to pesticide safety. It also defended itself in another, more subtle, manner. The union's challenge to the Committee's authority had arisen out of the 2,4,5-T conflict, in which the union disputed the ACP's decision over the safety of 2,4,5-T. In defending this decision the ACP was at the same time protecting its exclusive right to make decisions over the safety of 2,4,5-T and over pesticide safety matters in general. Thus, by continuing to insist that 2,4,5-T was safe to use in the face of the union's many arguments to the contrary, the ACP was repudiating the union's claims to have a valuable and legitimate contribution to make in the pesticide safety decision-making process. In this sense, the 2,4,5-T conflict took on a symbolic dimension, as it came to represent a far more profound conflict between the ACP and the NUAAW over the right to participate in decision-making. As long as the weedkiller continued to be declared officially safe to use, the ACP was able to assert its legitimate monopoly in pesticide safety decision-making and agenda-setting. Once that declaration of safety was reversed, the union would have proven that it, too, had an important contribution to make in pesticide safety clearance. It is this wider significance of the 2,4,5-T conflict which explains why the two sides became so deeply involved in what appeared on the surface to be a simple dispute over the safety of a single herbicide.

Power and the NUAAW: obstacles to achieving a ban

In seeking to understand how the ACP eschewed the NUAAW's arguments against the continued use of 2,4,5-T and thereby reaffirmed its exclusive authority to set the agenda and take decisions on the safety of pesticides, the researcher is confronted with an immediate problem. The ACP is not required to publish an account of its proceedings, one consequence of which is that there are no means by which to understand its decision-making procedures.[34] However, in spite of this limitation, it remains possible to analyse the NUAAW's powerlessness to influence the ACP over the questions of 2,4,5-T's safety and workers' representation, because this powerlessness was so much a result of (in)actions and circumstances located outside the boundaries of the ACP's formal decision-making.[35]

The dissemination of false information

It has been noted that although 2,4,5-T has been in use in the UK since the 1940s, the NUAAW did not begin to campaign against it until the 1970s. Moreover, even when the union began its campaign there was a gap of some seven to eight years before it felt able to take a high profile and to make bold assertions relating to the alleged dangers of 2,4,5-T. The time lags and stalling which thus characterise the 2,4,5-T campaign are explained below as being the result of insidious and long-term exercises of power which were carried out through the skilful control of information relating to 2,4,5-T.

In effect, the weedkiller was used in the UK for many years without its users being aware of its possible dangers. This ignorance was due to the manufacturers' and the safety regulators' failure to take adequate steps to test for the herbicide's safety and/or to publicise the results of any tests which may have been carried out. Their inaction led to the widely held assumption that 2,4,5-T was safe to use, and so led to the continued use of the potentially dangerous herbicide.

The farmworkers were thus in a situation of powerlessness in so far as they were unable to defend their interests in health and safety. To what extent can their powerlessness be attributed to an exercise of power over them? It has been established that farmworkers' inability to defend their interests was due to their ignorance, which, in turn, was the outcome of the 2,4,5-T manufacturers' and health regulators' inaction. This inaction constitutes an exercise of power as defined in Chapter 1 in so far as (i) action would have been a hypothetical possibility with determinate consequences for farmworkers' interests; and (ii) the failure to act influenced 2,4,5-T users' thoughts (and therefore actions) in a way which served the manufacturers' interests and prevented farmworkers from recognising and acting on their own objective interests. The successful control of farm-workers' thoughts and actions explains why the NUAAW's campaign to ban 2,4,5-T did not develop for so many years.

Whether or not the manufacturers and safety regulators were conscious of their power exercise is unclear. However, from the union's point of view this was scarcely a relevant issue. The inaction of the manufacturers and regulators, where acting was a hypothetical possibility, whether conscious or not, helped to prolong the extensive use of 2,4,5-T in Britain, and so to stall the union's campaign in defence of farmworkers' interests. The element of 'con-sciousness' or intention on the part of the manufacturers and regulators was incidental from the point of view of the outcome of their power exercise.[36]

Interestingly, similar inaction, with similar results, took place in the USA throughout the 1940s, 1950s and 1960s. Thomas Whiteside reports that

> The scientific history of the development and formulation of 2,4,5-T from the end of the Second World War to the end of the Vietnam War, is one of reckless effort and grossly inadequate test-ing. For example, the American military, having developed 2,4,5-T as part of its biological warfare program in the years following the Second World War, unhesitatingly employed it during the war in Southeast Asia, spraying twenty thousand tons over both populated and unpopulated areas of South Vietnam, without the Pentagon's scientists ever having taken the precaution of systematically testing whether the chemical caused harm to the unborn offspring of as much as an experimental mouse.[37]

Users of 2,4,5-T in the UK were only very gradually alerted to the herbicide's possible ill-effects. At first, it was their own experience of these alleged effects which drew their attention to the possible dangers of using 2,4,5-T. Slowly, information about the tragedies in Bolsover, Seveso and finally Vietnam became available, and this information appeared to corroborate the 2,4,5-T users' own impressions about the weedkiller. After thirty years of using 2,4,5-T, forestry and farmworkers were beginning to find out that continued use of the herbicide might constitute a threat to their interests.

However, even when the union and its members thus came to recognise that power had been exercised over them, they were still faced with considerable obstacles in the subsequent campaign to promote and defend their interests in occupational health and safety. These obstacles were related once again to the control of relevant information.

On this occasion the manipulation of information was an active, rather than passive, process in the sense that false information was actively propogated. The particular information which was controlled on this occasion did not directly concern the safety of 2,4,5-T as such, but rather the amount of 2,4,5-T in use in the UK. In practice these two issues were integrally related, for as long as the public believed that relatively little 2,4,5-T was being used in the UK, they would also regard the union's fears about the herbicide as being misplaced, if not hysterical. Thus, the control of information continued to stall the union's campaign, as a result of which the campaign did not develop fully until the late 1970s when the true extent of 2,4,5-T use in the UK was finally revealed. Acquiring that true information proved to be a long and arduous task.

In March 1979 the ACP published its Eighth Review of 2,4,5-T, in which it stated that an estimated 3 tonnes of 2,4,5-T were used annually in the UK. This, it claimed, represented barely 0·005 per cent of the amount of active ingredients used for UK crop protection. This estimated figure of 3 tonnes was widely circulated, so that most people who were concerned with the issue came across the figure and were led to believe it. For example, it was mentioned in September 1979 by the Royal Commission on Environmental Pollution when it published its inquiry into agricultural pollution in which the UK's 3 tonnes of 2,4,5-T was compared favourably with the 3,000 tonnes allegedly used in the USA each year. A few months later the ACP's figures were quoted once again, this time by the Junior Minister of Agriculture, Jerry Wiggin, who stated in the House of Commons in December 1979 that '. . . 2,4,5-T accounts for 0·005% of active ingredients used in crop protection in the United Kingdom'. And the 3 tonnes figure was reproduced once more when a BBC Horizon programme, transmitted in March 1980, claimed that in Britain 'a tiny 3 tonnes' of 2,4,5-T were sprayed each year, as compared to the USA's 3,000 tonnes.[38]

In spite of the frequent repetition of the 3 tonne figure, however, not everyone was equally convinced of its accuracy. In particular, Dr Roger Thomas, the Labour MP for Carmarthen, and his two assistants were suspicious of the 3 tonne figure, which appeared to them to be 'clearly absurd', given that at least twenty-five different weedkillers on the UK market contained 2,4,5-T.[39] Moreover, the frequent references to 2,4,5-T in the British Agrochemicals Association (BAA)'s 'virulent' defence of the herbicide made it difficult for Dr Thomas to believe that 2,4,5-T's market share was as small as had been alleged.[40] These suspicions, coupled with a concern over the possible health hazards involved in 2,4,5-T use, led Dr Thomas and his colleagues to pursue further the question of how much 2,4,5-T was being used annually in the UK.

Their pursuit proved to be more difficult than Dr Thomas and his assistants may have originally anticipated. Over a period of just a few months Dr Thomas tabled more than twenty questions in the House of Commons on the use of 2,4,5-T, but he was told repeatedly that '. . . only some 3 tonnes of 2,4,5-T was used in British agriculture in any one year (certainly in 1979, the latest year for which figures were available)—an amount so small as to be of no cause for concern'.[41]

Not satisfied with these answers, Dr Thomas decided to investigate the matter through other channels. Figures for 2,4,5-T imports seemed like a useful point to start from, given that the UK no longer manufactured 2,4,5-T and was consequently dependent on imports for its use of the herbicide. Yet when Dr Thomas requested information on 2,4,5-T imports he found that the conceptual categories used in the Overseas Trade Statistics were such as to obstruct his search, for the statistics did not list 2,4,5-T as a separate category.[42]

Dozens of letters were sent by Dr Thomas and his colleagues in their pursuit of information on the use of 2,4,5-T in the UK. Finally, in May 1980 they received information from the Statistical Office of H.M. Customs and Excise which showed that between 1975 and 1979 total UK imports of 2,4,5-T amounted to 677 tonnes, and that in

1979 alone 116 tonnes had been imported. This was forty times the amount of imports quoted by the ACP.

A few months later a letter from the Minister of State at MAFF, Earl Ferrers, notified Dr Thomas that

> The British Agrochemicals Association have just obtained for us details of the total supplies of herbicides containing 2,4,5-T which were marketed during 1977–79 for eventual use in the United Kingdom. These were in 1977 about 46 tonnes, in 1978 about 52 tonnes, and in 1979 about 58 tonnes of active ingredient.[43]

In other words, the amount of 2,4,5-T used annually in the UK was roughly twenty times greater than the quantity which had been repeatedly quoted by the ACP and other organisations.[44]

Where did the 3 tonne figure originate, and why was it so readily believed by the different groups involved in the debate over 2,4,5-T? Dr Thomas and his colleagues claim to have identified the 'conspirators' behind the propogation of this false information

> It seems clear to us that the Agrochemicals industry in this country has been guilty of a gross deception of the Government, of Members of Parliament and of the people of this country as to the scale of use of this particular herbicide.[45]

Whether or not the agrochemicals establishment consciously deceived the government and the British public over the use of 2,4,5-T has yet to be proved. It may be that the industry was in fact ignorant of the true total amount of 2,4,5-T being used, just as it may alternatively have been the case that the industry, as well as the government (and the ACP) were aware of the falsity of the 3 tonne figure. Yet, in an important sense the awareness of these different groups as to the 3 tonnes misrepresentation is not a relevant issue: regardless of whether it was known to be untrue, the very use of this figure had a detrimental impact on the NUAAW's campaign.

The 3 tonne figure was important primarily because it was instrumental in justifying the continued safety clearance and use of 2,4,5-T in the UK. According to Dr Thomas, 'Clearly the alleged scant use of 2,4,5-T was one of the main reasons for not banning the herbicide'.[46] And, just as the ACP may have cleared 2,4,5-T at least partly because of its alleged scant use, so too the Royal Commission on Environmental Pollution '. . . gave 2,4,5-T a clean bill of health, partly on the grounds that British useage was relatively small'.[47] By the same token, the NUAAW's public concern over 2,4,5-T's possible health hazards and its attempt at promoting a high profile campaign to have the herbicide banned were made to appear over-reactive and hysterical by the relatively small figure of 3 tonnes. The union's campaign could thus be discredited by those people who wanted to see 2,4,5-T in continued use in the UK, such as the Chair of the BAA, who had portrayed the union's campaign against 2,4,5-T as a 'witch hunt'.[48]

What is significant here is that the 3 tonne figure could be used to justify the continued clearance of 2,4,5-T and to discredit the NUAAW's campaign without the user necessarily being aware that the figure was wrong. Moreover, the continued reference to the 3 tonne figure, even without the purpose of justifying the herbicide's clearance, had the effect of strengthening the ACP's position and weakening the NUAAW's. For example, Christopher Riley in his BBC Horizon programme had used the 3 tonne figure in spite of the fact that the programme was intended to draw public attention to the supposed dangers of 2,4,5-T and dioxin. By publicising the '3 tonnes' he was unwittingly contributing to the union's difficulties in achieving a ban on 2,4,5-T.

The union attempted, without success, to determine whether the 3 tonne figure had been part of an intended act of obstruction to their campaign. Although they were unable to ascertain beyond doubt that it had been intentional, they used the incident to their best advantage. Firstly, they suggested that the ACP had been discredited by its use of such a grossly inaccurate figure, and that this 'mistake' made it difficult to have confidence in other statements the ACP made.[49] Secondly, the issue of freedom of information in connection with the pesticides clearance machinery was taken up and incorporated in the union's growing critique of the PSPS. Nonetheless, there was little doubt within the union that its efforts to promote and defend farmworkers' interests in occupational health had been seriously frustrated by thirty years' experience of using false information.

The mobilisation of dominant values

A second potential obstacle facing the NUAAW when it sought to challenge the ACP over the safety of 2,4,5-T related to the mobilisation of dominant social attitudes which associate scientific expertise with impartiality and correctness, often to the point of infallibility. This association enhanced the credibility of the ACP and its Scientific Sub-Committee, in contradistinction to which the union's image as a 'sectional interest' aiming to win 'political gain' from the 2,4,5-T case was used to discredit its case altogether. Implicit in each public reference to the ACP's great knowledge and expertise was a suggestion that the ACP was far better placed than the union to make pronouncements as to whether or not 2,4,5-T (or any other pesticide) was safe to use. The overall result of this power exercise was that it rendered the NUAAW powerless to influence official decisions concerning the safety of 2,4,5-T.

It is interesting to note in passing that similar attitudes and values were mobilised in the USA when popular opposition to the continued production of 2,4,5-T began to arise in response to the Agent Orange case. Dow Chemicals, at one time the principal American manufacturer of 2,4,5-T, took steps to juxtapose the scientific impartiality of its scientists with the allegedly jaundiced motives of the campaigners against 2,4,5-T. Thomas Whiteside explains how Dow insisted that

objective consideration of the whole 2,4,5-T issue has been obscured by 'emotionalism' and that, in effect, the company has been victimised by what purports to be scientific criticism but is essentially argument of a 'political' nature arising out of the vehement opposition of certain members of the scientific community to the Vietnam war.[50]

In Britain a variety of individuals involved in the 2,4,5-T conflict helped to construct the contrasting images of the 'objective experts' versus the 'politically motivated' union.

Between 1980 and 1982 the Minister of Agriculture, Peter Walker, repeatedly emphasised both privately and publicly his faith in the decisions of the ACP experts whose scientific abilities had gained them a 'worldwide reputation'. This was a clear indication that Walker considered the ACP, by virtue of its formal expertise, to be the best possible judge of the safety of 2,4,5-T and that he believed the union had little part to play in pesticide safety clearance. This preference for the ACP over the union in terms of their respective suitability to pass judgement on pesticide safety was reiterated on a number of occasions in Parliament. It was also stated clearly in a letter from Walker to the NUAAW's General Secretary, in which the Minister repeated what he claimed to have told the ACP's Chair, namely that '. . . the Government would not suspend or withdraw the use of any pesticide simply in response to sectional pressures, and without the benefit of a scientific appraisal of the available evidence'.[51]

A similar stance was taken in the House of Commons by the Junior Minister for Agriculture, Jerry Wiggin. After paying tribute to the country's pesticide safety record which, he said, owed a great deal to the PSPS, Wiggin assured the Commons that 2,4,5-T presented no cause for public concern: 'The world-wide opinion of those in the know is that we are worrying unnecessarily.'[52]

The same respect for the PSPS was expressed by the BAA, whose Chairman, Dr Hessayon, referred repeatedly to the 'competence', 'impartiality' and 'objectivity' of the ACP in his inaugural speech in 1980. In his speech Dr Hessayon argued that

> It is not the BAA's desire to discredit the circumstantial evidence and the unrelated facts put forward by the pressure groups. It would be as wrong for us, as an interested party, to try to be the judge on 2,4,5-T as it would be for the ecologist and the trade union researcher. What is required is an objective and impartial assessment and we as an Industry are happy to leave this to the Government's Advisory Committee on Pesticides.[53]

This message was repeated to me personally when I interviewed the Director of the BAA, Mr Tearleach Maclean. When I asked him whether the fact that 2,4,5-T use had been prohibited in eleven countries suggested that it ought to be banned in the UK, Mr Maclean replied

> Essentially, products should be permitted to be sold, or should be restricted, or banned, on the strength of the scientific evidence reviewed by people with no axe to grind, who are completely disinterested and unbiased—and that's what we have in the Advisory Committee on Pesticides.[54]

It is interesting to note how the ACP itself mobilised the values surrounding 'scientific expertise' in an attempt to justify and defend its own decisions concerning 2,4,5-T. The ACP drew on the popular values of independence, impartiality and specialist knowledge to build up its own credibility before it launched its attack on the NUAAW's claims. Thus, the ACP described itself in the Foreword of its Ninth Review of 2,4,5-T, which again cleared 2,4,5-T for safe use, in the following terms

> The Advisory Committee on Pesticides . . . is independent of commercial and sectional interests alike. Its independent members bring to the Committee's work not only knowledge built up within their specialist disciplines but also the benefit of close contacts with eminent colleagues in the professions and sciences.[55]

The ACP's expertise and independence were then used implicitly to add weight to its refutation of the NUAAW's case against 2,4,5-T.

In particular, the ACP members argued that the union's case had been based on circumstantial evidence which they, as scientific experts, classified as unscientific and therefore unacceptable.[56] Implicit in this rejection of the union's evidence was the suggestion that there was a single correct and scientific approach to the 2,4,5-T issue and that alternative approaches (such as the union's) were unscientific and incorrect. However, it has been seen that the basic disagreement between the ACP and the NUAAW was not in fact one which required technical expertise for it to be settled. The ACP and the union conflicted over the questions of how much proof of a chemical's danger was necessary to justify a ban, and what level of human risk would be acceptable to take or to impose on others. It has been seen that the two sides' answers to both of these questions were determined at least partly by their respective social priorities, not simply by their different scientific backgrounds. Nevertheless, by insisting on the 'scientific correctness' of their own position (which demanded absolute proof of danger before a ban could be recommended) the ACP members, as recognised experts in the field, were able to obscure the social dimension of the 2,4,5-T conflict. The dispute was thus made to appear as one between 'scientific right' and 'political wrong', rather than as one between two equally legitimate social interests.

The impact which this repeated mobilisation of values relating to scientific objectivity and infallibility could have on the public was illustrated for me in an interview with a practising farmer.[57] He explained that some years ago his farm, which had used 2,4,5-T, had been visited by the 'Government's Committee', which he described as '. . . a very august body of . . . very high-powered scientists, ranging from various medical people to chemists and botanists and so on. They were a pretty carefully selected committee'.

The Committee's visit had been part of a study of 2,4,5-T which later concluded that the herbicide was safe to use. The farmer explained, 'I rather took the view that they knew more about the job than I did; and if they're prepared to say that 2,4,5-T is safe, then it's probably safe . . . I feel protected by the Ministry's approval scheme.' When I asked him why he thought the union was campaigning for a ban on 2,4,5-T, the farmer replied, 'I think it has a political value in that it's a sort of winnable victory . . . I think it's just hard on poor, old 2,4,5-T.' The farmer's trust in the ACP expertise and his dismissal of the union's case as being invalid because it was politically motivated were borne out by his continued use of 2,4,5-T on his farm.

The repeated public references to the ACP as a group of educated, objective and creditable experts, in contrast to the sectional and biased union, had a clear impact on this farmer. Above all, the continued use of 2,4,5-T by him and by many other agriculturalists and domestic gardeners bears witness to the success of the ACP and its allies in exercising power over the NUAAW. By branding the union as amateur, unqualified, and politically motivated, the ACP and its allies invalidated the union's claims and thus rendered it powerless to defend its members' interests. As long as this situation continued, the ACP could carry on exercising its control over the entire agenda of pesticide safety.[58]

Silencing the union through the denial of representation

A third and related obstacle which the NUAAW encountered in its efforts to reverse the official clearance of 2,4,5-T was the membership bias of the pesticide safety decision-making machinery. It has been seen that this in itself became a point of bitter contention between the NUAAW and the government's ACP. The ACP and its Scientific Sub-Committee were staffed by MAFF-appointed scientific specialists who were trained in clinical toxicology, pathology, botany, pharmacology, agricultural science and other areas of scientific study, and who were employees of either MAFF or of academic institutions. The explicit exclusion of non-specialists from the ACP meant that those grievances which the specialists disregarded or overlooked would be prevented from emerging on to the decision-making agenda altogether. What were the consequences of this crude, but effective, exercise of power over the NUAAW and how was it sustained?

The NUAAW argued repeatedly in its 2,4,5-T campaign that any safety clearance of the weedkiller which depended upon it being used in the ACP's 'recommended way' was invalid, because this recommendation could not always be followed through in practice. For example, while the ACP recommended that workers avoid direct contact with the herbicide, the union insisted that this was far easier to say within the confines of a committee room than it was to carry out in the field.

The NUAAW maintained that

> There are so many ways of getting splashed or drenched by the chemical. Before use, the chemical has to be diluted. It is very difficult to pour from a five-gallon drum into a half-pint beaker without splashing. Then, while the diluted mixture is being carried in a knapsack sprayer, it can easily seep from the top and leak down the bearer's neck. Operators may well be walking forward through areas which have already been sprayed. Their boots, especially if they are leather, become saturated. It is difficult, often impossible, to detect where the spray has settled . . .[59]

Even when the worker was provided with protective clothing (which was not usually the case), the union claimed that contamination was possible.

> It is common for the spray to get under face masks, gloves and visors. It is also common for operators to transfer the herbicide to their ordinary clothes when they remove their protective gear after spraying. And what if the operator sneezes? Is there any way of using a handkerchief without putting themselves at risk?[60]

Moreover, although the official recommendation was to use 2,4,5-T when there is no wind blowing, 'Workers will tell you that in their experience the spraying is done on days when the weather is too bad for jobs like haymaking—which means in a lot of cases that it is windy.'[61]

Yet the ACP's make-up was such that there were no workers' representatives on the Committee to point out and to stress the extent of these practical difficulties to the experts while they were taking their decisions. Instead, the experts were able to overlook the daily events, such as sneezing or a sudden gust of wind, which made 2,4,5-T such a potentially dangerous chemical to use.

This oversight on the part of the ACP was critical, for its own clearance of 2,4,5-T was heavily dependent upon the provision that the chemical would be used 'in the recommended way'.[62] In the ACP's lengthy Ninth Review of 2,4,5-T there are repeated references to the ACP's view that people will not be harmed by 2,4,5-T, 'if it is used for the recommended purpose and in the recommended way',[63] a view which the committee had stated in its earlier, Eighth Review of 2,4,5-T.[64]

The NUAAW's concern over the problems inherent in this crucial provision which the ACP had applied to the alleged safety of 2,4,5-T led it to publicise as widely as possible its belief that, '. . . the conditions envisaged by members of the PAC [ACP] . . . are impossible to reproduce in the field'.[65] By emphasising this point the union hoped to prevent the ACP from shifting responsibility for 2,4,5-T related dangers from the committee itself on to the 2,4,5-T user. The union recognised that the ACP's repeated connection between safety and 'proper use' might enable the authorities to 'blame the victim' for any ill-effects which resulted from 2,4,5-T use: that is, the victim could be accused of not having handled the substance 'properly' and could thus be held responsible for his or her own suffering. By insisting instead that the 'recommended use' was impossible to follow in the 'real world' of pesticide application, the union hoped to redirect responsibility back onto the ACP.

However, the ACP was able to continue deflecting such responsibility, in spite of the union's manoeuvre. At the meeting held in August 1980 between the NUAAW and the ACP, the union had accused the Committee of not taking account of risks such as accidents, abuse or misuse of chemicals. The ACP replied to this allegation in its Ninth Review of 2,4,5-T in December 1980

> we are neither unaware of, nor indifferent to, problems which can arise from abuse, misuse or neglect. However, these are not problems for our Committee alone; nor does action in them necessarily fall within the scope of the PSPS.[66]

By first linking all possible 2,4,5-T related health problems to the user's misuse of the chemical, and then denying any responsibility for such misuse as might occur, the ACP was able to conclude its Review without fear of recrimination, by stating that 2,4,5-T was perfectly safe to use, as long as it was used 'in the recommended way'.

Thus, the main effect of the ACP's membership bias was to prevent the NUAAW from putting forward its views on 2,4,5-T in the decision-making arena and thereby to have an opportunity of influencing official decisions on the weed-killer's safety. The union attempted to overcome its power-lessness in this sphere by arguing at every opportunity that, not only did it have a legitimate contribution to make to debates and decisions on pesticide safety; but also that workers had a 'democratic right' to be represented on bodies such as the ACP. Yet these arguments failed to win any support from the government or ACP, as this chapter has shown.

Instead, the government responded to the union's demand to be represented in health and safety decision-making in two equally hostile ways. Firstly, as the last section has explained, the government undermined the union's claims to have a valuable contribution to make by labelling it 'biased', 'politically motivated' and 'amateur'. Secondly, the government disposed of the union's claim to have a 'demo-cratic right' to representation by ignoring the claim altogether. By nullifying the union's demand in these ways (and particularly through the second device) the government was able to prevent the demand from becoming an issue for resolution in the relevant decision-making institution, namely Parliament. This exercise of power over the union was made possible by the manner in which the relevant resources of power were distributed and used by the protagonists in the conflict.

The government's ability to define the terms of its conflict with the NUAAW—in terms of 'expertise' rather than 'democratic rights'—stemmed chiefly from its access to what Robert Dahl refers to as the resource of 'legality'. This resource derives from one's closeness to the law and to law-makers, which in turn can provide one with the ability to influence official policy-makers and policies. *Ceteris paribus*, the closer one is to the policy-makers, the greater will be one's influence over them.

By virtue of its location in Parliament, the government was able to a relatively large extent to set the policy-makers' agenda for debate: it could thus prevent any discussion over the non-issue of workers' claimed rights to representation in the ACP. Meanwhile, the NUAAW lacked the necessary resources for countering the government's influence in the Commons. It had neither economic nor electoral resources with which to capture the attention of Opposition or back-bench MPs (as seen in Chapter 5). Nor did the NUAAW have access to the resources of 'social standing' or popular credibility which would have provided it with an image of respectability which in turn would have made it an organisation 'to be reckoned with' in Parliament. Instead, the NUAAW represented the country's farmworkers, a labour force still regarded by many members of the public as a group of simple country bumpkins. This image of backwardness, combined with its lack of other resources, left the NUAAW unable to gain the necessary respect for its demands from the House of Commons. Thus, the inequality of resources between the government and the union meant that the demand for workers' representation scarcely became an issue in the parliamentary arena.

In spite of its powerlessness, the union continued to argue both for the need and the right of farmworkers to be represented on the ACP. Not surprisingly, these repeated demands failed to bring the union the desired opportunity to promote its members' interests. Moreover, and somewhat ironically perhaps, the more the NUAAW insisted upon its right to influence pesticide safety decisions, the more firm the ACP became over the alleged safety of 2,4,5-T, as though by insisting on this issue the ACP was asserting its sole right to decide on all such matters.

IV   NO APPLICATION WITHOUT REPRESENTATION: THE NUAAW's 'ALTERNATIVE' CAMPAIGN TO BAN 2,4,5-T

The leaders of the NUAAW recognised even before the publication of the Ninth Review of 2,4,5-T that as long as the PSPS remained intact and the ACP continued to be the sole arbiter of the weedkiller's safety, there would be little hope of promoting workers' interests relating to an official ban on 2,4,5-T. Consequently, the union decided to launch an 'alternative' campaign to end 2,4,5-T use in the UK, a campaign whose success would not depend upon the ACP's co-operation.

The NUAAW planned its campaign, which it ran concomitantly with its 'official' campaign via the ACP, with considerable care. In particular, it sought allies who would not have been expected to have associated the ACP's scientific expertise with infallibility or incontestability. This meant that the union would concentrate on its political and occupational allies; and on groups and individuals who had had direct or second-hand experience with 2,4,5-T and were of the opinion that, like other pesticides, it might be too dangerous to be used, irrespective of the ACP's 'informed' opinions. In seeking the assistance of these potential allies for its 'alternative' 2,4,5-T campaign, the union drew upon one of the few resources which were available to it, namely solidarity. Robert Dahl defines 'solidarity' as 'the capacity of a member of one segment of society to evoke support from others who identify him as like themselves'.[67] Dahl suggests that the basis for such identification might be similarities in occupation, social standing, religion, ethnic origin, or racial stock. In the case of the NUAAW's 2,4,5-T campaign the solidarity which was drawn upon was based upon shared experiences of 2,4,5-T, or similar substances and common occupational interests in health and safety. This resource, which drew a number of diverse groups into a defence of the NUAAW's position, proved to be the union's most effective power resource to have been uncovered in this study.

The first step in the union's attempt to ban 2,4,5-T unofficially was taken in November 1979 when the NUAAW Executive instructed its members in the Forestry Commission and strongly advised its farmworker members not to use 2,4,5-T, in spite of the ACP's eighth clearance of the weedkiller earlier that year. This gesture of defiance towards the expert ACP was relatively successful, mainly because so many of the workers involved had had first-hand or second hand experience of 2,4,5-T and did not require much convincing as to its potential hazards.

The union took the decision to pursue this unofficial ban on 2,4,5-T beyond the confines of its own membership in late 1979 when it received an unexpected fillip. As it began to prepare its dossier on the hazards of 2,4,5-T which it later presented to the Minister of Agriculture, the union found itself being 'bombarded' with telephone calls and letters of support. Some of these came from NUAAW members, but many also came from members of other unions, environmentalists, local authority workers, politicians, doctors and members of the general public—all of whom had experience, knowledge or an interest in 2,4,5-T. This unforeseen upsurge of popular interest in the 2,4,5-T issue influenced the NUAAW's approach towards the future of its campaign. It realised that a considerable section of the public at large who had been alerted to the 2,4,5-T issue by radio, television and newspaper reports would be sympathetic to the union's case, regardless of the ACP's pronouncements. In particular, the simultaneous publicity being given to the infamous Agent Orange case in the USA inspired many people to take note of the union's campaign and to support its efforts to bring an end to Britain's use of the 'deadly weedkiller'.

As a result of the campaign's reception, the union leaders decided to make full use of the support which it had so far generated, by spreading the campaign 'in all sorts of new directions'

> This meant, amongst other things, attempting to mobilise the weight of the labour movement, from branch, district and trades council level up to convincing the TUC General Council to call for a ban on 2,4,5-T. It meant also bringing the issue before parish, town, district and county councils, before the House of Commons and the European Commission and anywhere else where the case could be put for suspending the use of the weedkiller that may be killing more than weeds.[68]

The NUAAW began putting the 2,4,5-T issue forward through these various channels, concentrating particularly on the opportunities provided by its links with the rest of the labour movement. Following the NUAAW's instruction to its Forestry Commission members to stop using 2,4,5-T, the General and Municipal Workers' Union (GMWU) and the Transport and General Workers' Union (TGWU) adopted a similar position, with the former also pressing the TUC for a meeting of the unions affected to discuss 2,4,5-T. Sustained pressure for such a meeting came from the unions whose members were involved most closely with 2,4,5-T use: the NUAAW; the GMWU; the TGWU, all of whom had members in the forestry industry; the National Union of Railwaymen (NUR), some of whose members used 2,4,5-T to clear railway tracks of weeds; and the Association of Scientific Technical and Managerial Staff (ASTMS), whose laboratory staff had had possible contact with 2,4,5-T. By the time the TUC's Social Insurance and Industrial Welfare Department co-ordinated the meeting (29 January 1980) three more unions had joined the five mentioned above. These were the National Union of Public Employees (NUPE); the Fire Brigades Union (FBU); and the Institute of Professional Civil Servants (IPCS), some of whose members serviced the PSPS. The outcome of the subsequent meeting was a TUC

call for a further review of 2,4,5-T by the ACP, and a demand
that the HSE's Advisory Committee on Toxic Substances
(ACTS) carry out an independent investigation of the weedkiller.

It was at this point that the Junior Minister for Agriculture,
Jerry Wiggin, asserted his belief that the British public was
'worrying unnecessarily' about 2,4,5-T. He insisted that the
expert ACP had reviewed all of the available evidence on
2,4,5-T and had found the weedkiller to be safe; like the
ACP, Wiggin saw little reason to carry out yet another review,
given that there was no new evidence to be examined.

The TUC refused to be silenced by this rebuff, and decided
instead to add its voice to the NUAAW's call for a ban on the
use of 2,4,5-T in forestry work. Two weeks after the TUC
had taken this decision, the General Council agreed to extend
its demands even further. On the strength of the arguments
put forward by the NUAAW and by the GMWU which pointed
out that 2,4,5-T was not only a threat to farmworkers, but
also to workers in local authority parks and gardens, railway
workers and fireworkers, the TUC General Council committed itself to achieving a total ban on British use of 2,4,5-T.

Other influential groups and organisations joined in this
call for a ban on the herbicide, including the Labour Party
(after an initial reluctance to do so) and the Scottish TUC.
Assistance in the campaign extended beyond mere verbal
support, however, especially (although not only) among
those groups which had had contact with 2,4,5-T in one
form or another. Local authorities in Somerset, Avon,
Nottingham and South Yorkshire imposed bans on the use of
2,4,5-T within their areas. Railway workers and local authority
workers in areas which had not banned 2,4,5-T joined others
in refusing to handle 2,4,5-T. A short time later British Rail
suspended the use of 2,4,5-T pending further enquiries into
its safety; and the European Commission then announced
that it would launch a study of the substance, bringing the
issue on to a continental platform.

The number of local authorities which banned the use of
2,4,5-T rose steadily, reaching seventy-four by January 1981.
Their action was followed by British Rail's complete ban on
2,4,5-T use and similar action by the National Coal Board,
the national Water Authorities, and hundreds of private
gardeners. The impact of these localised bans on the use of
2,4,5-T in Britain was augmented considerably in December
1980, when the TUC General Council voted unanimously

to take steps to prevent 2,4,5-T from being imported by Britain. Given that the manufacture of 2,4,5-T had ceased in Britain in 1976, it was hoped that the TUC's embargo would have the effect of reducing the ACP's review and clearance of 2,4,5-T to the status of an academic exercise without any practical impact. As well as instructing dock workers to refuse to handle any 2,4,5-T imports, the TUC conducted an inquiry into which countries were manufacturing the weed-killer. The purpose behind this was to contact the relevant unions in 2,4,5-T manufacturing countries with the aim of convincing them to launch similar campaigns in their countries against the continued production and use of 2,4,5-T.

Britain's campaign against 2,4,5-T achieved two notable international successes. The first occurred in February 1981 when the European Federation of Agricultural Workers' Unions within the EEC (EFA), which represented some 2 million workers, responded to the NUAAW's lobbying by voting in favour of a ban on 2,4,5-T. The second achievement involved successful pressure by the TUC and in particular by the NUAAW in West Germany which was believed to be the largest supplier of 2,4,5-T to Britain. Following international publicity and campaigning on the 2,4,5-T, which West German environmentalists in particular took a great interest in, the West German government imposed a ban in September 1981 on the domestic sale and use of 2,4,5-T. This step did not, however, signify an end to West German production and export of the herbicide, which meant that the British unions continued putting their case forward in West Germany. Links were forged with West German unions which, in turn, pressed their government for a total ban on 2,4,5-T. Their pressure proved to be successful, for in September 1983 the TGWU was able to report that all European manufacture of 2,4,5-T had ceased. Only New Zealand remained as a significant supplier of 2,4,5-T to Britain.[69]

How successful was the NUAAW's defiance of the expert ACP? In spite of the union's vigorous campaigning and the TUC's supportive action, the herbicide continued to be used in Britain, particularly by domestic gardeners. The union remarked in 1983 that: '. . . as sales to industry dropped, the manufacturers, who did not produce but formulated the 2,4,5-T in Britain, began to concentrate their sales pitch onto domestic users. Many amateur gardeners continue to use products containing 2,4,5-T.'[70]

These remaining users of 2,4,5-T were able to obtain

supplies of the weedkiller in spite of the TUC's embargo for two reasons. Firstly, there were considerable stockpiles of 2,4,5-T in Britain. Secondly, although transport workers followed the TUC's instructions to black 2,4,5-T at the docks, the TUC was not able to bring all imports of the chemical to an end 'because of the ingenious way importers found to get the chemical through'.[71] This included the packaging of the pesticide in containers with misleading labels and the importing of it by light aircraft.

Yet the continued use of 2,4,5-T in Britain should not obscure the considerable successes of the campaign. The power which accrued to the union as a result of its access to and use of solidarity was unprecedented in its history. Major industrial users of 2,4,5-T, such as British Rail, bowed to the pressures of the growing number of campaigners against 2,4,5-T and the movement had achieved an international dimension within a few months. In sharp contrast to its campaigns for higher wages or for tied cottage abolition, the NUAAW's efforts to put an end to the use of 2,4,5-T met with a high level of support from a number of diverse and influential groups.

Confirmation of the NUAAW's wider success among the public at large was provided by the Director of the British Agrochemicals Association, Mr Tearleach Maclean. When I asked him whether the industry had been harmed by the campaign against 2,4,5-T he replied

> I would think yes, because I think the public . . . will see quite a bit written about the sale of a product which is alleged to be all these nasty things, while we're taking the line that the product continues to be cleared and therefore we'll continue to sell it. That, I think, will be seen by the public as a very hard-nosed, callous sort of attitude. To that extent, yes, I think the industry *has* been harmed.[72]

Nevertheless, in an important sense the NUAAW's campaign was a failure. For, although in the space of a few years and with the use of solidarity with other groups the union had successfully convinced numerous 2,4,5-T users to stop using the weedkiller, it nevertheless failed to achieve an *official* ban on 2,4,5-T. While the NUAAW may have brought a degree of discredit to the agrochemical industry and achieved a significant drop in 2,4,5-T sales in Britain,[73] the ACP was relatively unscathed by the campaign, to the extent that it remained steadfast in its decision over the safety of 2,4,5-T.

The ACP's firm refusal to ban 2,4,5-T in spite of popular attitudes towards the weedkiller was of crucial importance because it represented the ACP's persistent assertion of its authority in the field of pesticide safety. The 2,4,5-T issue had become a struggle between the union and the government-backed authorities over which of the two groups was best qualified to pass judgement on issues of occupational health and safety. The ACP's unequivocal safety clearance of 2,4,5-T, repeated in its Tenth Review in 1982, marked its continued insistence that it was the sole legitimate authority on pesticide safety. The union's continued publicity concerning 2,4,5-T's possible health hazards represented its equally unwavering challenge to the ACP's assumed monopoly of authority in deciding over pesticide safety. The fact that the union was unsuccessful in making this challenge suggests that its access to, and use of, solidarity in the 2,4,5-T campaign failed to bring with it access to other power resources which could have been used in the wider campaign for workers' representation. In particular, the union was unable to acquire the social standing which would have been necessary (given farmworkers' electoral and economic weakness) for convincing Parliament to give the union a voice in the pesticide safety decision-making process.

The symbolic importance of the 2,4,5-T conflict was not simply recognised in retrospect by the two sides. On the contrary, both sides were at all times highly conscious of the wider issues involved in their conflict—a factor which helps to explain why they had each been willing to take such strong measures over a single herbicide. The NUAAW for its part was convinced that the government

> simply dared not ban 2,4,5-T. The implications would be obvious. Other pesticides would be suspect, the whole rickety system of pesticide regulation and control in Britain would come under attack, the confidence placed in the system would be lost.[74]

The government commented similarly on the 2,4,5-T conflict in private correspondence between Minister of Agriculture Peter Walker and Geraint Howells MP. In his letter dated 27 May 1980, Walker wrote

> It would be very easy for me to ban 2,4,5-T in response to these pressures, but to do so would have important implications. Such action would undoubtedly lead to pressure upon Ministers to follow a similar course on every future occasion on which allegations were made against any particular pesticide. It would undermine the

credibility of our expert Advisory Committee upon which successive Ministers have relied heavily for many years. And it would virtually mark the end of our Safety Scheme which has ensured that our record in the safe use of pesticides is second to none.

When I asked Jerry Wiggin, MP (who was Junior Minister of Agriculture in 1980) why the government had not given way to the union's demands in order to avert the subsequent controversy, he replied in a similar vein

> For two very good reasons, the first being that if it had given in it would have admitted the system is in some way wrong, which it definitely didn't admit—in my view completely rightly. You have to have a system that enjoys the confidence of the user and the producer alike. I believe the system is very good, so If we had given in . . . we would have acknowledged that the system is not very good. *That's the first and most important thing.* Secondly, it would have been a serious hindrance, because the chemical is a very useful thing.[75] [my emphasis]

The most forthright depiction of the 2,4,5-T dispute as a conflict over much wider issues was offered in 1981 by the then Chair of the BAA, Dr Hessayon.

> If we give way on 2,4,5-T the unions will then go on to campaign against another chemical and then another. We are engaged in a power struggle for control over the industry which we cannot afford to lose.[76]

The two sides in the 2,4,5-T conflict—those in favour and those opposed to its continued use—were thus sharply aware of the high stakes involved in their dispute. If the authorities or the agrochemical industry had announced suddenly that there was sufficient evidence of 2,4,5-T's hazards to justify a ban or suspension on its use, then the ACP would have been discredited because of its clearance of the herbicide on as many as ten previous occasions. Such an event would call into question the reliability of the entire PSPS, thus adding force to the union's demand for an overhaul of the entire pesticides clearance system. In so far as the ACP did *not* reverse its previous judgements on the safety of 2,4,5-T, and thus did not relinquish its exclusive authority over pesticides safety matters, the NUAAW's campaign must be seen as a failure.

The union's inability to assert itself as a legitimate participant in pesticide safety decision-making has been underlined by the provisions contained in the new *Food and Environment Protection Act* (1985).

The union had developed a detailed critique of the PSPS during the course of its 2,4,5-T campaign which it publicised during the Bill's parliamentary passage with the intention of influencing the Bill's contents. In particular, the union criticised the non-statutory nature of the PSPS; the secrecy involved in the ACP's deliberations; the conflict of interests involved in MAFF's dual responsibility for agricultural efficiency and safety; and, most important of all, the absence of workers' representatives on the relevant decision-making bodies.

The *Food and Environment Protection Act* has, in fact, taken account of the first two of these four criticisms. The PSPS has become a statutory scheme due to the Act's provisions and results of agrochemical companies' safety tests on their products will become more widely available. However, neither of these two developments are attributable to the union's campaigning. The first is almost entirely the result of pressure on the British government by the EEC which objected to the voluntary nature of the PSPS on the grounds that '. . . it amounts to an informal cartel enabling the manufacturers to restrict price competition and unfairly block cheaper parallel pesticide imports from Europe'.[77]

The second reform, which improves public access to the information on which the ACP bases its decisions, is the outcome of successful pressure politicking by the Campaign for Freedom of Information in conjunction with a number of sympathetic MPs. The facts that the BAA itself was demanding greater 'openness' on the part of the industry[78] and that recent developments in the USA had resulted in the widespread availability of information on pesticide tests in that country contributed substantially to the success of this particular campaign.

However, from the point of view of the Agricultural and Allied Workers' National Trade Group (AAWNTG) of the TGWU, the *Food and Environment Protection Act* fails to address the most important issue of all, namely the creation of a system of workers' representation within the pesticide clearance scheme which would give them an opportunity to promote and defend their interests in securing adequate levels of occupational health and safety.[79] Throughout the Bill's parliamentary passage the union was unable to introduce such a measure into the legislation largely because it lacks social standing and other relevant sources of influence in the House of Commons.

It might be tempting to argue that the union ought to have by-passed Parliament in its campaign for workers' representation, just as it had by-passed the ACP in its earlier pursuit of an unofficial ban on 2,4,5-T. By appealing to selected sectors of the public at large, so the argument might go, the union could reproduce the successes that it achieved over 2,4,5-T. However, such an argument fails to take account of the fact that a major reason for the success of the 2,4,5-T campaign lay in the great publicity it received. In particular, the widely reported Seveso disaster and, even more so, the Agent Orange case, brought an awareness to the British public of the potential hazards and horrors involved in pesticide use, especially 2,4,5-T. The sensationalism which surrounded 2,4,5-T could not readily be reproduced and applied to the seemingly more mundane issue of workers' representation which, in any case, required the reasoned assent of political decision-makers rather than supportive piecemeal action by the wider public. For positive action to be taken on the demand for workers' representation in pesticide safety decision-making the union depended above all upon a sympathetic audience in Parliament. The absence of such an audience during the passage of the Food and Environment Protection Bill has meant that the farmworkers' union remains relatively powerless to protect the health and safety of its members, many of whom are daily exposed to potentially dangerous pesticides.

NOTES

1 Eva, D. and Oswald, R. (1981), *Health and Safety at Work*, Pan, London, p. 62; Health and Safety Executive (HSE), (1978), *Health and Safety: Agriculture 1976*, HMSO, London; HSE (1979), *Health and Safety: Agriculture 1977*, HMSO, London; HSE (1983), *Health and Safety: Agriculture 1980/1981*, HMSO, London; Winyard, S. and Danziger, R. (1984), *Hard Labour*, Low Pay Unit, London, pp. 3–5.
2 HSE, *Health and Safety: Agriculture 1978/1979*, p. 1.
3 Newby, H. (1979), *The Deferential Worker*, Penguin, Harmondsworth, p. 80; Newby, H. (1979), *Green and Pleasant Land?*, Penguin, Harmondsworth, p. 75.
4 HSE, *Health and Safety: Agriculture 1978/1979*, Appendix 5.
5 AAWNTG Document (1983), *Health and Safety Inspectors/ Representatives*, 21 October.
6 Farquhason, I. D. (1976), 'Pesticides: a guide to terminology', in

D. L. Gunn and J. G. R. Stevens, *Pesticides and Human Welfare*, Oxford University Press, p. 256.

7 Hansard, Volume 977, 31 January 1980, Col. 1597.

8 Stockbrokers Wood Mackenzie & Co., *Agrochemical Service*, December 1983. As well as British sales, there is a very lucrative export market with Britain being the third largest exporter of pesticides in the world. Britain supplies 15 per cent of all pesticides in international use and more than half of Britain's pesticides income derives from exports. *New Scientist*, 16 August 1984, 'Pesticides: exporting death'.

9 *Guardian*, 5 March 1985, 'ICI plans double sales'.

10 Body, R. (1984), *Farming in the Clouds*, Temple Smith, London, p. 21.

11 *Guardian*, 13 March 1985, 'Crop of ailments could be the price of farm spraying'.

12 Carson, R. (1965), *Silent Spring*, Penguin, Harmondsworth, p. 23.

13 The reluctance to pursue complaints concerning pesticides has been mentioned to me by a number of national and regional union officers, and was witnessed first-hand during my fieldwork in Suffolk in 1984. Cf. Gaventa, J. (1980), *Power and Powerlessness*, University of Illinois, Chicago, p. 92.

14 The *Food and Environment Protection Act* 1985 transformed the PSPS into a statutory system.

15 MAFF Information Sheet, (undated), *Safety and Efficacy Schemes for Pesticides*.

16 Doyal, L., Green, K., Irwin, A., Russell, D., Steward, F., Williams, R., Gee, D. and Epstein, S. (1983), *Cancer in Britain*, Pluto, London, p. 111.

17 *Ibid.*, p. 111.

18 Cf. William Durham, 'Pesticides in human health' in T. Sheet and D. Pimental (eds), (1979), *Pesticides: Contemporary Roles in Agriculture, Health and the Environment*, Humana, New Jersey, p. 92.

19 Whiteside, T. (1977), 'A reporter at large: the pendulum and the toxic cloud', *New Yorker*, 25 July.

20 McClure, B. (1984), *Veterans' Disability Compensation for Veterans exposed to Agent Orange or Atomic Radiation*, Congressional Research Service (CRS), Library of Congress, 25 October.

21 *New York Times*, 8 May 1984, 'Veterans accept $180 million pact on Agent Orange'; Merrill, S. and Simpson, M. (1985), *Agent Orange—Veterans' Complaints and Studies of Health Effects*, CRS, Library of Congress, 21 March.

22 See Cook, J. and Kaufman, C. (1982), *Portrait of a Poison*, Pluto, London, for a detailed narrative.

23 Advisory Committee on Pesticides, Pesticides Branch, MAFF (1979), *Review of the Safety for Use in the UK of the Herbicide 2,4,5-T*, London, March.

24 NUAAW (1980), *Not One Minute Longer*, NUAAW, London, March, pp. 12-13.

25 Irwin, A. and Green, K. (1983), 'The control of chemical carcinogens in Britain', *Policy and Politics*, 1, (4).

26 Cook and Kaufman, *op. cit.*, p. 70.

27 Advisory Committee on Pesticides, Pesticide Branch, MAFF (1980),

Further Review of the Safety for Use in the UK of the herbicide
2,4,5-T, London, December, p. 17. Also see Whiteside, op. cit.,
p. 35, who describes the position of Dow Chemicals Co. as similar
to that of the ACP when challenged over the safety of 2,4,5-T.

28   Further Review . . . , (ACP), p. 25.
29   This was made clear to me during an interview with Chris Kaufman
     (16 October 1984) who was the NUAAW's Research Officer during
     the union's 2,4,5-T campaign.
30   New Scientist, 8 September 1977, 'The political economy of risk',
     p. 598.
31   NUAAW internal memorandum (undated).
32   Cook and Kaufman, op. cit., p. 84; Irwin and Green, op. cit.,
     p. 440.
33   Crenson, M. (1971), The Unpolitics of Air Pollution, Johns
     Hopkins, Baltimore, Chapter 2; Lukes, S. (1974), Power: A Radical
     View, Macmillan, London, pp. 50-1.
34   Irwin and Green, op. cit., p. 451.
35   Cf. Polsby, N. (1980), Community Power and Political Theory,
     2nd edition, Yale University, London, and Dahl, R. (1961), Who
     Governs?, Yale University, New Haven, who posit that political
     power is exercised only within formal decision-making arenas.
36   Lukes, op. cit., pp. 23-4 and 50-2.
37   Whiteside, op. cit., p. 31.
38   Riley, C. (1980), Portrait of a Poison, transcript of a BBC Horizon
     Programme transmitted on 17 March, p. 4.
39   Thomas, R., Wardell, G. and Williams, A. (1980), '2,4,5-T cover-up
     by the MAFF', the Ecologist, 10 (6/7), July–September, p. 249.
40   Private correspondence from Dr Thomas to Mr Kaufman dated
     4 June 1980.
41   Cook and Kaufman, op. cit., p. 28.
42   Hindess, B. (1973), The Use of Official Statistics in Sociology,
     Macmillan, London.
43   Quoted in Thomas et al.'s article in the Ecologist, op. cit.
44   The difference between total imports and total sales is accounted
     for by exports of 2,4,5-T.
45   Thomas, et al., op. cit., p. 250.
46   Ibid., p. 249.
47   Hay, A. (1980), 'Red faces (and hot tempers) on 2,4,5-T', Nature,
     268, p. 97, 10 July.
48   Inaugural Address by Dr Hessayon, Chair of the British Agro-
     chemicals Assocaition 1980–81, 13 May 1980.
49   Minutes of the meeting held between the NUAAW and Scientific
     Sub-Committee on 12 June 1980.
50   Whiteside, op. cit.
51   Private correspondence between Peter Walker (Minister of Agri-
     culture) and Jack Boddy dated 15 April 1980.
52   Hansard, Volume 977, 31 January 1980, Col. 1679.
53   Inaugural speech by Dr Hessayon.
54   Interview with Mr Maclean held on 6 June 1985.
55   Further Review . . . , (ACP), Foreword.
56   Cook and Kaufman, op. cit., p. 34.
57   The farmer was a member of the AWB whom I interviewed on 22
     October 1984.

58 AAWNTG (1983), *How Many More?*, AAWNTG, London, p. 24;
    Bachrach, P. and Baratz, M. (1970), *Power and Poverty*, Oxford
    University Press, New York, p. 45.
59 Cook and Kaufman, *op. cit.*, p. 53.
60 *Ibid.*, p. 54.
61 *Ibid.*, p. 53.
62 Van den Bosch, R. (1978), *The Pesticide Conspiracy*, Doubleday,
    New York, p. 29.
63 *Further Review* . . . , (ACP), pp. 7, 17, 19, 25 and 28.
64 Cook and Kaufman, *op. cit.*, p. 51.
65 NUAAW, *Not One Minute Longer*, p. 3.
66 *Further Review* . . . , (ACP), p. 17.
67 Dahl, *op. cit.*, pp. 229–38 and 246–48.
68 Cook and Kaufman, *op. cit.*, p. 51.
69 *Landworker*, January 1981, March 1981, September 1981,
    December 1982, September 1983.
70 *Landworker*, September 1983.
71 *Ibid.*
72 Interview with Mr T. D. Maclean on 6 June 1985.
73 Stockbrokers Wood Mackenzie & Co., who are heavily involved in
    the agrochemical sector, suggest that 2,4,5-T herbicides' market
    share in 1985 is virtually negligible. (Telephone conversation June
    1985.)
74 Cook and Kaufman, *op. cit.*, p. 74.
75 Interview with Jerry Wiggin, MP, on 6 June 1985 (my italics).
76 Dr Hessayon, quoted in *How Many More?*, p. 6.
77 *Guardian*, 23 August 1984, 'For Safety's Sake . . . Makers Get
    Tough'.
78 BAA *Annual Report* 1983–84.
79 *Landworker*, September 1984.

Chapter 7

Power, powerlessness
and the agricultural workforce

There are two important conclusions to be drawn from the foregoing inquiry into political powerlessness. The first derives from the empirical study of post-war farmworkers' efforts to promote and defend their interests in high wages, non-tied housing and reasonable occupational health and safety. The conclusion must be that the farmworkers' union has been almost wholly powerless to satisfy these interests through its participation in formal policy-making institutions and through its use of the assistance offered by external allies of the agricultural work-force.

The second conclusion has ramifications which reach beyond the present case study. Political powerlessness, defined in Chapter 1 as Q's inability to promote or defend its interests in authoritative value-allocating institutions, was seen to be the outcome of T's exercise of power over Q within and, more importantly perhaps, beyond the formal value-allocating institution. T was shown to exercise power over Q in a multiplicity of ways, ranging from the relatively simple pluralist notion of prevailing in formal decision-making; to the more complex mobilisation of bias and nondecision-making; to the even more insidious and 'hidden' manipulation and control of information. This diversity of power exercises, and the implied effects which they have upon the powerless, leads one to a view of powerlessness as a multifarious phenomenon which pervades social and political life.

By adopting the approach to powerlessness put forward in Chapter 1 it has been possible to uncover and analyse dimensions of powerlessness and power which would have been neglected if a pluralist or 'two face' approach had been used instead. Whether or not the advocated approach can be applied successfully to further case studies can be determined only by carrying out further empirical analyses along similar lines.

The distribution of power resources was decisive in determining the relative power of the actors which were studied here. However, contrary to the pluralist belief that a lack of one type of power resource is compensated for by an abundance of another resource of power, the evidence is that power resources are cumulative and concentrated in such a way as to provide the farmworkers' union with access to far fewer significant power resources than its opponents, as a result of which the union has been unable to prevail in any of the issue areas looked at.

Although the National Union of Agricultural and Allied Workers (NUAAW) was not found to be 'entirely lacking in some influence resource',[1] its deprivation of power resources in four crucial areas was sufficient to prevent it from successfully promoting and defending each of the sets of interests which were considered in Chapters 4, 5 and 6. The union was seen to be badly off in its access to organisational resources; economic resources (in the sphere of job control or labour market strength); political resources (in the sense of parliamentary levers and allies); and social resources (in relation to farmworkers' collective social standing).

Chapter 3 examined the organisational weakness of the agricultural labour force, focusing on the low level of union membership among farmworkers, and the resulting poverty and relative impotence which has historically characterised the union. This organisational infirmity was attributed largely to farmworkers' inability to control or manipulate the labour market which, together with their physical isolation, has served to inhibit many farmworkers from joining the union or from participating in activities such as the Overtime Ban of 1984.[2]

Chapter 4 illustrated how the combination of farmworkers' organisational and labour market weaknesses has prevented the NUAAW from winning high wage increases through the Agricultural Wages Board (AWB). The lack of organisational and economic resources was related to the farmworkers' repeated low wage awards in the sense that their dual deficiency of power resources denies them one of the most important devices usually available to workers for the promotion and defence of their interests, namely strike action. It is the great unlikelihood of farmworkers' going on strike, combined with farmers' tight control over the labour market, which have led the independent members of the AWB to define 'reasonable' pay awards in terms of employers', rather than workers', interests.

Farmworkers' lack of parliamentary levers and allies was

studied in Chapter 5. During the period under examination, farmworkers' electoral marginality was compensated for by one parliamentary resource, namely the presence in the House of Commons of a handful of sympathetic MPs. The vulnerability of this resource to opposing forces explains why the Labour government's tied cottage reform was so limited. Moreover, the transitory nature of the resource in question means that even such limited reforms as the *Rent (Agriculture) Act* 1976 will not necessarily always be forthcoming from Parliament.

Finally, farmworkers' poor social standing was noted in Chapter 6. The image of farmworkers as being a backward and unsophisticated group of workers was seen to have prevented the NUAAW from influencing political decision-makers, especially in areas which allegedly require formal training and intellectual sophistication, such as pesticide safety.[3]

In contrast to farmworkers' paucity of power resources, agricultural employers were shown to have access to sufficient resources for the NFU to be able to promote and defend its members' interests with considerable success. The NFU's organisational strength, noted in Chapter 2, derives largely from its high membership level. The members, many of whom are wealthy farmers, provide it with solid financial support, which in turn is used for the NFU's many campaigns. Moreover, the members also confer collectively upon the NFU a legitimacy which is lacking in the NUAAW, which springs from the NFU's ability to claim to speak for the country's entire population of farmers.

Agricultural employers also have access to important economic resources. Firstly, the role of agriculture in the national economy and the part played by agricultural capital in preserving that role provide farmers with a significant degree of influence in political institutions such as Parliament and the AWB. Secondly, the farmers' tight control over the agricultural labour market (which is indirectly proportionate to farmworkers' ability to strike) has provided agricultural employers with a major power resource. At times they have benefited from this resource without having to take positive action to mobilise it; as, for example, in the regular and tacit influence over the AWB's independent members which this resource provides to the Employers' Side of the Board. At other times this resource has been mobilised overtly and successfully, as in the case of the farmworkers' Overtime Ban when employers' threats of dismissal prevented most farmworkers from taking action in support of their wage claim.

Employers' parliamentary resources contrast similarly with those of agricultural workers. Although both groups are electorally weak, the employers' access to organisational and economic resources combine to provide them with considerable parliamentary resources. These include strong and lasting contacts with local MPs in rural areas; social and political ties with the hundred or so agriculturally-oriented MPs at Westminster; and a more broadly based relationship with the many MPs of all parties who view maximum agricultural production as a crucial element for a healthy economy.

Thus, contrary to pluralist hypotheses, the conflict of interests that exists between agricultural employers and workers, as defined in Chapter 1, is built upon a highly unequal distribution of those power resources which are necessary for each side to promote and protect its respective interests.

A similar inequality of power resources was found to characterise the conflict of interests over pesticide safety regulation which divides farmworkers and the government (and, in particular, the government's Advisory Committee on Pesticides [ACP]). Chapter 6 showed that the inequality of resources that exists between these two groups is at least as vast as those inequalities located in Chapters 4 and 5. For example, the government was able to set the parliamentary agenda because of its access to the resource of 'legality', whilst the NUAAW's lack of economic, organisational and parliamentary resources, combined with farmworkers' low social standing, left the NUAAW with no means by which to influence Parliament over the issue of workers' representation in pesticide safety decision-making.

The one significant and effective resource which farmworkers were found to have access to was identified in Chapter 6. This was the resource of solidarity. However, although the union used this resource skilfully in the 2,4,5-T campaign, it is not a power resource which is often available to the union. Farmworkers can only draw upon solidarity when they are attempting to promote and defend interests which coincide with those of other groups, and when this coincidence of interests is recognised and acted upon by these other groups. The issue of solidarity between working-class groups is a subject to which an entire book could be devoted; here it can only be observed that the resource of solidarity is somewhat chimerical and, as such, it is not always a reliable resource of power.

A second weakness in the pluralist approach to power and powerlessness was that concerning the 'second face' of power. If this concept had been neglected in the present case study important experiences of powerlessness would have been overlooked entirely. As a result of such an oversight, farmworkers' apparent silence in formal institutions of value allocation, or their consent to pursuing only their limited interests, would have been mistaken for satisfaction with the status quo and consensus with the decision-makers, instead of being recognised as the outcome of diverse exercises of power.[4]

For example, in Chapter 4 it was seen that demands for 50 per cent pay increases were repeatedly mobilised off of the AWB's agenda. By referring to the union's demands as 'unreasonable' and 'unrealistic' at every available opportunity, the AWB's independent members forced the union to retreat from its original demands in the preliminary stages of each year's negotiating process. In certain years this mobilisation of values prevented the 50 per cent demand from being raised even during the Board's 'preliminary' discussions. This occurred when the union's Annual Conference voted to enter negotiations with a claim for a 'substantial increase' rather than for a specified target of 50 per cent in anticipation of certain defeat if the latter claim were made.

This anticipation of failure was strengthened further by the independents' frequent observation that the union had always failed in the past to achieve such high pay increases. By emphasising the union's history of powerlessness in this way the independents encouraged the NUAAW to desist from demanding high pay awards, for to continue to make these demands was portrayed as an unnecessary waste of everyone's time.

Similar values relating to 'realism' and 'reasonableness' were mobilised during the NUAAW's campaign for tied cottage abolition. Demands for the abolition of the tied cottage system were raised more often by radical Labour MPs than by the union because of the power which had been exercised for many years over the union by Labour Party 'moderates'. However, even this assistance from the union's more radical allies proved ineffective, for the radicals' demands were quelled, too, by prompt accusations of unreasonableness or political irresponsibility.

In Chapter 6 dominant values were once again shown to have been mobilised against the interests of farmworkers. The ACP's reputation for impartiality, expertise and virtual incontestability was strengthened by repeated references to these qualities by the government and by the ACP itself. Meanwhile, the NUAAW was tainted with labels such as 'amateur', 'politically motivated' and 'hysterical', which discredited its case against the ACP's monopoly of decision-making rights in matters relating to pesticide safety.

The mobilisation of values explored in Chapters 4, 5 and 6 was not the only form of nondecision-making that was located in the study. Further types of nondecision-making were examined, including the use of procedural biases—for example, the practice of keeping AWB members apart from one another throughout negotiations so as to keep conflict covert and thus to facilitate 'compromise'. Devices such as this were found to have been employed, like the mobilisation of values, in order to keep certain issues off of the agendas of relevant institutions. The prevalence and effectiveness of this sort of power exercise suggests that the pluralist approach is wrong to concentrate exclusively on 'who prevails in formal decision-making', and to dismiss as part of the 'background' the power exercises which determine which issues will be formally discussed and decided upon within a given institution.[5]

These non-formal exercises of power are not confined to the mobilisation of specifically institutional biases. As Chapter 4 illustrated, power can be exercised altogether outside of an institution and yet have serious implications for the power relations which exist within it. The use of parliamentary power resources to secure Professor Dickson's removal from the AWB, as well as the agricultural employers' assertion of their power in the marketplace during the workers' overtime ban were examples of how this might occur. In neither case could the NFU's actions be deemed a 'background' to the AWB's operations: instead, they were distinct exercises of power which, by enabling the employers to set the AWB's agenda, profoundly influenced the power which was then exercised within the AWB.

Although the pluralist approach is criticised here for its refusal to acknowledge the existence of a 'second face' of power, this does not signify a wholesale rejection of the pluralist argument in favour of studying 'who prevails' in formal decision-making. For example, by looking at the process of prevailing in the AWB's formal decision-making, it was possible to establish that farmworkers were often powerless to defend even their limited interests (for example, in 10 per cent wages increases) because they lacked access to the relevant power resource, which in this case was information. Pluralists are criticised here not because they point to the significance of the formal decision-making process, but because they fail to recognise that there are *other* important loci of political power which warrant academic inquiry.

The present study has thus used the notion of a 'second face' of power to discover the nature of farmworkers' powerlessness and at the same time to highlight specific weaknesses in the pluralist view of power and powerlessness. However, in doing this it has identified a serious problem in the 'second face' approach as it has been put forward by Peter Bachrach and Morton Baratz. In particular, their refusal to include unobservable phenomena in a study of powerlessness was found to be an unhelpful constraint. The case study revealed that if the student of powerlessness begins with a heuristic conception of what constitutes Q's 'objective' interests (as opposed to Q's subjective desires) then s/he will be able to include in his or her study important power relations which otherwise would be overlooked.

This point was illustrated most clearly in Chapter 6. If the 2,4,5-T controversy had been approached solely from the perspective of farmworkers' subjective (i.e. observable) desires, then it would have been necessary to argue that for thirty years it was in farmworkers' interests to use 2,4,5-T despite its possible health hazards, for this is what their (observable) behaviour and desires between 1940 and 1970 would suggest. Conversely, having begun with a recognition that subjective desires do not necessarily correspond with objective interests, it was possible to discover that farmworkers' behaviour, as well as their very thoughts concerning 2,4,5-T, were the outcome of exercises of power. This view of the situation developed from the heuristic premise that regardless of farmworkers' actions, their *objective* interests are in refraining from pesticide use until the given pesticide is proven safe. Having noted the discrepancy between farmworkers' behaviour and their objective interests, it became necessary to seek out the specific form of power which had apparently been exercised to prevent farmworkers from acting on their interests. Historical analysis revealed that power had been exercised over the 2,4,5-T users through the withholding of information concerning the possible dangers relating to the use of 2,4,5-T.

Chapter 6 was also able to explore other ideas raised in Chapter 1, in particular the notion that power can be exercised unconsciously and through inaction. It was argued that the withholding of information on 2,4,5-T constituted an exercise of power over farmworkers, irrespective of whether it entailed any positive action on the part of the 2,4,5-T manufacturers and safety regulators (who hypothetically could have provided the relevant information), and regardless of whether these groups were conscious of their power exercise. This contention was based upon a view of power which embraces any (in)action by T which contributes significantly to the harming of Q's interests. Chapter 6 demonstrated that one advantage of using this perspective on power in a study of powerlessness is that it enables the observer to understand more fully the obstacles which prevent Q from satisfying its interests, and so to recognise steps which would have to be taken for the future promotion and defence of these interests.

The empirical study also explored the relationship between power and responsibility which was discussed in Chapter 1. This relationship was studied most closely in Chapter 5, in connection with the Labour government's reluctant exercise of power over the NUAAW. The government was portrayed as having little option but to moderate its proposals for tied cottage reform, chiefly because of the procedural constraints under which it operated and the skilful exploitation of these constraints by the NFU. In the absence of any significant 'free will' on the part of the government, it could not be held morally responsible for its exercise of power over the NUAAW. In spite of this, the government can be attributed with causal responsibility; regardless of its 'inability to do otherwise', the government effectively assisted the NFU in preventing the NUAAW from promoting farmworkers' interests in achieving extensive tied cottage reform. To the extent that the government contributed significantly to the frustration of farmworkers' interests in this way, and acting differently was a hypothetical, although not actual possibility, the government is regarded as having exercised power and must be held (causally) responsible for so doing.

The evidence of the second part of this study suggests that farmworkers' work-place powerlessness, as identified by Howard Newby, has been compensated for neither by any significant strength in formal institutions of value allocation, nor by farmworkers' alliances with external agents such as the Labour Party. Indeed, to a large extent farmworkers' powerlessness on the farm is the direct cause of their powerlessness in formal arenas. Most notably, the powerlessness of the Workers' Side of the AWB is a direct consequence of farmworkers' organisational and labour market weaknesses. Given this relationship between occupational and institutional powerlessness, it would be misleading to suggest that farmworkers can hope to gain dramatic improvements in their conditions of work by concentrating on formal political action rather than, for example, on direct action.

This is not to suggest that the union has failed to achieve any gains through its participation in political decision-making. The NUAAW concluded its sixty-year old tied cottage campaign with the introduction of a significant measure of reform which, while leaving many problems intact, did bring a new sense of security to the lives of many farmworkers. Similarly, although the 2,4,5-T campaign failed to bring about a formal ban on the herbicide, the NUAAW achieved a significant reduction in Britain's use of 2,4,5-T through its informal links and alliances with external groups. The important point, however, is that successes such as these are not attributable to farmworkers' access to long-term and durable resources of power. On the contrary, in a sense these successes were something of a fluke, in that they were achieved through the fortuitous presence in Parliament of two sympathetic MPs at the time when tied cottage reform was being discussed; and through the development of the tenuous resource of solidarity, involving groups who happened to share farmworkers' interests in banning 2,4,5-T because of their own experiences with the weedkiller.

It may be that the NUAAW's merger with the Transport and General Workers' Union (TGWU) will improve farmworkers' access to longer term power resources over the coming years by underpinning the two resources mentioned above. Firstly, the merger with the TGWU has brought farmworkers access to over twenty-five sponsored MPs, which marks a clear numerical advancement over the one MP which the NUAAW had previously sponsored. Although the twenty-five TGWU MPs may not be committed as intensively to promoting farmworkers' interests as was the NUAAW's MP (for the simple reason that they have to concern themselves with the interests of all TGWU workers) their presence in Parliament may provide the Agricultural and Allied Workers' Trade Group with an opportunity to develop stronger parliamentary links than it has hitherto enjoyed.

The second possible resource which may be developed and deployed following the merger of unions is that of solidarity. The union's new organisational links with other groups of workers belonging to the TGWU has provided it with a formal and lasting basis upon which to build a resource of solidarity. The development of this resource, in co-operation with transport workers, dock workers, local authority workers and other TGWU members, might prove to be of great use to farmworkers in future years, particularly given the occupational interests shared by some of these groups. Whether or not this potential resource can be developed and used remains to be seen.

Until now the history of the farmworkers' union has been one of outstanding powerlessness, interspersed with occasional successes and minor breakthroughs. This powerlessness has been experienced for the greatest part of a century, as a result of which it has formed a large part of the image and self-image of the agricultural labour force and its union.

Recent developments in the social and economic make-up of Britain suggest that the powerlessness with which farmworkers have become so closely identified has begun to spread to other groups of manual workers. In what appears to be a bitter parody of Marxist analysis, the agricultural labour force may have become the 'vanguard' of the British working-class in so far as its experiences of labour market weakness, isolation, poverty and insecurity are becoming a new way of life for many British industrial workers.[6] Just as the role of the agricultural worker in the British economy was superceded in the eighteenth and nineteenth centuries by that of the industrial worker, so now the industrial workforce is being weakened by economic trends which are forcing Britain away from its 200-year old industrial base and towards a service economy. One result of this development has been an apparent movement towards 'deference' and docility among a substantial section of the traditionally militant industrial working class.

If the supercession of industrial workers by service workers is part of a long-term trend, rather than being a temporary phenomenon caused by current government policies, then industrial workers will have much to learn from the farmworkers' experiences of powerlessness. But the question of whether or not industrial workers will follow in the agricultural workers' footsteps cannot be answered within the confines of this study. The main concern here has been to analyse the nature of political powerlessness and, in so doing, to contribute in some small way towards the improvement of farmworkers' conditions of work.

NOTES

1   Dahl, R. (1961), Who Governs?, Yale University Press, New Haven, p. 228.
2   This work-place powerlessness of the agricultural work-force has been studied in detail by Howard Newby. In particular see Newby, H. (1972), 'Agricultural workers in the class structure', SR, 20; Newby, H. (1974), 'The changing sociological environment of the farm', Farm Management, 2 (9); Newby, H. (1979), The Deferential Worker, Penguin, Harmondsworth; Newby, H (1972), 'The low earnings of agricultural workers', JAE, 23.
3   There is a certain irony here: while there are too many farmworkers for the agricultural work-force to enjoy a significant degree of labour market control, there are too few of them to wield 'indirect' political clout through an electoral resource.
4   Bachrach, P. and Baratz, M. (1963), 'Decisions and nondecisions', APSR, 57; Bachrach, P. and Baratz, M. (1970), Power and Poverty, Oxford University Press, New York; Bachrach, P and Baratz, M. (1962), 'The two faces of power', APSR, 56.
5   Nelson Polsby in particular adopts this approach; Polsby, N. (1980), Community Power and Political Theory, second edition, Yale University, London, pp. 120–1.
6   Carr, S. (1984), Changing Patterns of Work, Workers' Educational Association, London.

Bibliography

PRIMARY SOURCES

Advisory Committee on Pesticides (ACP), (1979), *Review of the Safety for Use in the U.K. of the Herbicide 2,4,5-T*, Pesticides Branch MAFF, London, March.
—— (1980), *Further Review of the Safety for Use in the U.K. of the Herbicide 2,4,5-T*, Pesticides Branch MAFF, London, December.
Agricultural and Allied Workers' National Trade Group (1983), *How Many More?*, London.
—— (1983), *Statement Submitted by the Workers' Side of the Agricultural Wages Board*, March.
—— (1983), *Statement Submitted by the Workers' Side of the Agricultural Wages Board*, April.
Association of District Councils (1975), *Comments on Consultative Document—Abolition of the Tied Cottage System in Agriculture*, 2 October.
Commission of the European Communities (1981), *The Common Agricultural Policy*, revised edition, November.
Congressional Research Service, (1984), *Veterans' Disability Compensation for Veterans Exposed to Agent Orange or Atomic Radiation*, Library of Congress, USA, 25 October.
—— (1985), *Agent Orange—Veterans' Complaints and Studies of Health Effects*, Library of Congress, USA, 21 March.
Co-operative Programme of Agro-Allied Industries, Food and Agriculture Organization and other United Nations organizations (1972), *Pesticides in the Modern World*, Newgate Press, London.
Department of Employment (1985), *New Earnings Survey 1984 Part A*, HMSO, London.
Department of the Environment and Ministry of Agriculture, Fisheries, and Food (1975), *Abolition of the Tied Cottage System in Agriculture: Consultative Document*.
—— (1977), *Some Questions and Answers About the Rent (Agriculture) Act 1976*, Dept of Environment and MAFF Welsh Office.
Lund, P. J., Morris, T. G., Temple, J. D. and Watson, J. M. (1982), 'Wages and employment', in *Agriculture: England and Wales 1960–1980*, Government Economic Service Working Paper Number 52, MAFF, March.
Ministry of Agriculture, Fisheries, and Food (MAFF), *Annual Review and Determination of Guarantees*, 1952–1973.
—— *Annual Review of Agriculture*, 1973–84.
—— (1968), *A Century of Agricultural Statistics: Great Britain*

1866-1966, London.
—— (1970), *The Changing Structure of Agriculture,* London.
—— (1979), *Farming and the Nation,* February.
—— (1983), *Earnings, Hours and Numbers of Persons Including the Report on the Wages and Employment Enquiry,* 1982, March.
—— *Report on Safety, Health, Welfare and Wages in Agriculture,* 1962-75.
—— *Report on Wages in Agriculture,* 1976-84.
National Board for Prices and Incomes (1967), *Pay of Workers in Agriculture in England and Wales,* HMSO, London.
—— (1969), *Pay of Workers in Agriculture in England and Wales,* Report No. 101, HMSO, London.
National Council of Social Service and National Consumer Council (1978), *The Right to Know: a review of advice services in rural areas.*
National Farmers' Union, *Annual Report,* 1977, 1983.
—— (undated), *The National Farmers' Union of England and Wales,* Speakers' Brief 4-982.
—— (undated), *The National Importance of British Agriculture.*
—— (1983), *The NFU in the '80s,* Cyclo 259/83, February.
—— (1984), *The Way Forward: New Directions for Agricultural Policy.*
National Union of Agricultural and Allied Workers, *Annual Report,* 1953-81, London.
—— (1980), *Not One Minute Longer,* London, March.
Riley, C., *Portrait of a Poison,* BBC Horizon Programme, transcript of programme which was transmitted on 17 March 1980.
Royal Institute of Chartered Surveyors (1975), *The Agricultural Tied Cottage—Discussion Papers.*
Rural Voice and the Bus and Coach Council (1983), *The Country Would Miss the Bus,* London, February.

SECONDARY SOURCES

Books and pamphlets

Abercrombie, N. and Turner, B. S. (1982), 'The dominant ideology thesis', in A. Giddens and D. Held (eds), *Classes, Power and Conflict,* Macmillan, Basingstoke.
Bachrach, P. and Baratz, M. (1970), *Power and Poverty: theory and practice,* Oxford University Press, New York.
Bell, C. and Newby, H. (1975), 'The sources of variation in agricultural workers' images of society', in M. Bulmer (ed.), *Working Class Images of Society,* Routledge & Kegan Paul.
Beresford, T. (1975), *We Plough the Fields,* Penguin, Harmondsworth.
Bloch, M., Heading, B. and Lawrence, P. (1979), 'Power in social theory: a non-relative view', in S. C. Brown (ed.), *Philosophical Disputes in the Social Sciences,* Harvester Press, Brighton.
Blythe, R. (1969), *Akenfield: Portrait of an English Village,* Allen Lane, London.

Body, R. (1982), *Agriculture: the triumph and the shame*, Temple Smith, London.
—— (1984), *Farming in the Clouds*, Temple Smith, London.
Britton, D. K. (1983), 'Is there a case for farm income support', in *Agriculture: the triumph and the shame: An Independent Assessment*, Centre for Agricultural Strategy, University of Reading.
Brown, M. and Winyard, S. (1975), *Low Pay on the Farm*, Low Pay Unit, London.
Buchanan, S. (1982), 'Power and planning in rural areas: preparation of the Suffolk County Structure Plan', in M. J. Moseley (ed.), *Power, Planning & People in Rural East Anglia*, Centre of East Anglian Studies, University of East Anglia.
Capstick, M. (1970), *The Economics of Agriculture*, Allen & Unwin, London.
Carr, S. (1984), *Changing Patterns of Work*, Workers' Educational Association, London.
Carson, R. (1965), *Silent Spring*, Penguin, Harmondsworth.
Clark, D. (1982), 'Rural housing: problems and solutions—an overview', in *Rural Housing: Problems and Solutions*, A Seminar Report organised by Peak National Park Study Centre, NCVO and the Development Commission.
Clark, G. (1982), *Housing and Planning in the Countryside*, Research Studies Press, Chichester.
Clutterbuck, C. and Lang, T. (1982), *More than We Can Chew*, Pluto Press, London.
Coates, D. (1980), *Labour in Power? A Study of the Labour Government 1974-1979*, Longman, London.
Connolly, W. E. (1983), *The Terms of Political Discourse*, 2nd edition, Martin Robertson, Oxford.
Cook, J. and Kaufman, C. (1982), *Portrait of a Poison*, Pluto Press, London.
Craig, C., Rubery, J., Tarling, R. and Wilkinson, F. (1982), *Labour Market Structure, Industrial Organisation and Low Pay*, Cambridge University Press.
Crenson, M. (1971), *The Unpolitics of Air Pollution: a study of Non-decisionmaking in the Cities*, Johns Hopkins Press, Baltimore.
Dahl, R. A. (1961), *Who Governs? Democracy and Power in an American City*, Yale University Press, New Haven.
—— (1969), 'The concept of power', in R. Bell, D. Edwards and R. Harrison Wagner (eds), *Political Power*, Free Press, New York.
Day, G. (ed.) (1982), *Diversity and Decomposition in the Labour Market*, Introduction, Gower Publishing, Aldershot.
Donaldson, J. G. S. and Donaldson, F. (1969), *Farming in Britain Today*, Allen Lane, London.
Doyal, L., Green, K., Irwin, A., Russell, D., Steward, F., Williams, R., Gee, D. and Epstein, S. (1983), *Cancer in Britain: the politics of prevention*, Pluto Press, London.
Dunbabin, J. P. D. (1974), *Rural Discontent in Nineteenth Century Britain*, Faber, London.
Dunlop, O. J. (1913), *The Farm Labourer: the history of a modern problem*, Fisher Unwin, London.
Durham, W. F. (1979), 'Pesticides and human health', in T. J. Sheets

and D. Pimentel (eds), *Pesticides: Contemporary Roles in Agriculture, Health and the Environment*, Humana, New Jersey.

Edwards, A. and Rogers, A. (eds), (1974), *Agricultural Resources*, Faber, London.

Evans, G. E. (1975), *The Days that We Have Seen*, Faber, London.

Farquhason, I. D. (1976), 'Pesticides: a guide to terminology', in D. L. Gunn and J. G. R. Stevens (eds), *Pesticides and Human Welfare*, Oxford University Press.

Field, P. (1977), *Are Low Wages Inevitable?*, Spokesman, London.

Fisher, A. and Dix, B. (1974), *Low Pay and How to End It: a union view*, Pitman, Bath.

Flathman, R. E. (1980), *The Practice of Political Authority*, University of Chicago, Chicago and London.

Fussell, G. E. (1948), *From Tolpuddle to T.U.C.: a century of farm labourers' politics*, Windsor Press, Slough.

Galbraith, J. K. (1984), *The Anatomy of Power*, Hamish Hamilton, London.

Gasson, R. (1974), *Mobility of Farmworkers: a study of the Effects of Towns and Industrial Employment on the supply of farm labour*, University of Cambridge, Department of Land Economy, Occasional Paper No. 2.

―― (1975), *Provision of Tied Cottages*, University of Cambridge, Department of Land Economy, Occasional Paper No. 4.

―― (1976), *Tied Cottages on Large Farms*, University of Cambridge, Department of Land Economy.

Gaventa, J. (1980), *Power and Powerlessness: Quiescence and Rebellion in an Appalachian Valley*, University of Illinois Press, Chicago.

Giles, A. K. and Cowie, W. J. C. (1964), *The Farmworker: his training, pay and status*, Department of Agricultural Economics, University of Reading.

Giles, T. and Stansfield, M. (1980), *The Farmer as Manager*, Allen & Unwin, London.

Goffe, R. and Scase, R. (1982), ' "Fraternalism" and "paternalism" as employer strategies in small firms', in Graham Day (ed.), *Diversity & Decomposition in the Labour Market*, Gower Publishing, Aldershot.

Gold, M. (1983), *Assault and Battery: What Factory Farming means for Humans and Animals*, Pluto Press, London.

Grant, W. (1983), 'The National Farmers' Union: the classic case of incorporation?', in D. Marsh (ed.), *Pressure Politics*, Junction Books, London.

Grigg, D. (1982), *The Dynamics of Agricultural Changes*, Hutchinson, London.

Groves, R. (1981), *Sharpen the Sickle!*, Merlin Press, London.

Heath, C. E. and Whitby, M. C. (1970), *The Changing Agricultural Labour Force: Implications for Training*, Agricultural Adjustment Unit, University of Newcastle.

Hindess, B. (1973), *The Use of Official Statistics in Sociology*, Macmillan, London.

Hobsbawm, E. J. (1968), *Industry and Empire: an Economic History of Britain Since 1750*, Weidenfeld and Nicolson, London.

Hobsbawm, E. J. and Rudé, G. (1969), *Captain Swing*, Lawrence and Wishart, London.

Holman, R. (1978), *Poverty: Explanations of Social Deprivation*,

Martin Robertson, London.
Hunter, L. C. and Mulvey, C. (1981), *Economics of Wages and Labour*, 2nd edition, Macmillan, London.
Hyman, R. (1971), *The Workers' Union*, Clarendon Press, Oxford.
Irving, B. and Hilgendorf, L. (1975), *Tied Cottages in British Agriculture*, Tavistock Institute of Human Relations, London.
Irwin, A. (1984), 'Controlling technological risks: the case of carcinogenic chemicals', in M. Gibbons and P. Gummett (eds), *Science, Technology and Society Today*, Manchester University Press.
Jones, A. (1975), *Rural Housing: the Agricultural Tied Cottage*, Occasional Papers on Social Administration No. 56, York.
Jones, G. E. (1973), *Rural Life*, Longman, London.
Larkin, A. (1979), 'Rural housing and housing needs', in J. Martin Shaw, *Rural Deprivation and Planning*, Geo Abstracts, Norwich.
Lockwood, D. (1973), 'The distribution of power in industrial society— a comment', in J. Urry and J. Wakeford, *Power in Britain*, Heinemann Educational Books, London.
Lukes, S. (1974), *Power: A Radical View*, Macmillan, London.
—— (1977), 'Power and structure', in S. Lukes, *Essays in Social Theory*, Macmillan, London.
—— (1978), 'Power and authority', in T. Bottomore and R. Nisbet, *A History of Sociological Analysis*, Heinemann, London.
—— (1979), 'On the relativity of power', in S. C. Brown (ed.), *Philosophical Disputes in the Social Sciences*, Harvester Press, Brighton.
Madden, M. (1956), 'The NUAW 1906-1956', unpublished B.Litt Thesis, Oxford University.
Mann, M. (1973), *Consciousness and Action Among the Western Working Class*, Macmillan, Hong Kong.
Martin, E. W. (1965), *The Shearers and the Shorn: A Study of Life in a Devon Community*, Routledge & Kegan Paul, London.
Martin, R. (1977), *The Spciology of Power*, Routledge & Kegan Paul, London.
Martin, R. and Fryer, R. H. (1973), *Redundancy and Paternalist Capitalism: a Study in the Sociology of Work*, George Allen and Unwin, London.
Maynard, J. (ed.), (1974), *A Hundred Years of Farmworkers' Struggle*, Institute for Workers' Control, Nottingham.
McEachern, D. (1980), *A Class Against Itself: Power and the Nationalisation of the British Steel Corporation*, Cambridge University Press.
Miliband, R. (1973), 'The power and the capitalist enterprise', in J. Urry and J. Wakeford (eds), *Power in Britain*, Heinemann Educational Books, London.
Mingay, G. E. (1972), 'The transformation of agriculture', in R. Hartwell, G. Mingay, R. Boyson, N. McCord, C. Hanson, A.W. Coats, W. Chaloner, W. O. Henderson and M. Jefferson, *The Long Debate on Poverty*, The Institute of Economic Affairs.
Mokken, R. J. and Stokman, F. N. (1976), 'Power and influence as political phenomena', in Brian Barry (ed.), *Power and Political Theory*, John Wiley, London.
Morriss, P. (1980), 'The essentially uncontestable concept of power', in M. Freeman and D. Robertson (eds), *The Frontiers of Political*

Theory, Harvester Press, Brighton.
Moynihan, D. P. (ed.), (1968), *On Understanding Poverty*, Basic Books, New York.
Newby, H. (1977), 'In the field: reflections on the study of Suffolk farmworkers', in C. Hell and H. Newby (eds), *Doing Sociological Research*, George Allen and Unwin, London.
—— (1977), 'Paternalism and capitalism', in R. Scase (ed.), *Industrial Society: Class, Cleavage and Control*, George Allen and Unwin, London.
—— (1979), *The Deferential Worker*, Penguin, Harmondsworth.
—— (1979), *Green and Pleasant Land?*, Penguin, Harmondsworth.
Newby, H., Bell, C., Rose, D. and Saunders, P. (1978), *Property, Paternalism and Power*, Hutchinson, London.
Nix, J. (1984), *Farm Management Pocketbook*, Wye College, Farm Business Unit.
Norton-Taylor, R. (1982), *Whose Land Is It Anyway?*, Turnstone Press Ltd., Wellingborough.
Orr, J. (1916), *Agriculture in Oxfordshire*, Oxford University Press.
Parenti, M. (1978), *Power and Powerlessness*, St. Martins Press, New York.
Phillips, D. and Williams, A. (1982), *Rural Housing and the Public Sector*, Gower Publishing, Aldershot.
—— and —— (1982), *Rural Britain: a Social Geography*, Blackwell, Oxford.
Polsby, N. (1980), *Community Power and Political Theory*, 2nd edition, Yale University Press, London.
Pond, C. (1980), 'Low pay', in N. Bosanquet and P. Townsend (eds), *Labour and Equality*, Heinemann, London.
Pond, C. and Winyard, S. (1983), *The Case For a National Minimum Wage*, Low Pay Unit, London.
Rogers, A. (1976), 'Rural housing', in G. Cherry (ed.), *Rural Planning Problems*, Leonard Hill, London.
Rose, D., Saunders, P., Newby, H. and Bell, C. (1978), 'Land ownership and the politics of rural areas', in Alan Walker (ed.), *Rural Poverty: Poverty, Deprivation and Planning in Rural Areas*, Child Poverty Action Group, London.
——, ——, ——, ——, (1979), 'The economic and political basis of rural deprivation: a case study', in J. Martin Shaw (ed), *Rural Deprivation and Planning*, Geo Abstracts, Norwich.
Rossi, H. (1977), *Shaw's Guide to the Rent (Agriculture) Act 1976*, Shaw and Sons Ltd, London.
Roth, A. (1975), *The Business Background of MPs 1975–1976*, Parliamentary Profiles, London.
—— (1981), *The Business Background of MPs: 1981*, Parliamentary Profiles, London.
Rowntree, B. S. (1914), *The Labourer and the Land*, J. M. Dent & Sons Ltd, London.
Russell, N. P. (1985), *An Analysis of the Distribution of Farm Incomes in England and Wales*, Manchester University, Department of Agricultural Economics Bulletin No. 200, April.
Saunders, P. (1979), *Urban Politics: A Sociological Interpretation*, Hutchinson, London.
Schattschneider, B. E. (1960), *The Semisovereign People*, The Dryden

Press, Illinois.
Scott, J. (1982), *The Upper Classes: Property and Privilege in Britain*, Macmillan, Hong Kong.
Self, P. and Storing, H. (1962), *The State and the Farmer*, Allen & Unwin, London.
Selly, C. (1972), *Ill Fares the Land*, Andre Deutsch, London.
Shelter (1974), *Report on Tied Accommodation*, Shelter, London.
—— (1979), *The Forgotten Problem: a Study of Tied Accommodation and the Cycle of Insecurity*, Shelter, London.
Shoard, M. (1980), *The Theft of the Countryside*, Temple Smith, London.
Therborn, G. (1982), 'What does the ruling class do when it rules?', in A. Giddens and D. Held (eds), *Classes, Power and Conflict*, Macmillan, Basingstoke.
The Times Guide to the House of Commons: June 1983, Times Newspapers Ltd, London.
Townsend, P. (1979), *Poverty in the United Kingdom*, Penguin, Harmondsworth.
—— (1980), 'The problem of the meaning of poverty', in A. B. Atkinson (ed.), *Wealth, Income and Inequality*, 2nd edition, Oxford University Press, New York.
Van Den Bosch, R. (1978), *The Pesticide Conspiracy*, Doubleday and Co. Inc., New York.
Venn, J. A. (1923), *Foundations of Agricultural Economics*, Cambridge University Press, London.
Wellstone, P. D. (1978), *How the Rural Poor Got Power*, University of Massachusetts Press, Amherst.
Westergaard, J. H. (1972), 'Sociology: the myth of classlessness', in R. Blackburn (ed.), *Ideology in Social Science*, Fontana, Glasgow.
Westergaard, J. H. and Resler, H. (1975), *Class in a Capitalist Society— a Study of Contemporary Britain*, Heinemann Educational Books, London.
Wilson, G. (1977), *Special Interests and Policymaking: Agricultural Policies and Politics in Britain and the U.S.A. 1956–1970*, John Wiley, London.
—— (1978), 'Farmers' organisations in advanced societies', in H. Newby (ed.), *International Perspectives in Rural Sociology*, John Wiley, Chichester.
Wilson, H. (1971), *The Labour Government 1964–70: a Personal Record*, Weidenfeld and Nicolson and Michael Joseph, London.
Winyard, S. (1982), *Cold Comfort Farm*, Low Pay Unit, London.
Winyard, S. and Danziger, R. (1984), *Hard Labour*, Low Pay Unit, Birmingham.
Wootton, B. (1955), *The Social Foundations of Wage Policy*, George Allen & Unwin, London.
Wormell, P. (1978), *Anatomy of Agriculture: a Study of Britain's Greatest Industry*, Harrap, London and Kluwer, London.
Worsley, P. (1973), 'The distribution of power in industrial society', in J. Urry and J. Wakeford, *Power in Britain*, Heinemann Educational Books, London.
Wrong, D. (1979), *Power: Its Forms, Bases and Uses*, Blackwell, Southampton.

Articles

Abbreviations

APSR   *American Political Science Review*
ASR   *American Sociological Review*
BJLS   *British Journal of Law and Society*
JAE   *Journal of Agricultural Economics*
PS   *Political Studies*
S   *Sociology*
SR   *Sociological Review*

Apart from the more scholarly articles cited below, articles from the following newspapers have been used: *Landworker*, the *Financial Times*, the *Guardian*, and, *Farming News*. The articles used from these publications are too numerous to be listed here; but the most helpful ones have been acknowledged in the footnotes of the main text.

Bachrach, P. and Baratz, M. (1962), 'The two faces of power', *APSR*, 56.
—— , and —— , (1963), 'Decisions and nondecisions: an analytic framework', *APSR*, 57.
—— , and —— , (1975), 'Power and its two faces revisited: a reply to Geoffrey Debnam', *APSR*, 69.
Balbus, I. (1970-71), 'The concept of interest in pluralist and Marxian analysis', *Politics and Society*, 1.
Barry, B. (1975), 'The obscurities of power', *Government and Opposition*, 20.
Bell, C. and Newby, H. (1974), 'Capitalist farmers in the British class structure', *Sociologia Ruralis*, 14 (1-2).
Benton, T. (1981), 'Objective interests and the sociology of power', *S*, 15 (2).
Blake, D. (1984), 'Land of Milk and . . .', *New Statesman*, 18 May.
Bottini, R. (1977), 'End of tied cottages', *Labour Monthly*, June.
Bradshaw, A. (1976), 'A critique of Steven Lukes' "Power: a Radical View" ', *S*, 10.
Britton, D. K. (1977), 'Some explorations in the analysis of long-term changes in the structure of agriculture', *JAE*, 28 (3).
Clark, D. M. (1981), 'Rural council house sales', *The Village*, 36 (4).
Clements, L. M. (1978), 'The "demise" of tied cottages', *The Conveyancer and Property Lawyer*, 24.
Cowie, W. J. G. and Giles, A. K. (1956), 'An inquiry into reasons for "the drift from the land" ', *Selected Papers in Agricultural Economics*, 5, University of Bristol.
Debnam, G. (1975), 'Nondecisions and power: the two faces of Bachrach and Baratz', *APSR*, 69.
European Documentation, 'The agricultural policy of the European Community', *Periodical 6/1982*, 3rd edition.
Frey, F. (1971), 'Comment: on issues and nonissues in the study of power', *APSR*, 65.
Gasson, R. (1969), 'The occupational immobility of small farmers', *JAE*, 20 (2).
—— (1974), 'Turnover and size of labour force on farms', *JAE*,

25 (2).

Giles, A. K. and Cowie, W. J. G. (1960), 'Some social and economic aspects of agricultural workers' accommodation', *JAE*, 14 (2).

Goldthorpe, J. (undated), 'Social Structure, Interests and Political Partisanship', xerox.

Hay, A. (1980), 'Red faces (and hot tempers) on 2,4,5-T', *Nature*, 268.

Hindess, B. (1976), 'On three-dimensional power', *PS*, 24.

—— (1982), 'Power, interests and the outcomes of struggles', *S*, 16 (4).

Howarth, R. W. (1969), 'The political strength of British agriculture', *PS*, 17.

Irwin, A. and Green, K. (1983), 'The control of chemical carcinogens in Britain', *Policy and Politics*, 11 (4).

Lloyd, D. H. (1982), 'The leadership function in agricultural management', *Agricultural Manpower*, 4.

Mackel, C. J. (1975), 'A survey of the agricultural labour markets', *JAE*, 26 (3).

Mackintosh, J. R. (1970), 'The problem of agricultural politics', *JAE*, 21 (1).

Mann, M. (1970), 'The social cohesion of liberal democracy', *ASR*, 35.

Mann, S. A. and Dickinson, J. M. (1978), 'Obstacles to the development of a capitalist agriculture', *Journal of Peasant Studies*, 15 (4).

McIllroy, J. (1984), 'No strike, no say', *Marxism Today*, November.

Mills, F. D. (1964), 'The NUAW', *JAE*, 16 (2).

Mooney, P. H. (1982), 'Labour time, production time and capitalist development in agriculture', *Sociologia Ruralis*, 22 (3-4).

Morriss, P. (1972), 'Power in New Haven: a reassessment of "Who Governs?" ', *British Journal of Political Studies*, 2.

Newby, H. (1972), 'Agricultural workers in the class structure', *SR*, 20.

—— (1972), 'The low earnings of agricultural workers: a sociological approach', *JAE*, 23 (1).

—— (1974), 'The changing sociological environment of the farm', *Farm Management*, 2 (9).

—— (1977), 'Tied cottage reform', *BJLS*, 4.

Norriss, G. M. (1978), 'Industrial paternalist capitalism and local labour markets', *S*, 12 (3).

Partridge, P. H. (1963), 'Some notes on the concept of power', *PS*, 11.

Pennock, J. R. (1959), 'The political power of British agriculture', *PS*, 7.

Pettigrew, A. (1972), 'Information control as a power resource', *S*, 6.

Phillips, D. and Williams, A. (1981), 'Council house sales and village life', *New Society*, 28 November.

Pierson, R. (1978), 'What about the farmworkers?, a trade union view', *JAE*, 29 (3).

Posel, D. (1982), 'The Dimensions of Power', xerox.

Ravetz, J. (1977), 'The political economy of risk', *New Scientist*, 8 September.

Rogers, A. (1981), 'Rural housing—the necessity of choice', *The Village*, 36 (3).

Rogers, S. J. (1970), 'Farmers as a pressure group', *New Society*, 5 February.

Rose, D., Newby, H., Saunders, P. and Bell, C. (1977), 'Land tenure and official statistics: a research note', *JAE*, 28 (1).

Self, P. and Storing, H. (1958), 'The farmers and the state', *Political Quarterly*, 29 (1).

Sharp, G. and Capstick, C. W. (1966), 'The place of agriculture in the national economy', *JAE*, 17 (1).

Shoard, M. (1980), 'Public money and private vandalism', *New Statesman*, 10 October.

Thomas, R., Wardell, G. and Williams, A. (1980), '2,4,5-T cover-up by the MAFF', *The Ecologist*, 10 (6/7).

Whiteside, T. (1977), 'A reporter at large: the pendulum and the toxic cloud', *New Yorker*, 25 July.

Index

DATE DUE

1-20-04			